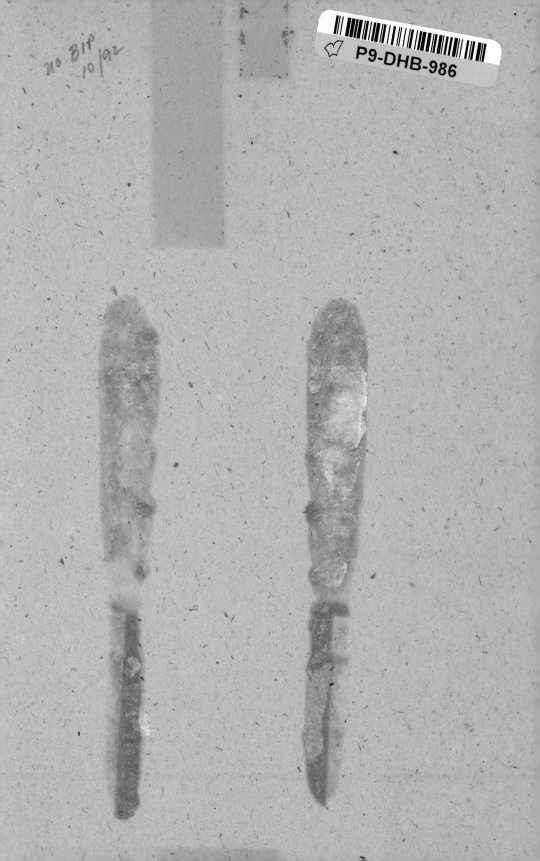

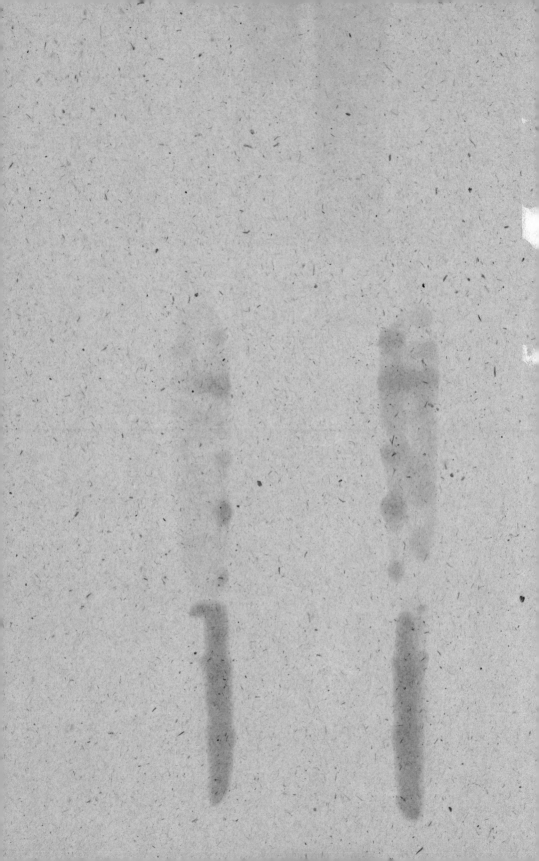

FRIEND AND FOE

**Aspects of French-Amerindian Cultural Contact
in the Sixteenth and Seventeenth Centuries**

Treatment of the Enemy. From De Bry, Theodore, America, Part II
(Courtesy British Museum).

Veue de Quebec (1699) by J.B.L. Franquelin, in Pinart, A.L. *Recueuil de cartes, plans et vues relatifs aux Etato-Unis et au Canada...* Pares, 1893. No. 11 (Courtesy Public Archives of Canada, Paintings, Drawings and Prints).

Iroquois, Hurons, Algonquins, et Divers Peuples en Canada, et en la Lousiane. Gravé par P.M. Ogier d'après P. Sevin. (Courtesy Public Archives of Canada, Paintings, Drawings and Prints).

Division of Agriculture. From De Bry, Theodore, America, Part II (Courtesy New York Public Library).

CORNELIUS J. JAENEN
FRIEND AND FOE

**Aspects of French-Amerindian Cultural Contact
in the Sixteenth and Seventeenth Centuries**

**Winner of the Sainte-Marie prize in History, 1973
Historical Sites Branch,
Ontario Ministry of Natural Resources**

**Columbia University Press
New York   1976**

Winner of the Sainte-Marie prize in history, 1973
Historical Sites Branch,
Ontario Ministry of Natural Resources

Copyright © 1976 by the Historical Sites Branch,
Ontario Ministry of Natural Resources.

Published in 1976 in Canada by
McClelland and Stewart Limited and
in the United States of America
by Columbia University Press.

Printed in Canada

Library of Congress Cataloging in Publication Data

Jaenen, Cornelius J.
  Friend and foe.

  Bibliography: p.
  1. Indians of North America—Canada—Government
relations. 2. Canada—History—To 1763 (New France)
I. Title.
E92.J33   1976   323.1'197'071   75-44212
ISBN 0-231-04088-1

Contents

Jurors Statement/5

Preface/6

Introduction/7

I   Amerindian Nature/12
II   Efforts at Evangelization/41
III   Social Problems and Differences/84
IV   Barbarism and Cruelty/120
V   Integration and Segregation/153

Conclusion/190

Bibliographical Note/198

Juror's Statement

As jurors, we unanimously select the manuscript **Friend and Foe** as the winner of the 1973 Sainte-Marie Prize Series, for its original research and contribution to the knowledge and understanding of seventeenth century Canada.

John Moir
University of
Toronto

Bruce Trigger
McGill University

Marcel Trudel
University of
Ottawa

PREFACE

This book makes a new and exciting contribution to our knowledge of French-Amerindian relations in 16th and 17th century Canada. Professor Jaenen has analyzed the contemporary documentary sources from a new perspective. In his assessment of these sources he has striven to place them in the context of the beliefs and assumptions of the French culture of the time. Further, he has drawn wisely from recent approaches in ethno-history, psychology and anthropology to glean from the existing record a more accurate view of the Amerindian reaction to the French presence. Through this process he has challenged some of the long-standing interpretations of the contact experience, producing new insights into that experience.

The Sainte-Marie Prize is offered annually and is awarded for excellence in original research and/or interpretation of 17th century Canadian history, or international circumstances and events directly influencing Canada's development in that hundred year period.

The Sainte-Marie Prize in History is a programme which reflects the intention of the Ontario Government that operational historic sites play a broad role in the on-going educational and cultural life of the community. Sainte-Marie among the Hurons has pioneered many of the attempts to make historic sites more relevant to the concerns of an ever-widening spectrum of the population.

Professor Jaenen's book is admirably suited for the Sainte-Marie Prize in History. It maintains the high academic standards set by previous winners and adds significantly to our knowledge of the contact experience. Equally important, there is no doubt that a major value of this work will be in the stimulation it gives to further research.

The author has noted that the greatest obstacle facing the contemporary historian in analyzing French-Amerindian relations has been the difficulty of comprehending the beliefs and conduct of the Amerindians. And, of course, this inability to comprehend the ways of a very different culture was a constant problem to the French and Amerindians themselves. Professor Jaenen, through his investigation, has offered us new perspectives on the French and Amerindians of the 17th century, and, perhaps, on ourselves as well.

Robert Bowes
Director
Historical Planning and Research Branch
Ontario Ministry of Culture and Recreation
July 1975

INTRODUCTION

Few aspects of French colonization in North America have been more commented upon and less well understood than the meeting of the French and the Amerindians. Most historians have accepted Parkman's now threadbare dictum: "Spanish civilization crushed the Indian; English civilization scorned and neglected him; French civilization embraced and cherished him."[1] The suggestion that the English and Spanish experiences were quite different from the French experience has become part of accepted history. The French in the seventeenth and eighteenth centuries were themselves anxious to leave the impression that their contacts with the Amerindians were mutually satisfactory both in the pursuit of the fur trade and in the cultural context of missionary work, and that in their military alliances they were "equal partners in a great North American empire." The effectiveness of this propaganda among the Amerindians themselves is well-illustrated by Pontiac's call to arms:

> And as for these English,—these dogs dressed in red, who have come to rob you of your hunting grounds, and drive away the game, — you must lift the hatchet against them. Wipe them from the face of the earth, and thus you will win my favour back again, and once more be happy and prosperous. The children of your great father, the King of France, are not like the English. Never forget they are your brethren. They are very dear to me, for they love the red men, and understand the true mode of worshipping me.[2]

The accuracy of this view can be tested only by a careful examination of the contacts between the French and the Amerindians.

The Amerindians have usually been considered in the context of the fur trade, colonial warfare and missionary activity. They were, for the most part, depicted as part of the North American environment that European colonists had to overcome in the cause of progress and in the task of nation-building. Herein lies one of the essential differences between European man and American man at the time of contact: the red man lived in harmony with his environment to the point that to outsiders he seemed to be an integrated part of the New World, but the white man felt a need to conquer and dominate the new environment and to remould it to his Old World conceptions. It has been said that the Amerindians were part of the "background of Canadian history" because they figured so prominently in public policy during the seventeenth, eighteenth and early nineteenth centuries; but throughout most of the nineteenth and twentieth centuries they were only peripheral to the main themes of national development and history.[3]

While it is true that in the seventeenth and eighteenth centuries the native peoples were very much in the foreground and involved in most of the significant activities of colonial life and affairs, it is essential to recall even earlier contacts. Their first contact with Europeans came at the close of the tenth century with the arrival of Viking explorers and exploiters. The sagas and scant religious archives leave the details of the Viking retreat before apparently hostile Amerindians lost in the mediaeval mists. After more enduring contacts had been established between European fishermen along the Atlantic Coast and American aborigines in the fifteenth century, the period of exploration began. A dominant idea in this period of exploration was that the New World was populated by peoples with different languages and cultures who conducted the European explorers and discoverers on tours along the well-known water routes and trails to the various centres of population. Explorers were fed, sheltered, offered the amenities of social life, and provided with multilingual guides. Even in this context Europeans saw themselves and their activities as being at the centre of the historical stage.

Several new approaches to the initial contacts between Europeans and Amerindians and to the early Amerindian background to Canadian history have been suggested.[4] The Amerindians are now being examined in such conceptual frameworks as European assimilationist policies, the ramifications of Catholic apocalypticalism, and national cultural superiority complexes. The contributions and insights of a variety of social scientists — anthropologists, archaeologists, ethnohistorians, psychologists — and other specialists — linguists, medical doctors, geographers, psychiatrists — are shedding new light on old problems for historians. New hypotheses are burgeoning as a result of a renewed general interest in Amerindian history and new insights from a variety of disciplines. One very striking feature is the emergence of the professional anthropologists as historians.[5] Clark Wissler, Harold Driver, Edward Spicer, Wilcomb Washburn, Anthony F. C.

Wallace, Bruce Trigger and William Fenton are becoming familiar names to today's historians. It yet remains for the historians in the field of Amerindian history and civilization to make any scholarly impact on the anthropologists and ethno-historians.

Within the compass of traditional history there are still exciting possibilities awaiting exploration. Can one go so far as to reassert the Bolton thesis that the European-Amerindian experience in the Americas was a common one and the so-called "Indian policy" in New England, New Spain and New France was based on a common fund or reservoir of Western European ideologies which were neither peculiarly national nor specifically Catholic or Protestant? If there was such a common source of Western European Renaissance views should not the study of cultures in contact be conducted entirely on comparative lines?

If the myth of the noble savage and the concept of depraved barbarians represent a polarization of views in all European experiences, how does one explain the presence of both views in each experience of cultural contact? In what circumstances does one view predominate over the other? Is it not possible that when the French were dependent on the aboriginal tribes for safety and sustenance, as were the English and Dutch at certain stages of their contact experience, the dominant view of the red man was necessarily one of the noble, generous, unsophisticated aborigine? Was not the environmental factor the determining element with the agricultural English finding it necessary to displace the settlements of the agricultural littoral tribes, whereas the French, in the pursuit of the fur trade and in establishing interior posts, did not need to displace aboriginal settlements? Did not the French become more dependent upon the native population than the English settlers to the south? If so, did not both dominant views grow out of the frontier experiences so that Turner's frontier thesis is capable of explaining very divergent attitudes and policies?

An even more important point is the question whether the study of French-Amerindian relations highlights the whole problem of America's impact on Europe. The discovery and colonization of the New World was, for centuries, seen in terms of European expansion and of widening the circle of Renaissance European man's awareness of the world. More recently, decolonization has led historians to reassess the European legacy, and this at a time when anthropologists and archaeologists have greatly increased our knowledge of the precontact past of the aborigines. Was not a myth of America created in the sixteenth and seventeenth centuries? What role did this impact of the New World play in the subsequent spiritual and intellectual, not to mention the political and economic, developments of Europe? What credibility can be ascribed to O'Gorman's theses that America was not discovered but was invented by sixteenth-century Europeans?

This study purports to consider briefly the nature of France's contact with the Amerindian peoples in the sixteenth and seventeenth centuries in terms of the challenges and repercussions contact brought to each of the participants. Much has been written about the economic and political consequences of the discovery of the Americas. Less has been written about the intellectual prelude and aftermath. Many traditional European assumptions and beliefs about history, geography, theology and the sciences were challenged and modified or refined. As Louis Le Roy wrote in 1570:

> Do not believe that there exists anything more honourable to our or the preceding age than the invention of the printing press and the discovery of the new world; two things which I always thought could be compared not only to Antiquity, but to immortality.[6]

More has been written about the Spanish experience than about the French experience, although there is much to recommend a study of the latter.

A final word of explanation is needed about the nature of this study. It was the French who sailed to America and established contact with the aborigines, not the Micmacs or Iroquois who sailed to Europe and established contact with the Bretons, Normans and Rochelais. The direction of this historical event underlines the ideological context of the contact between Frenchmen and Amerindians in the sixteenth and seventeenth centuries. Europeans invariably assumed, and it never seemed to have been questioned, that Europe was the centre of the world and of civilization, that its culture was older than any other cultures, that America was a new continent and that her peoples were relatively recent immigrants.[7] History, like society, was Europocentric.

1. Francis Parkman, *The Jesuits in North America in the Seventeenth Century* (Toronto: 1899), vol. I, p. 131.
2. Francis Parkman, *The Conspiracy of Pontiac* (New York: 1962), p. 169.
3. George F. Stanley, "The Indian Background to Canadian History," *Canadian Historical Association Annual Report, 1952* (Toronto: 1952), pp. 14-31.
4. Wilcomb E. Washburn, "Relations between Europeans and Amerindians during the Seventeenth and Eighteenth Centuries: The Epistemological Problem" (Unpublished paper read at International Colloquium on Colonial History, University of Ottawa, November 27-28, 1969), pp. 1-20; also "A Moral History of Indian-White Relations: Needs and Opportunities for Study," *Ethno-history* IV, 1 (Winter, 1957), pp. 47-61; Cornelius J. Jaenen, "The Frenchification and Evangelization of the Amerindians in Seventeenth Century New France," *Canadian Catholic Historical Association, Study Sessions, 1968*, 35 (1969), pp. 57-71.
5. Wilcomb E. Washburn, "History, Anthropology, and the American Indian," *American Studies* XI, 1 (Autumn, 1972), pp. 29-33.

6. Loys Le Roy, *De La Vicissitude ou Variété des Choses en l'Univers* (Paris: 1579), fs. 98-99, cited in J. H. Elliott, *The Old World and the New, 1492-1650* (Cambridge: 1970), pp. 9-10.
7. For a consideration of the parochial conceit and conceptual confusion of European discovery see Wilcomb E. Washburn, "The Meaning of 'Discovery' in the Fifteenth and Sixteenth Centuries," *American Historical Review* LXVIII (October, 1962), pp. 1-21.

CHAPTER I

AMERINDIAN NATURE

The first contacts between Frenchmen and Amerindians were made by the fishermen who had fished the Grand Banks at least since the fifteenth century, and who for a variety of reasons from time to time landed in the New World. The circumstances of these initial contacts can only be deduced from the reactions of the aboriginal peoples to later recorded expeditions to North America. The first European fishermen would appear to have been interested in furs, particularly in the well-worn and greasy beaver cloaks, as Cartier's expedition of 1534 was offered furs in barter for trinkets. That Europeans may also have been interested in the Amerindian women is suggested by the fact that the younger women were usually safely retired to the woods during bartering encounters with French crews. Verrazano reported in 1524:

> Every day the people came to see us at the ship, bringing their women of whom they are very careful; because, entering the ship themselves, remaining a long time, they made their women stay in the barges and however many entreaties we made them, offering to give them various things, it was not possible that they would allow them to enter the ship.[1]

The Amerindians had reason to fear not only that their women might be molested, but that they themselves might be kidnapped and taken to France. Amerindians were taken to France for a variety of reasons: to provide visible proof of landings in the New World; to serve as curios for public, and especially Court, spectacles; to be educated as interpreters and catechizers in the service of Europeans; to stimulate religious zeal and obtain financial support for the missions; to cement alliances with specific tribes; and, in a few instances, to serve in the galley fleet or as slaves.

The arrival in 1503 of a Brazilian native called Essomericq, who had been brought by Captain Binot Paulmier de Gonneville and who reportedly lived in France until 1538, marked the beginning of a long succession of such Atlantic crossings. It was a great-grandson of the sea captain, abbé Jean Paulmier de Gonneville, who sent a long memorandum to Pope Alexander VII arguing convincingly for a French mission in the New World. The capture of "wild woodmen," probably Tupinamba and Guarani tribesmen, and their public exhibition in Rouen in 1509 aroused much speculation about the nature of these "savages." Henri Estienne reported that "seven human savages have been brought from that island (which one calls the Terre-Neuve) to Rouen, along with their piraque, their clothes, and their arms." The missionary Biard wrote six years later that "Captain Thomas Aubert, of Dieppe, sailed in the year 1508, and brought back from there some of the Natives, whom he exhibited to the wonder and applause of France."[2] Some of these unwilling visitors were depicted in bas-reliefs in a parish church in Dieppe and in a hotel in Rouen.

This taking of captives became part of the pattern of early contact, paralleling the enthusiasm of the times for collecting curios. In 1524 a young Amerindian woman captured by Giovanni de Verrazano's crew resisted captivity so vigorously that she was given her freedom, but a young boy captured at the same time was taken to Europe. In July, 1528, at Saint-Malo, Jacques Cartier's wife stood as godmother at the baptism of a Brazilian girl, apparently brought to France the previous year. In 1534 Jacques Cartier took Domagaya and Taigoagny, sons of the Laurentian Iroquois chieftain, Donnacona, back to France. They returned to the St. Lawrence with his expedition in 1535, having learned French during their eight months' sojourn in Europe. They did not appear to have been greatly impressed by their hosts, or captors, in spite of their complimentary statements immediately upon arrival at Stadacona, as they had not prepared themselves for baptism and soon after landing in Canada they began to intrigue against Cartier's expedition.

A year later, in May, 1536, Cartier captured Donnacona, his two sons, and a few warriors and sailed for Saint-Malo with them and the four children he had been offered in the autumn of 1535. One of these girls whom Donnacona appears to have offered Cartier subsequently escaped from the French vessel where she was held. Donnacona intervened and had her returned with the explanation "that they had not advised her to run away, but that she had fled because the ship's boys had beaten her . . . ." Barcia provided an additional piece of information concerning this expedition; he wrote:

> . . . he put into St. Malo with his Indians who were travelling contentedly in the hope of returning quickly to Canada with a good store of wealth. The French, however, showed the opposite attitude . . . . Cartier maintained the land was not fit for Europeans to live in . . . ."[3]

Donnacona was received at Court by a curious Francis I. André Thévet was among those who met the Laurentien chieftain at Court. Shortly thereafter he published some of the information he had obtained from the chieftain in his *Singularitez de la France antarctique*. The ten captives whom Cartier had brought to France, with the exception of a young girl of about ten years of age, were all dead before Cartier returned to Canada in 1541. Upon returning to Stadacona, Cartier admitted that Donnocona had died but he maintained that all the others "had remained in France where they were living as great seigneurs; that they were married, and that they did not wish to return to their country."[4]

Even after the ill-fated colonization attempts of Cartier and Roberval the interest in captive and visiting aborigines was not only sustained, but increased. Both of the predominantly Huguenot colonization ventures in Brazil and Florida resulted in more natives being transported to France in circumstances bordering on abduction or slavery. Villegagnon brought a number of young boys from the Tupinamba tribe and presented them to Henry II, who in turn distributed them among his favourite courtiers. Jean Ribaut sought to comply with a royal request to provide the Queen with two Floridian natives, and Jean Mocquet, the royal geographer, had considerable difficulty in bringing the King a Carribbean youth. In 1583 Etienne Bellenger, with the help of Malouin fishermen, brought back natives to be trained as interpreters. Rabelais saw Amerindians in Saint-Malo, and Montaigne formed many of his impressions of the New World from speaking to a Brazilian native in Rouen in 1563. Even François Gravé Dupont presented Henry IV with a Montagnais in 1602, following the example of De Monts. In short, almost every French navigator and colonizer satisfied the desires of the Court for Amerindian captives.[5]

Equally popular with the French was the display of New World men at public festivals and celebrations. In 1550, to celebrate the entry of Henry II and Catherine de Medici into Rouen, an entire Tupinamba village was reconstructed, complete with log and thatched huts, hammocks, canoes, and even parrots and monkeys in trees which had been painted red to resemble the prized brazilwood. The three hundred "Brazilians", of whom only fifty were actually Tupinambas brought to France by ships engaged in the lumber trade, played their roles so well in a mock battle with their supposed enemies, the Tabagerres, that they terrified the townspeople. Four years later, a similiar exotic festival with Amerindians in feather skirts and headdresses, which had become their standard costume for such presentations, was staged at Troyes for the entry of Charles IX into that city. But no spectacle equalled that staged in Bordeaux on April 9, 1565, when three hundred soldiers directed twelve captive nations. Among those represented were "American and Brazilian savages whose captains declaimed before the King, each in his tongue which was interpreted for His Majesty."[6]

The seventeenth-century festivals were no less spectacular than the earlier ones. Henry IV was entertained at Fontainebleau in 1605 by Amerindians lighting a fire using only dry sticks. In 1612, the *fête* in Paris for the wedding of Louis XIII and Anne of Austria included captive Amerindians in the cortège. At the celebrated carnival of 1626, presented at the court of Louis XIII, representations of the four continents played a leading role in the ballet. They had been added to the four elements, four seasons, four temperaments, four gospels, and four times of day which had traditionally made up the interwoven allegorical themes. The Jesuits at Pont a Mousson celebrated the canonization of their founder, Ignatius Loyola, six years later with a similar festival in which befeathered natives again represented America. In 1645 the Queen Mother attended a *divertissement* in which eight natives in feathered skirts and headdresses, carrying a cage full of parrots, performed their native dances and then released the birds which symbolized exotic America. In 1662 a great carrousel was put on in front of the Louvre for Louis XIV in which, for three days, five horse brigades paraded in elaborate costumes to the delight of the Parisians. The fifth brigade represented the Amerindians and was led by the Duke of Guise. Louis XIV later was entertained by watching Iroquois captives row their bark canoes on the ponds of Versailles. These occasions[7] did much to arouse and sustain general curiosity in the New World, but they also raised thorny problems of a historical, scientific and theological nature as well.

Most Frenchmen who showed any interest in America quickly became either indiophiles or indiophobes. However, it is not easy to demarcate schools of thought as opposed to the personal reactions and beliefs of those who expressed their views on Amerindian nature and character. The Spanish experience had already acquainted French scholars with some of the initial problems posed by the New World, and the French always tended to be influenced by Spanish writings on the subject.

In 1510, John Major, a Scottish professor living in Paris, published a justification of Amerindian enslavement and military conquest on the basis of the Aristotelian theory of natural slavery, which greatly influenced Spanish theorists.[8] The jurist, Juan Ginés de Sepulveda, seized on the theory that the imperfect must be subject to the perfect, and that the superior must rule the inferior to justify Spain's title to America. He expanded the argument to assert that the threefold baseness of the aboriginal tribes — their idolatry, their paganism, and their barbarism — demanded their subjugation by a superior civilization.[9] Spain's claim to the Americas, sanctioned by the *Requerimiento* of 1514, asserted she had been given the Indies just as the Jews had been given the Promised Land and that if the inhabitants would not submit to Spanish rule and accept Catholicism, war might justly be waged against them. This idea that Amerindian idolatry justified conquest had mediaeval roots and was not easily erased from European minds.[10] The French were quick to discount the Spanish claims on the grounds that "the popes hold spiritual jurisdiction but cannot distribute lands to kings,"[11] and proceeded to assert their own claims. Major's remarks on the conquest of New Spain constituted the first extended theoretical treatment of Spain in America; he conceded complete temporal power to neither pope nor emperor, and declared that mere infidelity could not deprive a people of dominion, although opposition to the preaching of the faith justified punitive action.

In opposition to these views of Amerindian character and cultures there stood the indiophile view of aboriginal innocence and perfection, the optimistic view that the New World peoples offered an opportunity to build a new and ideal civilization superior to that of Europe. The chief opponents of Sepulveda's thesis were Bartolomé de Las Casas, Antonio de Montesinos, Juan de Zumarraga and Domingo de Betanzos. The polarization of views and the bitter attacks the two schools of thought launched against each other came to a climax in the Las Casas-Sepulveda public debate at Valladolid in 1550-51.[12] The temptation to characterize the opposing viewpoints as Dominican and Franciscan, or more recently as the views of the reformed orders versus the more flexible and worldly *conventuels*, oversimplifies the complexity of the reactions.[13] Those who held favourable views of Amerindian qualities might still justify their enslavement, their segregation, or their exclusion from holy orders. So also, those who had a very low opinion of Amerindians' intellectual capacity and character might advocate humane treatment and equitable political and economic accommodations.

Information about the French contact with "another world" came from travellers such as Cartier, Roberval, Saintonge, Villegagnon and Ribaut, but it was the French thinkers and writers who tried to interpret the facts and in doing so raised many questions and problems. Ronsard wondered if the Amerindians might not regret their contact with Villegagnon; Rabelais' Pantagruel was made to visit the valley of the St. Lawrence; Henri de la Popelinière, who advocated Huguenot colonization, was troubled about disturbing the way of life of the American natives. In 1579 an account of the Spanish massacre of the French colonists in Florida, and a French edition of Las Casas' *Brief Account of the Destruction of the Indies,* gave new and vigorous support to the Black Legend, which maintained that there were no redeeming qualities in the Spanish exploitation of the New World.[14] Montaigne's reaction is probably the clearest warning that was sounded:

> I am afraid that we shall have very greatly hastened the decline and ruin of this new world by our contagion, and that we will have sold it our opinions and our arts very dear. It was an infant world; yet we have not whipped it and subjected it to our discipline by the advantage of our natural valor and strength, nor won it over by our justice and goodness, nor subjugated it by our magnanimity. Most of the responses of these people and most of our dealings with them show that they were not at all behind us in natural brightness of mind and pertinence.[15]

One aspect of the problem facing early travellers and travel writers was how to comprehend the New World and its peoples, which were all completely new to them; another aspect of the problem was how to relate what was observed and understood in terms intelligible to their European readers. Jean de Léry concluded a description of the natives he met with the following advice:

> Their gestures and countenances are so different from ours, that I confess to my difficulty in representing them in words, or even in pictures. So, to enjoy the real pleasures of them, you will have to go and visit their country.[16]

The basic question was sometimes framed in terms of whether or not the Amerindians were "true men" possessing the full range of human capacities, and whether they were descendants of Adam and part of that humanity for which Jesus Christ had offered Himself. The reaction in some quarters to the discovery of New World man was to doubt that he was fully human like the inhabitants of the three known continents. The debate was not unlike what might ensue were twentieth-century man to be confronted suddenly by beings from outer space; the greatest difference in such a comparison might be that in the sixteenth century the problems were more theological than scientific. In Spain and Mexico there had been some doubt not only about the intelligence of the Amerindians, but also about whether they could be considered to share in common humanity and what was their spiritual potential. French translations of Ovieda and Gomara, which were published in Paris in 1555 and 1568 respectively, introduced French readers to the view of the Amerindians as sub-human beings possessing *ni foi, ni roi, ni loi.*[17]

Pope Paul III's bull *Sublimus Deus* affirmed, among other things, that they were indeed "truly men" who should not "in any way be enslaved" and who were "capable of understanding the Catholic faith." [18] The bull was aimed at satisfying the two traditional European ways of defining man: the classical, in terms of his rationality; and the Christian, in terms of his receptivity to divine grace. Jean Bodin wrote that Moses had been divinely inspired to write of man's origins "that all men whom his story might reach should understand clearly that they are of the same blood and allied by the same bond of race." [19] Even Lafitau, a Jesuit missionary to the Iroquois in the early eighteenth century, recalled that the first reported reaction to the discovery of the Amerindians was to wonder if they were of the race of Adam. [20]

The implication was that there had been some acceptance of a sub-human classification of beings who were "brutish" and "bestial." Hermaphrodites, cannibals, devils and witches were regarded as being somewhere between the human world and the animal world, whereas creatures like mermaids and mermen, centaurs, acephali, and unicorns were more than ordinary beasts. The theme of the bestiality of the Amerindians, alternating strangely with the theme of primeval innocence, continued to find expression in the seventeenth century. Pierre d'Avity, for example, classified the Amerindians as savages just one rank above the brutish beasts, but lower than the barbarians of the Orient. Five alleged qualities of brutishness seemed to confirm this low classification: their exclusive concern with earthly affairs and with the present; their restriction to hunting, fishing and collecting food supplies and their culinary limitations; their nudity; their lack of permanent housing; their lack of government and civic administration. Eméric de Crucé wrote about "cannibals and saveges who have nothing of man but the countenance." [21] The Jesuits, along with Marie de l'Incarnation and Bishop Laval, revived the theme when describing the Iroquois menace in mid-century. It was a view that came to dominate and terrorize the inhabitants of New France almost as much as the actual raids of the Five Nations, and has continued to dominate the historiography of the period.

The missionaries accepted, in general, the common humanity of the natives and in some cases this view gave them an important advantage in propagating their doctrines. It was reported in 1683, for example, that among the Miamis and Illinois, Allouez had found the natives preferred the French to other Europeans:

> I think that these are the english, from whom They receive no tokens of friendship, and who take no trouble to Instruct Them. In fact, those heretics pay no heed to their salvation, saying that they look upon Them only As beasts; and that Paradise is not for that sort of people. The Father did not fail to Show

them that he was animated with very different sentiments toward them; that he looked upon Them as men, in Whom he recognized The image of a God who had Created them, who had died for them, and who destined them to The same happiness as the Europeans.[22]

Although they accepted the ecclesiastical pronouncements on the humanity of the Amerindians, Europeans still wrestled with the speculative problem of accounting for them in the chain of being. Man, according to Aristotelian, Thomist and Neo-Platonic views, occupied the middle rungs of the ladder or chain of being, between sub-human wild men and divine beings. Catholic thought asserted the possibility of men becoming like gods, or, on the other hand, of degenerating to the level of animals through sin.

The problem of diffusion and of human migrations became important in attempting to reconcile the new discoveries with the Biblical accounts of the creation, the deluge, and the multiplication of Noah's descendants. Numerous writers in the sixteenth and seventeenth centuries, among them only a small proportion of French, were preoccupied with the origins of American natives. Two Spanish writers dominated seventeenth-century theorizing. Joseph de Acosta, who was sometimes quoted by his fellow Jesuits labouring in New France, in his *Historia natural y moral de las Indias* published in 1590, presented a critical view of existing theories; whereas Gregoria Garcia, a Dominican, in his *Origen de los Indios* published in 1607, tended to accept most theories and transformed the possible into the probable.[23] The theories of Amerindian origins ranged all the way from indigenous and Oriental sources to Jewish, Carthaginian, Canaanite, Ophiric, Phoenician, Trojan and Egyptian transoceanic migrations. Some of these had their advocates in France, and most were well-known to the élite that was concerned with America in the mid-seventeenth century. The Atlantis origin theory, for example, which had been expounded by the Spaniard Agustin de Zarate, appeared in a French edition in 1570. It was rejected by Lescarbot as pure and unfounded myth.[24] Giralmo Benzoni's popular history which advanced a Carthaginian origin was published in French before 1600, but of it Lescarbot made only passing mention. Surprisingly, Lescarbot was much more in favour of a Canaanite theory, which had been enunciated first in Spain by Juan Suarez de Peralta circa 1580.[25]

Lescarbot followed the widely disseminated sixteenth-century idea that the ancients had visited the New World:

Whoever will weigh these words will find them to be by no means untrue; and will conclude that in the first centuries men had knowledge of America and of other lands adjoining it, and that on their ceasing to go thither, owing to the length of the journey, this knowledge was lost, and only a vague tradition remained.[26]

Although the possibility of European and African trans-Atlantic voyages were not ruled out as a way in which some connection had been maintained with the New World in the mediaeval period, it is rather astonishing that no direct link was made by any of the writers between the earliest fishing voyages and the last recorded and documented Viking expeditions to the New World. As for the animal population of the New World, Lescarbot resorted to Joseph de Acosta's argument, which had theological implications that troubled many writers, that land bridges and interlocking continents in antiquity could account for inter-continental migrations. The French debt to Spanish theory was great for the general outline of the now-accepted theory of the peopling of the New World was taken from Spanish writers and was well-established in France by the late sixteenth or early seventeenth century.

The French were also aware of the public controversy between Jan de Laet and Hugo Grotius in Holland in the years 1641-44. Grotius, when serving as Swedish ambassador to Paris, prepared a manuscript dealing with the question of the origins of the Amerindians which he sent to his brother in order to obtain the comments of Jan de Laet, a director of the Dutch West India Company who had published a history of the New World in 1625.[27] De Laet sent Grotius critical notes and a copy of Acosta's book; Grotius proceeded to publish his manuscript without taking any account of De Laet's commentary or the Acostan thesis, arguing for a Norwegian origin of the northern Amerindians, an Ethiopic origin for those of the Yucatan, and a Chinese origin for those of Peru.[28] De Laet published a point-by-point refutation and the debate became acrimonious and public.[29] In 1644 Jean-Baptiste Poissons published a pamplet arising out of this controversy in which he supported an Ophiric origin, whereas Robert Comte published a pamphlet affirming Phoenician and Carthaginian origins. But the French never demonstrated as much interest in the question of Amerindian origins as did the Spaniards, the English and the Dutch.

The theory that the Amerindians were descendants of the Hebrews, and more particularly of the Lost Ten Tribes of Israel, originated in published form with Joannes Lumnius in Antwerp in 1567.[30] The theory became widespread through Gilbert Genebrard's *Chronographia in duos libros distincta,* published in Paris in the same year. Lamothe Cadillac, in 1695-96, prepared a long memorandum attempting to prove that the tribes around Michilimackinac were "descended from the Hebrews and were originally Jews, which may also be observed from the terms they use in conversation and in their speech and customs."[31] Hennepin summarized the principal arguments for such a hypothesis:

> One would be apt to suspect that these Savages of America originally sprung from the Jews, some of whom might casually have been wreckt, and cast upon that Part of the World; for they have several Customs not unlike theirs; they make their Cabins in the form of Tents, like as the Jews did; they anoint themselves with Oil, and are superstitiously addicted to Divination from Dreams. They bewail over the Dead with great lamentation. The Women go into mourning for their near Relations a whole Year, during which time they abstain from dancing and feasting, and wear a sort of a Hood upon their Heads, and commonly the Father or Brother of the Deceas'd take care of the Widow. Besides it seems as if God had laid a particular Malediction upon 'em, as he did upon the Jews: They are brutish, and persist unalterably in their Opinions; they have no certain fix'd Place of Abode; they are very lascivious, and have such gross Conceptions that when we tell 'em Souls are immortal and immaterial, they ask what they eat in the other World. Moreover we may observe some Conformity between Moses's Relations of the Creation of the World, and the belief of these Savages about it, as I observed above.[32]

Although such views were generally accepted, Western Europe was shocked by the publication in 1655 of the provocative thesis of a Huguenot writer, Isaac de la Peyrère. He argued in his *Prae-Adamitae* that men probably existed before Adam, hence the two accounts of creation in Genesis and the obscure references to the "daughters of men" and to giants; he also suggested that these Gentiles of the first creation spread over the world, even to America, and escaped the deluge which destroyed the "sons of God."[33] La Peyrère was a Huguenot who, in the furious reaction aroused by his book, was forced to convert to Catholicism, abjure his theory, and spend the remaining years of his life in a monastery. His work, however, served to broaden the field of discussion on the origins of all mankind, not just of the Amerindians. His polygenetic hypothesis advanced the view that diversity had been the state of mankind since the beginning of time. This contradicted two supposedly unique features of Amerindian civilizations which had been emphasized as differentiating them from the Old World civilizations with which parallels and even direct communication had been suggested: firstly, the Amerindians were almost completely isolated from life on the other continents; secondly, they differed from other primitive civilizations in that their tribes were not pastoral.[34] Orthodox thinkers believed this diversity had developed or evolved in isolation; La Peyrère implied that the Amerindians as observed in the sixteenth century were what they had always been since their creation.

Eventually, there arose the suggestion that the Amerindians were the living representatives of ancient Europeans who had been retarded in their development.[35] Etienne Pasquier, a Parisian lawyer writing in the 1560s, asserted that from the information he had acquired from his contemporaries it appeared that the Amerindians were really new peoples, rude in manners and like the ancestors of Europeans.[36] Jean Bodin concluded, therefore, that the Golden Age was not in the past:

> No one, looking closely into this matter, can doubt that the discovery of our men ought to be compared with the discoveries of our elders; many ought to be placed first.[37]

The idea that the Amerindians were living representatives of European ancestral peoples assumed that every tribe and nation passed through identical stages of development. This raised arguments among anthropologists over diffusion of culture and cultural evolution.[38] Anthropologists have all now accepted the monogenetic thesis, and it has been argued recently that the discovery of the Amerindians evoked in the minds of Europeans both the memory of the savage heritage from which they had emerged and the consciousness of the continuing obstacles which had to be overcome in order to create a New France, a New England, or a New Spain.[39]

The colour or racial factor was not important in the period of early contact in the way that obvious cultural or civilizing differences were considered important. It has been asserted that the colour factor became important only after there evolved a "European predilection for dividing the world's population into 'white man and coloured peoples'."[40] There are few references in French literature, technical works and correspondence to colour as a means of distinguishing Amerindians. Indeed, Roberval asserted in 1542 that they were white:

> To declare to you what is the condition of these Savages, it is necessary to say on this subject: That these people are of good stature and well proportioned. They are white, but go about completely naked; and if they were dressed in the fashion of our French, they would be just as white, and would look as well; but they paint themselves with diverse colours, because of the heat and strength of the Sun.[41]

Roberval expressed the popular Europocentric theory that variation in pigmentation was caused by differences in exposure of originally white skins to the rays of the sun.

Henri Estienne, on the other hand, said in 1509 that the Amerindians brought to France were "of the color of soot, have very large lips, and have some tattoing on the face."[42] Verrazano reported that the natives in the region of the present-day Carolinas were "of dark color not much unlike the Ethiopians, and hair black and thick, and not very long," but farther north he found the natives "lighter colored than those past."[43] Charles Lalemant described them as "strongly inclined to black"; Le Jeune as "naturally white" and having "nothing savage about them but their tanned color"; Bressani as "not very dark, especially in their youth"; other Jesuit writers as "the same complexion as the French," "not very swarthy," "olive-colored," "a swarthy complexion," or "an olive tint" like the Portuguese. Only Bressani made a comment which might indicate some unfavourable association between colour and moral qualities and this was not uncomplimentary to the Amerindians: " . . . they are hardly Barbarians, save in name. There is no occasion to think of them as half beast, shaggy, black, and hideous."[44] Generally, the question of colour was of minor concern. Certainly there is nothing in the literature parallel to Oviedo's crude biological theory basing Amerindian inferiority on the size and thickness of their skulls. As long as man, even Amerindian red man, was regarded as monogenetic in origin and homogeneous in descent he was not classified in racial terms. During initial contact there was even a lack of distinction made among aboriginal tribes.

More useful than the concept of colour equated with race, is a recent sociological definition of the SNI or somatic norm image.[45] Each group, according to this approach, has its own SNI, or "complex of physical characteristics which are accepted by a group as its norm and ideal," by which it can evaluate and analyse other societies. Thus, as the French considered themselves aesthetically superior to the Amerindians, in terms of modern sociological and political definitions they were racist.[46] Chauchetière's narrative of 1680 contained the following judgement:

> These savages were indeed given to understand that the French did not resemble them, and were not so base as they, who derive their strength only from lying; and that the black gowns, who had no interest in telling them lies, — against which they inveigh and preach every day, — were not deceivers.[47]

The Amerindians, for their part, considered the French inferior to themselves; in other words, they had their own somatic norm image and considered themselves aesthetically superior. Pierre d'Avity wrote in 1637 that "although they lack police, power, letters, acts, wealth and other things they despise other nations and esteem themselves highly."[48] He was merely echoing the sentiments of Father Gabriel Sagard who had spent the winter of 1623-24 among the Hurons. The Hurons thought the French possessed "little intelligence in comparison to themselves" and although they did respect the wisdom of the Récollet missionaries they "did not have this opinion or belief concerning other Frenchmen in comparison with whom they estimated their own children wiser and more intelligent."[49] Except for their scientific knowledge, the Jesuits were no more highly esteemed than the Récollets. Even the children sometimes scorned them and ridiculed them "because they do not see in a Frenchman any of the perfections of a savage and cannot recognize the virtues of a generous Christian."[50] The Amerindians generally regarded the French as physically weaker than themselves, ugly, especially because of their excessive hairiness, and subject to deformities and infirmities. The French were not entirely ignorant of Amerindian tastes and opinions as, for example, the missionary Garnier, in ordering suitable "holy pictures" from France in 1648, specified the need for full facial views, no beards or frizzy hair, and preferably bright primary colours, not greens or yellows, in clothing. Sagard related how "one of the ugliest savages in his district" laughed at the Frenchmen with beards and wondered how they could be so ugly and how any woman could look favourably on them. He added:

> They have such a horror of a beard that sometimes when they try to insult us they call us Sascoinronte, that is to say, Bearded, You have a beard; moreover, they think it makes people more ugly and weakens their intelligence.[51]

Lahontan, who was usually very generous in his appraisal of aboriginal nature, remarked on "their fanatical Opinions of things, which proceeded from their Prepossession and Bigotry with reference to their own customs and ways of living."[52]

Many of the first impressions of Amerindians recorded by travellers were very favourable. They were not only physically handsome and virtuous, but also reasonable, alert and apparently capable of intellectual development. Often they were depicted as superior to Frenchmen in physical stature, in strength, agility, and speed. This superiority was said to result from the natural benefits of the climate, land and water rather than from any innate native superiority. These descriptions placed them almost between men and angels in the great chain of being along with giants, who were superior in size and strength, Amazonian women, who were superior in strength and independence, and nature nymphs, who were superior in beauty. Sieur de Cobes, who visited New France in 1605, gave a correspondent his impressions in a letter dated February 13, 1608 and subsequently published:

Now to describe the nature of those who inhabit it, you should know that they are very handsome men, white as snow, who let their hair grow down to their waists (both men and women), with high foreheads, eyes burning like candles, strong in body and well proportioned. The women too are very beautiful and graceful, well formed and dainty, so much so that given the fashion of their clothes which is somewhat strange one would say they were Nymphs or some goddesses, very charming and tractable, but apart from that prepared to be massacred rather than consent to their dishonour, or have knowledge of any other man besides their husbands. Apart from that, in their manner of living they are very brutish . . . ."[53]

Pierre d'Avity took the consensus of those who had visited the New World in the 1630s to be as follows:

Moreover, they are as handsome young men and beautiful young women as may be seen in France. They are great runners and swimmers, and the women too have a marvellous disposition. They are usually more slim and nimbler than we and one finds none who are paunchy, hunchbacked, deformed, niggardly, gouty or stony among them . . . . The majority of them are not at all malicious, but liberal, have a good mind and clear one so far as discerning common and sensible matters, deducing their reasons with gracefulness, always employing some pleasing comparison. They have a very good memory for material matters, such as having seen you, the qualities of a place where they have been, or what one did in their presence some twenty or thirty years ago . . .[54]

They were characterized by such traits as emotional restraint, stoicism, practicality, personal resourcefulness, individualism and bravery. A commonly misunderstood trait was the Algonkian value placed on deference in interpersonal relationships. The French sometimes concluded that the Algonkians had no leadership, whereas in fact the band could take united action rapidly because of the kinship and clan ties. Father Le Jeune observed that the Montagnais could not "endure in the least those who seem desirous of assuming priority over others."[55] As in all stateless societies, problems were resolved in accordance with a set of overt rules. One might say that instead of decisions there were compromises.

Hennepin concluded that there were traits of aboriginal intelligence common to all the cultures of North America. He based his observations on the early Récollet encounters with the Montagnais, Hurons, Iroquois and Neutrals, as well as later encounters with the

Micmacs, Illinois, Miamis, Kickapoos, Sioux and tribes of the south. He wrote:

> I observed, as my Predecessors, that the Savages don't want good Sense in what concerns the general and particular Interest of their Nation. They pursue their Point, and take right Methods to come to the end of their designs: but 'tis what I am astonish'd at, that whilst they are so clear sighted in their common Affairs, they should have such extravagant notions of the concerns of Religion, the Manners, Laws, and Maxims of Life.[56]

For seventeenth-century Frenchmen it was inexplicable that a people who seemed to be intelligent, rational and superstitious should not also come to the same conclusions they had reached on matters of social and religious concern. The problem was one of attempting to reconcile native reasonableness and intelligence with what Frenchmen conceived to be "right reason" and "right religion."

There was, therefore, a qualifying conviction among some travellers and writers that the Amerindians were like immature children who required European tutelage in order to realize their full capacities.[57] This childishness was, according to some early reports, redeemed by their docility and passivity. The abbé de Belmont summarized three-quarters of a century of missionary experience in these terms:

> . . . it is necessary to know that these people are naturally cold, and the women timid and modest — be it that this reserve comes from the climate or their education; they do not fight readily; that they quarrel little; that excess and imprudence are decried among them more than "what will be said" or being gossiped about; finally, that unless they are withdrawn from their cool temperament by a strange principle, or by being supported by some custom, they have difficulty in overcoming modesty.[58]

Docility was a quality among sedentary converts living on the *réserve* that most appealed to Mother Marie de l'Incarnation. She wrote to a friend:

> As for the settled Savages, they dwell in the fervour of the first Christians of the Church. One could not see souls purer or more zealous in observing God's law. I am full of wondering admiration when I see them submissive as children to those who instruct them.[59]

On the other hand, Marie de l'Incarnation disclosed some rather disconcerting thoughts about the aborigines. In 1635, after having read the Jesuit *Relations* of 1634 describing the killing of two hundred Hurons and the enslavement or adoption of another one hundred by the Iroquois, she reaffirmed her ardent desire to go to Canada although she imagined "what it is to live with Barbarians; the danger there is of dying of starvation, or of the cold; the frequent chances of being captured." [60] The journey to Canada was envisaged as a pilgrimage of suffering and self-denial, perhaps of martyrdom:

> Crosses and sufferings are more agreable to me than all the delights of the world; let them send me to the depths of the most cruel Barbarism, there will be my delights, and I shall cherish my little Savage girls more than if they were Princesses. I go gladly to follow my dear Jesus and suffer all he will require for his love. [61]

She, like a number of her contemporaries, saw the Amerindians in the familiar literary framework of the monstrous and physically abnormal world of Mandeville or of the enchanted isles of mediaeval fantasy.

As late as 1650 the necessity to exaggerate in order to be believed was demonstrated in an imaginative account of why the French had failed to find precious treasure in New France. Le Fevre wrote:

> The great horrible and frightful monster is on the passage leading to this mine, some savages calling him Gougon, others the evil mother; because he has the face of a woman and eats all those he can catch. He is of such a frightening height that the top of the highest masts of the tallest ships would not come up to his waist, also having a pouch where he could put a whole ship. It is remarked that where gold mines, or silver, or of treasures, have been discovered there also have been perceived demons in the environs who guarded them and did harm to those who approached them. [62]

These two very different traditions, the monstrous and physically abnormal world of Mandeville and the enchanted isles of fantasy, on which Europeans could draw to explain the aborigines also help to explain the seemingly contradictory reactions discernible even in the works of a single author.

Many of the early descriptions of the aborigines were written in wholly negative terms, the authors stressing at considerable length the absence of some conventional elements of European civilization — no letters, no laws, no government, no navigation, no agriculture, no foreign exchange, no organized warfare. Montaigne characterized the Amerindians he had heard about and whose artifacts he had examined with great interest and care in the following terms:

> This is a nation, I should say to Plato, in which there is no sort of traffic, no knowledge of letters, no science or numbers, no name for a magistrate or for political superiority, no custom of servitude, no riches or poverty, no contracts, no successions, no partitions, no occupations but leisure ones, no care of any but common kinship, no clothes, no agriculture, no metal, no use of wine or wheat.[63]

Louis Le Roy expressed identical negative sentiments in 1575 when he attributed to "those who have navigated there" the observation that the natives discovered were "living still as the first men, without letters, without laws, without kings, without commonwealths, without arts, but nevertheless not without religion."[64] Pierre d'Auity remarked that the Amerindians were "without commanders, without laws, without any forme of civilitie, or policie," then identified five levels of cultural privation or brutishness. There were first those who had no religion; those who had no agriculture; those who had no clothing; those who had no constructed homes; those, the most uncivilized of all, who had no government.[65] Champlain, while favourable in his comments about tribes with whom the French had intercourse, described the tribes unfriendly to his enterprises as "brute beasts having neither faith nor law, living without God and religion."[66] It was, incidentally, these tribes that had the highest levels of civilization among the cultures that the French met in the Canadian area. These negative comments reveal the Europocentric approach which represented Amerindian barbarism as cultural because the natives did not conform to a French order of life and conduct. The differences between French civilization and Algonkian and Iroquoian cultures were essentially the features which set a state or civilized society apart from a stateless tribal society.

The most enduring myth concerning Amerindian nature was that of the "noble savage."[67] The origins of this myth of the child of nature, the *buon selvaggio*, as an idealization of primitive man, has been traced back to the concept of the primeval paradisiacal condition of man in the Garden of Eden, the fall and the beginning of a degeneration characterized by corrupting civilization.[68] Montaigne was among the first to give expression to the sentiment in France:

> Those people are wild, just as we call wild the fruits that Nature has produced by herself and in her normal course; whereas really it is those that we have changed artificially and led astray from the common order, that we should rather call wild.[69]

Montaigne maintained that the aborigines of America seemed barbarous to him in the sense that "they have been fashioned very little by the human mind, and are still very close to their original naturalness." He admired them for being ruled by "the laws of nature" and for being "little corrupted by ours." Montaigne was certain the ancient philosophers and sages "could not imagine a naturalness so pure and simple as we see by experience."[70] Du Tertre saw the tribes he met as "the most content, the happiest, the least vicious" because "they are as nature produced them, that is to say, in a great simplicity and natural naiveté."[71] Lescarbot qualified what he regarded as French superiority with the following observations:

> And yet I would not so greatly depreciate the condition of the tribes whom we are to describe as not to avow that there is much good in them. For, to put it briefly, they have courage, fidelity, generosity, and humanity, and their hospitality is so innate and praisworthy that they receive among them every man who is not an enemy. They are not simpletons like many people over here; they speak with much judgment and good sense, . . . So that if we commonly call them Savages, the word is abusive and un-merited, for they are anything but that, as will be proved in the course of this history.[72]

This supposed felicity of the aborigines was the result of their comparative liberty, their equality among themselves, and their spirit of brotherhood. Such observations by travellers, missionaries, and their commentators tended to produce rather revolutionary ideas about European governments and institutions. Clodoré observed, for example, that not only were the natives of the French Antilles living in complete liberty, but also the French colonists enjoyed much more liberty than was accorded their class in France.[73] Claude d'Abbeville wrote in 1614 of the Tupinamba tribe that "they have no law or police for public order, apart from some portion of the law of nature."[74] Gabriel Sagard depicted Huron life as characterized by a freedom un-known in the absolutist France of Cardinal Richelieu, by a simplicity and sincerity uncorrupted by European civilization and sophistication, and by crude but uncorrupted virtues. Realizing some of the implica-tions of his laudatory comments he hastened to qualify his judgements with the phrase that, however, they were "deprived of the knowledge of God and of the light of the faith."[75]

The Amerindians were not, however, as free and unfettered as these writers thought them to be, or as Rousseau's imagination would depict them in the eighteenth century. They knew a law and order which differed from the constraints of French society. Every Amer-indian was bound by the customs of his people and by the chains of age-old traditions. These constraints governed his behaviour not merely in his social relations but also in his religion, his occupational tasks, his warfare, his medicine and his art.

Observers were certain they saw more equality in Amerindian life than in French society. This equality may have impressed them even more than did the liberty of aboriginal societies. The exotic delights of America which the Huguenot pastor, Jean de Léry, experienced may be explained in part by the fact that he wrote his account some twenty years after his Brazilian sojourn and after he had suffered much persecution and cruel discrimination in France. Paul Boyer wrote enthusiastically of the equality of the peoples he encountered in the New World:

> They do not know what are extortions, or subsidies, nor brigandry; no avarice, no cupidity, no lawsuits, no quarrels, no servants, no masters, no unfortunates, no beggars, not so much as an inkling of coveteousness, which things should make us blush with shame. No distinctions of estates among them, and they consider men only by the actions they accomplish.[76]

The inequalities and inequities of French society were often attacked through the literary device of an account of Amerindians visiting Paris or Rouen and commenting on the extremes of wealth and poverty which they noticed there. Montaigne said that the astonished natives "thought it strange that these needy halves could endure such an injustice, and did not take the others by the throat, or set fire to their houses."[77]

Lescarbot and Denys extended the idealization of the noble savage to an idealization of the New World as a land of opportunity. Lescarbot noted that in many cases in France children were becoming a burden on their parents but now a way of escape has been opened to the nation. If navigation remained reasonably safe to New France "whoever finds himself oppressed over here will be able to pass over there and there pass his days at rest and without poverty."[78] Sixty years later, Denys took up the same argument. He observed that he did not advocate the forcible removal to the colony of people who were happy and at ease in Old France, but "so many poor unfortunates who are healthy and who could work would they not be happier in that country than over here begging their living?"[79]

With liberty and equality there seemed to come a unity and brotherhood social critics did not find in metropolitan France. Abbeville commented:

> I am still astonished at the so great concord and unity which are found in all the families of these savage nations . . . . It is a good lesson to many Catholic families.[80]

Biard spoke of fraternity as a fact and living reality among the Canadian tribesmen and he regretted it would be impossible to assemble the French in like numbers without outbreaks of quarrelling, backbiting and reproaches.[81] The virtues of the primitive Amerindians were likened to those of primitive Christians because in the religion of nature, where God was the god of nature, goodness and creedlessness were equated. Lahontan's Adario has been called the best known *sauvage de bon sens,* yet the author had to defend himself against the charge that he praised the savages because he was one himself. He retorted that his enemies complimented him by giving him "the character of the honestest Man in the World." He urged his critics to read other travel books which would convince them, he believed, in stronger terms than he had used of aboriginal liberty and goodness.[82]

Was the myth of the noble savage invented and used to castigate wayward Europeans? The literature would seem to indicate that the myth came from a search for the earthly paradise, the ideal state. In finding simple, albeit rather crude virtues among the pagan Amerindians it was possible to draw unfavourable comparisons with Frenchmen who, enlightened by the teachings of Catholicism, should have surpassed the aborigines in virtue as well as in knowledge. Montaigne mused over the meaning of barbarity in tribes which "retain alive and vigorous their genuine, their most useful and natural, virtues and properties, which we have debased . . . in adapting them to gratify our corrupt taste. . . ."[83] Sagard, as a result of a winter spent with the Hurons, differentiated between licence and the spirit of liberty — a distinction which not all authors were able to make. The sexual laxity of the Hurons, for example, he could accept as part of their untutored and uncivilized barbarism; and their pressures to have him set aside his vow of chasity he rationalized with the comment "they could not understand our manner of Religious life."[84] But the liberties enjoyed by Huron youths when taken by French traders became licence, revolt against authority and rejection of the civilized code because these "renegade Frenchmen" experienced sinful joy and sometimes shame and repentance. Du Tertre held up the example of natural savages to more enlightened, but unfortunately less righteous, Europeans:

> They have good reasoning, and the mind as subtle as persons can have who have knowledge of letters, and who have never been sophisticated and polished by human knowledge, which very often in sophisticating our minds fills them for us with malice; and I can say in trut hthat if our Savages are more ignorant than we, they are much less vicious, indeed that they scarcely know malice except what our French teach them . . . . They are naturally benign, quiet, affable and very compassionate, to the point of tears, at the hurt of our French, being cruel only to their sworn enemies.[85]

The Jesuits also seem to have fostered the image of the noble child of nature for reasons other than Molinist views, or a too facile moral outlook which stressed God's grace in human nature. For the success and progress of their missions they had to oppose the ruthless exploitation of the natives by traders and traffickers, and at the same time they had to present the readers of their *Relations* with optimistic reports of their evangelical labours and to rationalize the conversion of natives who were obviously not being assimilated. In these circumstances, it has been suggested, the missionaries used the myth of the noble savage as a scourge for the civilized, as a "rhetorical figure with which to reproach the wayward European."[86]

On the other hand, there is much to commend the acceptance of these initial comments at face value for they were frequent and almost unanimous. The greatest of all myths, indeed, may be the interpretation that the favourable reports of aboriginal life and society were an idealization and a form of utopianism.[87] There is much to recommend an acceptance of the records for what they purported to be — *bona fide* evaluations and comparisons.

Concomitant with the appraisal of aboriginal nature was the attempt, by Jean Bodin in particular, to clarify the relationship between history and contemporary life and the geographical environment. Bodin parted company with the strictly institutional historians at this juncture:

> Since that is so, let us seek characteristics drawn, not from the institutions of men, but from nature, which are stable and are never changed unless by great force or long training, and even if they have been altered, nevertheless eventually they return to their pristine character. About this body of knowledge the ancients could write nothing, since they were ignorant of regions and places which not so long ago were opened up; instead, each man advanced as far as he could by inference of probabilities.[88]

Environmental theories raised the familiar mediaeval question about the degree to which people could be held responsible for their good or evil qualities. Bodin, for his part, sought to avoid any extreme interpretations and suggested a relative and contextual evaluation of each particular case:

> Since these vices are, as it were, innate in each race, history must be judged according to th ecustoms and nature of each people before we can make unfavourable comments.[89]

An outgrowth of the concept of the noble savage was the convictions expressed by a number of writers that mothers ought to nurse their children as did the Amerindian women. Lescarbot lauded the aboriginal women for recognizing the functional rather than merely the attractive qualities of their breasts, and deplored the French custom of employing "vicious nursemaids" from whom the infants "sucked in with their milk corruption and bad nature."[90] Native women showed love for their offspring, calling French mothers callous "porcupines" for parting so readily with their children. Abbeville reported:

> They take care not to do like many mothers here, who scarcely can await the birth of their children to put them out to nursemaids . . . . The Savage women would not want to imitate them in that for anything in the world, desiring their children to be nourished with their own milk.[91]

Fifty years later, Biet repreated the observation that "they do not know what it is among them, to give their children out to be nursed by another."[92] It is interesting that nature and nurture were so closely related in these early writers' conceptualization.

The absence of differentiation on the basis of race or pigmentation tended to blur the differences among the Amerindian cultures. Nevertheless, on the basis of differences in language and sometimes in observable beliefs and customs, the French had some awareness of the great cultural diversity of the Amerindians. The term "nation" was commonly employed to designate identifiable groups. Thomas Le Febvre, basing his ideas on information gleaned from sea captains who knew the New World well, included in a treatise on French trade the following description:

> These people number as many as forty nations speaking diverse languages, living under different laws and diverse customs, most of them waging cruel warfare on one another, some being sedentary and settled in villages and others nomadic and wandering from one country to another like migratory birds. Some live in warmer climes than others, regions which are better populated and where there is more hope of conversion and settlement than elsewhere.[93]

Sagard, in his differentiation among tribal groups, thought the Micmacs were superior to the Hurons or Montagnais.

Although the travellers and missionaries noted many dissimilarities between aboriginal customs and their own customs they also noted cultural correspondences. In describing aspects of Huron and Montagnais life it was common procedure, growing out of unquestioned mental habit, to compare such practices with classical or contemporary, literary or actual, practices. The device was probably necessary to communicate to French minds, which had not had the benefit of eyewitness experience in Canada, in commonplace and readily understandable language. Consequently, Lescarbot could compare aboriginal clothing to that of the Greeks and Romans as a way of making his description understandable. Champlain, Lescarbot, Moquet, Du Tertre and Le Jeune set the pattern for French interpretation of the aborigines. The *Relation* of 1648 said:

> It seems as if innocence, banished from the majority of the Empires and Kingdoms of the World, had withdrawn into these great forests where these people dwell. Their nature has something, I know not what, of the goodness of the Terrestrial Paradise before sin had entered it. Their practices manifest none of the luxury, the ambition, the avarice, or the pleasures that corrupt our cities.[94]

The noble savage served as a symbol of perfectibility, although the order of achieving this became in this case the reverse of the idea of progress. The Amerindian represented a return to nature, to a primitive stage of existence from which the world had declined. The image of the good and simple peoples was firmly established by the mid-seventeenth century, enabling literary romanticism to develop a cult of nature, of unbridled emotions and passionate love of primitive and unsophisticated emotions and passionate love of primitive and unsophisticated men, of humanitarianism, and an anti-intellectual distrust of the educated and sophisticated with its concomitant admiration for uncouth peasants, innocent children and untutored aborigines.[95]

In summary, the opinions of the French were circumscribed by three factors: tradition, experience, and expectations. On first contact, the French saw virtues and good qualities in the Amerindians which suggested to them the Golden Age and the lost Paradise of their literary and philosophical tradition. What they saw was a living reality which was soon coloured by their assumptions and conventions. Tradition and expectations, while influencing their comments, were shaken by sustained contact which brought a realization of the divergence between their image of the New World and the reality of that world. Standard images and inherited concepts became less dominant. Writers began to stress the French experience in the New World, even to the point of criticizing accepted views and contemporary French customs.

1. Alessandro Bacchiani, "Giovanni da Verrazzano and His Discoveries in North America, 1524, According to the Unpublished Contemporaneous Cellère Codex of Rome, Italy," *Fifteenth Annual Report, 1910, of the American Scenic and Historic Preservation Society* (Albany: 1910), Appendix A, p. 192.
2. Henry Harrisse, *Découverte et Evolution cartographique de Terre-Neuve et des Pays circonvoisins* (Paris: 1900), pp. 162-3, citing Henri Estienne, ed., *Eusebii Caesariensis Episcopi Chronicon* (Paris: 1512), p. 172; R. G.

Thwaites, ed., *The Jesuit Relations and Allied Documents,* 73 vols. (Cleveland: 1896), Vol. III, p. 39.

3. Anthony Kerrigan, ed., *Andrés Gonzáles de Barcia: Chronological History of the Continent of Florida containing the Discoveries and Principal Events which came to Pass in this Vast Kingdom* (Gainsville: 1951), p. 20.

4. These events in the Cartier vogages are recorded in (Société littéraire et historique de Québec), *Voyages et Découverte au Canada, entre les années 1534 et 1542, par Jacques Quartier, le Sieur de Roberval, Jean Alphonse de Xanctoigne, &c.* (Québec: 1843), pp. 19, 52-53, 63-65, 70, 72. Paul Gaffarel, ed., *André Thevet: Les Singularitez de la France antarctique, autrement nommée Amérique* (Paris: 1878), p. 407 gives an account of Donnacona's interviews. Thevet's book is currently receiving more favourable judgement from historians.

5. Margaret T. Hodgen, *Early Anthropology in the Sixteenth and Seventeenth Centuries* (Philadelphia: 1964), p. 112; Carolyn T. Foreman, *Indians Abroad, 1493-1838* (Ottawa: 1943), passim.; P. Villey, *Les sources et les évolutions des Essais de Montaigne* (Paris: 1908), Vol. II, pp. 156, 510; Arthur A. Tilley, "Rabelais and Geographical Discovery," *Studies in the French Renaissance* (New York: 1968), p. 50. Some travel books were merely imaginary or plagiarized accounts; for example, Sieur de Cobes' *Lettre envoyée de la Nouvelle-France* was based largely on Champlain, while Jean Alphonse's *Cosmographie* was taken from a Spanish book of 1519 by Fernandez de Enciro. It is not an exaggeration to say that anthropology had its origins in the geographical explorations of the Renaissance. Cf. Michele Duchet, *Anthropologie et histoire au siècle des lumières* (Paris: 1971), pp. 25-47; Annemarie de Wall Malefijt, *Images of Man: A History of Anthropological Thought* (New York: 1974), pp. 36-58; Wilhelm E. Mühlmann, *Geschichte der Anthropologie* (Frankfurt-am-Main: 1968), pp. 34-38; John Howland Rowe, "The Renaissance Foundations of Anthropology," *American Anthropologist* 67 (1965), pp. 1-20.

6. Margaret M. McGowan, "Form and Themes in Henry II's Entry at Rouen," *Renaissance Drama,* New series, Vol. I (1968), pp. 199-251; Ferdinand Denis, *Une Fête brésilienne célébrée à Rouen en 1550* (Paris: 1850); Théodore Godefroy, *Le Cérémonial François* (Paris: 1619), t. I, p. 917. The role of Amerindians in festival presentations is studied at some length in James H. Hyde, "The Four Parts of the World in Old-Time Pageants and Ballets," *Apollo* 4 (1926), pp. 232-238; 5 (1927), pp. 19-27; Marcel Paquot, *Les Etrangers dans les divertissements de la Cour de Beaujoyeux à Molière* (Paris: 1933); and Roy Strong, *Splendor at Court* (Boston: 1973).

7. Louis Wapy, *Sacra atque hilaria Mussipontana* (Pont à Mousson: 1623), p. 21; C. Perrault, *Courses de Testes et de Bagues faittes par le Roy, 1662* (Paris: 1670); Claude-François Menestrier, *Des Ballets anciens et modernes selon les Règles du théâtre* (Paris: 1682), pp. 104-110; Emile Magne, *Les Fêtes en Europe au XVIIe siècle* (Paris: 1930), p. 36; Marie-Françoise Christout, *Le Ballet de Cour de Louis XIV, 1643-1672* (Paris: 1967), pp. 42-47, 197-204; Margaret M. McGowan, *L'Art du ballet de Cour en France, 1581-1643* (Paris: 1963), pp. 149-153, 292. The feather skirts and elaborate headdresses had become the identifying characteristics of Amerindians on stage. Menestrier, *op. cit.,* p. 252 said: "the Americans wear a feather bonnet of many colours, a sash of the same kind which covers their nakedness; they also have a collar of these same feathers of which also they carry a bouquet in each hand when dancing."

8. Pedro Leturia, "Major y Vitoria ante la conquista de América," *Estudios eclesiasticos* II (1932), pp. 44-82. Although the French avoided "forced acculturation" as a conscious political policy, the context of cultural interaction between French and Amerindians often imposed on the natives

35

changes which were unwanted or enigmatic. Cf. Edward P. Dozier, "Forced and Permissive Acculturation," *American Indian* VII (Spring, 1955), p. 38.

9. M. Menendez y Pelayo and M. Garcia-Pelayo, eds., *J. G. de Sepúlveda: Tratado sobre las justas causas de la guerra contra los Indios* (Mexico: 1941), pp. 101-105, 151. A useful study is Robert E. Quirk, "Some Notes on a Controversial Controversy: Juan Ginés de Sepúlveda and Natural Servitude," *Hispanic American Historical Review* XXXIV (1954), pp. 357-364.

10. Alfred Vanderpol, *Le droit de guerre d'après les théologiens et les canonistes du moyen-âge* (Paris: 1911), pp. 207-222; Alfred Vanderpol, *La doctrine scolastique de droit de guerre* (Paris: 1911), pp. 161-170. Raymond Lull's argument for "la possibilité de l'emploi de la force contre les infidèles — non pas pour les convertir, mais pour rendre possible la prédication" was resurrected: Ramon Sugranyes de French, *Raymond Lull: Docteur des Missions* (Fribourg: 1954), p. 80.

11. H. P. Biggar, ed., *A Collection of Documents relating to Jacques Cartier and the Sieur de Robreval* (Ottawa: 1930), Bonvallot to Charles V, December 27, 1540, p. 170. French rejection of Spanish claims in the sixteenth century is treated in C. de la Roncière, "Notre première tentative de colonisation au Canada," *Bibliothèque de l'Ecole de Chartes* LXXIII (1912), pp. 283-300, and in Henry Folmer, *Franco-Spanish Rivalry in North America, 1524-1763* (Glendale: 1953), pp. 1-30. The Spaniards did not base their territorial claim on the papal grant exclusively; they used it as a reinforcement of rights won by conquest and always invoked "and other just and legitimate titles."

12. Richard Morse, *Introduction to Contemporary Civilization in the West* (New York: 1954), Vol. I, pp. 489-511.

13. R. P. Canedo, "Différentes attitudes face à l'Indien," in M. Bellestra-Gaibros *et al.*, eds., *La Découverte de l'Amérique* (Paris: 1968), pp. 195-196. It would seem that Lewis Hanke, *Aristotle and the American Indians: A Study in Race Prejudice in the Modern World* (Chicago: 1959) invented a few Franciscans to substantiate his thesis of Dominican-Franciscan rivalry.

14. Pierre Chaunu, "La légende noire antihispanique," *Revue de Psychologie des Peuples* (Université de Caen) (1964), pp. 188-223.

15. Ronald H. Frame, ed., *The Complete Works of Montaigne. Essays, Travel Journal, Letters* (Stanford: 1957), Book III, p. 693.

16. Jean de Léry, *Histoire d'un Voyage fait en la Terre du Brésil, autrement dite Amérique* (La Rochelle: 1578), p. 127. Passages cited throughout have been translated.

17. Lewis Hanke, "The Contribution of Bishop Juan de Zumarraga to Mexican Culture," *The Americas* V (1949), pp. 275-284; Gonzalo Fernandes de Oviedo, *L'Histoire naturelle et généralle des Indes* (Paris: 1555), p. 20; Lopez de Gomara, *Histoire généralle des Indes Occidentales* (Paris: 1568), pp. 163, 236, 442, 438.

18. Lewis Hanke, "Pope Paul III and the American Indians," *Harvard Theological Review* XXX (April, 1931), pp. 65-102.

19. Beatrice Reynolds, ed., *Jean Bodin: Method for the Easy Comprehension of History* (New York: 1945), p. 335.

20. Joseph François Lafitau, *Moeurs des Sauvages Ameriquains, comparées aux Moeurs des Premiers Temps*, 2 vols., (Paris: 1724), Vol. I, pp. 27-29.

21. Eméric de Crucé, *Nouveau Cynée* (Paris: 1623), t. vi, pp. 5-6; Amerindians were identified with the hairy wild men of mediaeval illustrative art in François Desperpz, *Recueil de la diversité des habits, qui sont de présent en usage, tant es pays d'Europe, Asie, Affrique, & Isles Sauvages, le tout fait après le naturel* (Paris: 1564). The standard references on the wild man in European art and literature are Edward Dudley and

Maximillian E. Novak, eds., *The Wild Man Within: An Image in Western Thought from the Renaissance to Romanticism* (Pittsburgh: 1974), and Richard Bernheim, *Wild Men in the Middle Ages* (Cambridge, Mass.: 1952).

22. Thwaites, *op. cit.,* Vol. LXI, pp. 209-211.
23. Lee Eldridge Huddleston, *Origins of the American Indians. European Concepts, 1492-1729* (Austin: 1967), pp. 48-76 sets forth the Acostan and Garcian traditions which dominated northern Europe and Spain respectively. The best treatment of the concept of the great chain of being is Arthur O. Lovejoy, *The Great Chain of Being, A Study of the History of an Idea* (Cambridge: 1950).
24. W. L. Grant, ed., *Marc Lescarbot: The History of New France* (Toronto: 1907), Vol. I, pp. 48-49.
25. *Ibid.,* Vol. I, pp. 43-44.
26. *Ibid.,* Vol. I, p. 49.
27. Joannes de Laet, *L'Histoire du Nouveau Monde ou Description des Indes Occidentales* (Leyden: 1640) is the French edition.
28. Edmund Goldsmid, ed., *Hugo Grotius. On the Origin of the Native Races of America. A Dissertation* (Edinburgh: 1884), pp. 10-19.
29. Huddleston, *op. cit.,* pp. 118-128.
30. Huddleston, *op. cit.,* p. 34. There has been a tendency to attribute a Jewish origin theory to most pre-1600 writers but this is not borne out by a close examination of the sources. Cf. Robert Wauchope, *Lost Tribes and Sunken Continents. Myth and Method in the Study of American Indians* (Chicago: 1962), pp. 3-53 tends to overdo the theory; also Don Cameron Allen, *The Legend of Noah* (Urbana: 1949), pp. 125-128.
31. Milton Quaife, ed., *The Western Country in the 17th Century. The Memoirs of Antoine Lamothe Cadillac and Pierre Liette* (New York: 1962), p. 53.
32. Louis Hennepin, *A New Discovery of a Vast Country in America* (London: 1968), Vol. II, p. 58.
33. The first English edition was *Man before Adam* (London: 1656). David R. McKee, "Isaac de la Payrère, a Precursor of Eighteenth Century Critical Deists," *Publications of the Modern Languages Association* LIX (1944), pp. 456-485. For the course of the controversy in Europe see Allen, *op. cit.,* pp. 133-137.
34. Daniel G. Brinton, *The Myths of the New World. A Treatise on the Symbolism and Mythology of the Red Race of America* (New York: 1876), pp. 21-22.
35. Joseph-François Lafitau, *Moeurs des Sauvages amériquains* (Paris: 1724) was written from this premise. Cf. Kenneth E. Bock, "The Comparative Method of Anthropology," *Comparative Studies in Society and History* VIII, No. 3 (April, 1966), pp. 269-280.
36. J. H. Elliott, *The Old World and the New, 1492-1650* (Cambridge: 1970), pp. 50-51, citing *Les Oeuvres d'Estienne Pasquier* (Amsterdam: 1723), Vol. II, Bk. iii, letter iii, p. 55.
37. Reynolds, *op. cit.,* p. 301.
38. Leslie A. White, "Diffusion vs. Evolution: An Anti-Evolutionist Fallacy," *American Anthropology* 47 (1945), pp. 339-356.
39. This is the thesis of Roy Harvey Pearce, *The Savages of America. A Study of the Indian and the Idea of Civilization* (Baltimore: 1953).
40. Winthrop Jordan, *White over Black: American Attitudes toward the Negro, 1550-1812* (Baltimore: 1969), p. 253. Alden T. Vaughan, *New England Frontier: Puritans and Indians, 1620-1675* (Boston: 1965), pp. 62-3, while critical of attributing cultural conflicts to racial or colour factors, deserves the criticism of Francis Jennings, "Virgin Land and Savage People," *American Quarterly* 23, No. 4 (October, 1971), pp. 540-541, for an insufficiently critical portrayal of settler-native relations.

41. "Voyage du Sieur de Roberval au Canada, 1542," *Voyages et Découverte au Canada* (Québec: 1843), p. 94.
42. Henry Harrisse, *Découverte et Evolution cartographique de Terre-Neuve et des Pays circonvoisins* (Paris: 1900), p. 162.
43. Bacchiani, *op. cit.*, Appendix A, pp. 180, 186.
44. Thwaites, *op. cit.*, Vol. XXXVIII, p. 257. The hairy black man of mediaeval art was the uncivilized wild sub-human creature who inhabited the outer limits of the known world.
45. Harry Hoetink, *The Two Variants in Caribbean Race Relations* (New York: 1967), pp. 120-159. I am grateful to Professor Donald G. Baker of Southampton College for first drawing this to my attention.
46. Pierre van den Berghe, *Race and Racism* (New York: 1967), pp. 9-11; also Donald G. Baker, "Color, Culture and Power: Indian-White Relations in Canada and America," *The Canadian Review of American Studies* III, No. 1 (Spring, 1972), pp. 4-5.
47. Thwaites, *op. cit.*, Vol. LXIII, p. 221.
48. Pierre d'Avity, *Description générale de l'Amérique, troisième partie du Monde* (Paris: 1637), p. 30.
49. Gabriel Sagard-Théodat, *Le Grand Voyage au Pays des Hurons* (Paris: 1632), pp. 176-177.
50. Thwaites, *op. cit.*, Vol. XXVII, p. 215.
51. Georges M. Wrong, ed., *The Long Journey to the Country of the Hurons by Father Gabriel Sagard* (Toronto: 1939), p. 137.
52. R. G. Thwaites, ed., *New Voyages to North America by Baron de Lahontan* (Chicago: 1905), Vol. II, p. 471.
53. Sieur de Cobes, *Coppie d'une Lettre Envoyée de la Nouvelle-France ou Canada, par le Sieur de Cobes, Gentilhomme Poictevin a un sien amy* (Lyon: 1609), p. 13.
54. d'Avity, *op. cit.*, pp. 30-31.
55. Thwaites, *op. cit.*, Vol. VI, p. 165.
56. Hennepin, *op. cit.*, Vol. II, p. 65.
57. Thwaites, *op. cit.*, Vol. II, p. 155; V, pp. 55, 189; VIII, p. 27; XIV, pp. 95-97; XVI, p. 217; XVIII, pp. 141, 151.
58. abbé de Belmont, "Histoire de l'eau-de-vie en Canada," *Collection de Mémoires et de Relations sur l'Histoire ancienne du Canada* (Québec: 1840), pp. 2-3.
59. Dom Guy Oury, *Marie de l'Incarnation, Ursuline (1599-1672), Correspondance* (Solesmes: 1971), letter from Marie de l'Incarnation to Mother Ursule de Ste. Catherine, September 13, 1640, p. 119. The translation follows closely that given in Joyce Marshall, ed., *Word from New France. The selected Letters of Marie de l'Incarnation* (Toronto: 1967), p. 84.
60. Oury, *op. cit.*, XII, Marie de l'Incarnation to S. Bernard, Feuillant, April, 1635, p. 27.
61. *Ibid.*, XXXVIII, Marie de l'Incarnation to her brother, April 15, 1639, p. 81.
62. Thomas LeFevre, *Discours sommaire de la Navigation et du Commerce* (Rouen: 1650), p. 210.
63. Donald H. Frame, ed., *Montaigne's Essays and Selected Writings* (New York: 1963), p. 93.
64. Loys Le Roy, *De la vicissitude ou variété des choses en l'univers* (Paris: 1575), p. 118.
65. Pierre d'Avity, *Les Etats, empires et principautez du Monde* (Paris: 1614), cited from the English translation of Edward Grimstone, *The Estates, Empires & Principalities of the World* (London: 1615), pp. 252, 266-67.
66. Samuel de Champlain, *Voyage et Descouvertes faites en la Nouvelle*

France depuis l'année 1615 jusques à la fin de l'année 1618 (Paris: 1620), p. 1.

67. Oliver la Farge, "Myths that Hide the American Indian," in Abraham S. Eisenstadt, ed., *American History: Recent Interpretations* (New York: 1969), pp. 17-32. Other works dealing with the subject are H. N. Fairchild, *The Noble Savage, A Study in Romantic Naturalism* (New York: 1928); René Gonnard, *La légende du bon sauvage* (Paris: 1946); Guiseppe Cocchiara, *Il mito del buon selvaggio. Introduzione alla storia della teorie ethnologice* (Messina: 1948); Henry B. Jones, *The Death Song of the "Noble Savage": A Study in the Idealization of the American Indian* (Chicago: 1924); Mircea Eliade, "El mito del buen salvaje o los prestigios del origen," *La Torre*, (Universidad de Puerto Rico) III, No. 11 (1955), pp. 49-66; Althea E. Currie, "The American Indian as portrayed by Montaigne, Voltaire and Chateaubriand," Master's Thesis, University of Illinois, 1930.

68. Henri Baudet, *Paradise on Earth. Some Thoughts on European Images of Non-European Man* (New Haven: 1965), pp. 10-12, 36.

69. Frame, *op. cit.*, p. 89.

70. *Ibid.*, pp. 91-93.

71. Jean-Baptiste Du Terte, *Histoire générale des Antilles habitées par les François* (Paris: 1667), Vol. II, p. 357.

72. Lescarbot, *op. cit.*, pp. 32-33.

73. J. de Clodoré, *Relation de ce qui s'est passé dans les Isles et Terre Ferme de l'Amérique, pendant la dernière Guerre avec l'Angleterre* (Paris: 1671), Vol. I, p. 235.

74. Claude d'Abbeville, *Histoire de la Mission des Pères Capucins en l'Isle de Maragnan et terres circonvoisines* (Paris: 1614), p. 328.

75. Gabriel Sagard, *Le Grand Voyage du Pays des Hurons* (Paris: 1632), p. 343.

76. Paul Boyer, *Véritable Relation de tout ce qui s'est fait et passé au voyage que Monsieur de Bretigny fit à l'Amérique Occidentale* (Paris: 1654), p. 227.

77. Frame, *op. cit.*, p. 117. The account is given in much more detail in an unlikely source: Michel Baudier, *Histoire de la Religion des Turcs* (Paris: 1625), p. 122.

78. Marc Lescarbot, *La Conversion des Sauvages qui ont esté baptisez en la Nouvelle France, cette année 1610* (Paris: 1610), pp. 33-34.

79. Nicolas Denys, *Description géographique et historique des costes de l'Amérique septentrionale* (Paris: 1672), Vol. II, p. 26.

80. Abbeville, *op. cit.*, p. 280.

81. Pierre Biard, *Relation de la Nouvelle France, de ses Terres, Naturel du Pais, et de ses Habitans* (Lyon: 1616), p. 57.

82. Louis Armand de Lom d'Arce, baron de Lahontan, *Journal of a Voyage to North America Undertaken by Order of the French King, containing the Geographical Description and Natural History of that Country, particularly Canada* (London: 1761), Vol. I, p. 8.

83. Frame, *op. cit.*, p. 89.

84. Sagard, *op. cit.*, p. 165.

85. Du Tertre, *op. cit.*, pp. 358-359.

86. Jack Warwick, *The Long Journey. Literary Themes of French Canada* (Toronto: 1968), pp. 104-105.

87. Wilcomb E. Washburn, "Relations between Europeans and Amerindians during the Seventeenth and Eighteenth Centuries: The Epistemological Problem," Unpublished paper read at the International Colloquium on Colonial History, University of Ottawa, November, 1969, p. 4.

88. Reynolds, *op. cit.*, p. 85.

89. *Ibid.*, p. 128; Cf. Marian J. Tooley, "Bodin and the Mediaeval Theory of Climate," *Speculum* XXVIII (1953), pp. 64-83.

90. Marc Lescarbot, *Histoire de la Nouvelle France* (Paris: 1609), p. 667.
91. Abbeville, *op. cit.,* p. 281.
92. Antoine Biet, *Voyage de la France Equinoxiale en l'Isle de Cayenne* (Paris: 1664), p. 399.
93. Thomas LeFebvre, *Discours sommaire de la Navigation et du Commerce* (Rouen: 1650), p. 208. Translation is that given in J. M. Bumsted, ed., *Documentary Problems in Canadian History* (Georgetown: 1969), Vol. I, p. 10.
94. Thwaites, *op. cit.,* Vol. XXXII, p. 283.
95. "Certain characteristics of the noble savage cult bear a close relationship to romantic naturalism: the belief in the beneficent influence of nature upon the sensitive soul; the belief, perennially popular, in simple, passionate, and unconventional love, unsanctioned by civilised institutions; the belief in the religion of nature; and the belief in the superiority of primitive poetry." Edna L. Steeves, "Negritude and the Noble Savage," *Journal of Modern African Studies* II, No. 1 (1937), p. 100.

CHAPTER II

EFFORTS AT EVANGELIZATION

Among devout religious activists the conviction persisted that the discovery of the New World was not an accident nor without previous design.[1] There was an eternal and immutable purpose not only in the discovery of the Amerindians but also in their eventual incorporation into the known Christian world. Therefore, eveything that could be learned about these native peoples and their continent had its place in the universal scheme.

The most abundant information about the New World and its peoples came to France through the annual *Relations* of the Society of Jesus. The Jesuit missionaries tended to collect information which it was assumed might arouse interest in their evangelical labours in North America. Two important points should, however, be remembered: firstly, the factual relations the Jesuits saw and described were not miscellaneous assortments of strange practices, but were organized categories of rites and beliefs associated with religion, marriage customs, family life, disposition of the dead, customs of political organization, and customs of dress, shelter and diet; secondly, the discovery of Canada had aroused more curiosity about the New World and its peoples than real interest and therefore propaganda was necessary to arouse concern and organize support in France for the missions.[2] The information which was provided, besides achieving in a limited way its stated objective, became a valuable source of information for men of letters.[3]

The early missionaries and travellers often seem to have assumed that Amerindian hearts were filled with innocence and predisposed to goodness, and that Amerindian minds were *tabulas rasas* on which the Catholic religion could easily be inscribed. Experiences in the New World, sometimes bitter and cruel, showed that conversion was, to a large extent, dependent on understanding native life and modes of thought in order to root out traditional beliefs and use certain of their superstitions and preconceptions to the advantage of the new religion. There was an overriding determination to extirpate abominable and idolatrous practices, but to do this a knowledge of native society would help in changing native beliefs into an acceptance of Catholicism.

The idea that the Amerindians had no religion, and therefore could not be opposed to Catholicism but were merely ignorant of it, was widespread in the sixteenth century and persisted for some decades into the seventeenth century. Jacques Cartier in letters to Francis I had called for missionary activity to win "savage peoples living without a knowledge of God and the use of reason" to the Catholic church.[4] Thévet considered that the natural primitiveness of these aborigines augured well for missionary activity:

> America is inhabited by marvellously strange and savage people without faith, without laws, without religion, without any civilities, but living like unreasoning beasts as nature has produced them, eating roots, men as well as women remaining ever naked, until perhaps such time as they will be frequented by Christians, from whom they will little by little learn to put off this brutishness to put on more civil and humane ways.[5]

Champlain described tribes unfriendly to him as "brute beasts having neither faith nor law, living without God and religion."[6] Biet premised a number of defects in aboriginal society upon their ignorance of the Divinity:

> As they have no religion, they have whatsoever no political law, observing nevertheless some ways of living which they have received from father to son, and keep these inviolably; hence it comes they live in great liberty.[7]

Abbeville said they had "neither faith nor any shadow of religion"; Le Jeune said they had "no ordinance concerning the service of the superior being, each doing as he himself sees fit."[8] The missionaries must have been aware, at times, that their reports contained implications about the aboriginal lack of knowledge of God and, on the other hand, the merits they saw in aboriginal society. How could one be enthusiastic about the life and behaviour of savages who were ignorant of the faith? Happiness and the good life were seemingly not conditions of true religion. Aware of this contradiction, writers soon added to their descriptions of the felicity of primitive men the redeeming phrase "I leave aside their lack of religion." So the belief was firmly established that the Amerindians on religious grounds deserved good treatment because in the absence of an elaborated native religion they could not be accused of being devil-worshippers, idolaters, or heretics.

The Jesuits added much to French knowledge of Amerindian religions. Charles Lalemant said in 1627 that although the tribesmen had neither divine worship nor formal prayers they did believe in a divine creator, in an immortal soul, and in a hereafter.[9] In 1632, Paul Le Jeune affirmed the earlier belief that "the Canadians are attached to no worship whatever of any Divinity";[10] nevertheless, the following year he corrected himself by adding that he had been mistaken in this earlier report and had now discovered that they did have a concept of a divinity. In 1650 Thomas Le Febvre published a treatise on trade and navigation in which he summarized this information for French readers in terms which they could understand:

> Several of these people of Canada already believe that there is a God the Father, a Mother, an immortal soul, a son and Sun which is the author and preserver of all things, that the Father is above all, that since he has had to be stern with mankind the mother devours them but the son is good to them, preserves them and gives them life.[11]

Algonkian religion stressed man's harmony with nature. Living and non-living components, superhuman and supernatural forces, animals, birds, plants, and physical features of the environment all formed a balanced whole. Even hunting was governed by spiritual rules and considerations, which the French regarded at first as meaningless taboos. The Amerindians believed the animal allowed itself to be taken for food and clothing if it were hunted in a manner appropriate to its fate. Religion was concerned with the material welfare of all members of the tribe. Yet it stressed spiritual individuality because each man had to live in harmony with superhuman forces and beings, with animals who could talk to him, with mystical and medicinal herbs, and even with inanimate objects which possessed spirits. On the other hand, the French Catholics stressed collective spirituality. Their ethic emphasized such qualities as humility before God and dependence upon Him for supernatural grace, other-worldly orientations with a passive resignation to poverty and misery as states that could bring special blessings, and complete subservience to a universal church and its clergy which claimed a monopoly on supernatural power and grace.

Nicolas Perrot affirmed that the tribes of the western interior, like the coastal tribes and Iroquoian groups, believed in the immortality of the soul, in eternal reward or an eternal country of departed souls, in a divine creation and in the efficacy of prayers. He added:

> The savages — I mean those who are not converted — recognize as principal divinities only the Great Hare, the Sun, and the

devils. They most often invoke the Great Hare, because they revere and adore him as the creator of the world; they reverence the Sun as the author of light; but if they place the devils among their divinities, and invoke them, it is because they are afraid of them, and in the invocations which they make to the devils they entreat them for life. Those among the savages whom the French call "jugglers" talk with the demon, whom they consult for success in war and hunting.[12]

The French missionaries' and explorers' progressive realization of the high development of Amerindian religions is shown by such statements. From a belief in the total absence of any religion to an awareness of animism, French consciousness moved to an acknowledgment of polytheism.

When an appreciable pagan resistance to Catholic missionary efforts made itself felt, the missionaries concluded that the Amerindian resistors worshipped the devil. As early as 1611 the natives of Acadia were branded as "servants of Satan." The *Relation* of that year said:

> Of the one supreme God they have a certain slender notion, but they are so perverted by false ideas and by customs, that, as I have said, they really worship the Devil.[13]

Jérome Lalemant called the Hurons "Slaves of the Devil." Other missionaries concluded that these native religions resembled some of the old pagan religions of Europe and of classical times. Allouez reported that the beliefs of the Ottawas resembled "in many respects the beliefs of some of the ancient Pagans."[14]

On the other hand, there were practices and beliefs that were reminiscent of Christianity or Judaism. The deluge tradition among the aborigines was frequently reported.[15] Le Jeune's *Relation* of 1636 drew a detailed parallel between the Huron myth of Tawiscaron and Isouskeha and the Biblical account of Cain and Abel.[16] Given the willingness to accept pre-Columbian contacts and the possibility of an earlier introduction to the worship of the One True God, there was no hesitation in identifying aboriginal practices with Catholic belief and practice. The best-known example of such a cultural association was Chrestien Le Clercq's enthusiasm about the cult of the cross among the natives of Gaspesia. Whether their reverence for the cross had Christian origins, dating perhaps from the Vikings, or Celtic expeditions, or the fishing fleets, or was a case of independent cultural development he did not resolve conclusively. It must be remembered also that the swastika was known to Amerindians although there has been no direct link established between the recent use of that symbol in Finland and Germany and its American origins. Le Clercq was more interested in the possibility that the cult of the cross could facilitate the conversion of these Micmacs to Catholicism:

> The use of the Cross, and the honour which our Gaspesians rendered to this sacred sign of our salvation, gave me the very subject for explaining to them the holy mysteries of which in the darkness of their errors and blindness they were ignorant. Thus I had them conceive that this Cross, which they shared with others through the singular favour of Heaven, should bring them to the worship of the One who had taken it to himself because of his love for us . . . . I leave to the Reader the freedom to judge as he pleases the origin of the cult of the Cross among this Pagan Nation . . . .Here, in any case, in abridged form, are some of the main reasons which oblige me to belivee that the Cross had been venerated among these Barbarians before the first arrival of the French in this country . . .[17]

Le Clercq repeated that the Micmac chieftain insisted they "did not receive from strangers the use of the Cross" but that it had been transmitted "from the tradition of his forefathers."

There were also indications of Jewish survivals in Amerindian religion. Cadillac singled out the Jewish and Amerindian practices of honouring the dead, of periodic feasts and festivals, of formal intercessions, of attention to dreams, and of parallel beliefs in creation and the deluge. He wrote:

> The Jews prayed to God to take the souls of their relatives to Eden, that is, to the garden or paradise of delight. The Indians pray to the Sun to guide and light the spirits of their tribe during their journey until they reach the happy dwelling-place of their ancestors . . . . So I believe, from the observations I have just set forth that many people will be convinced that they are descended from the Jewish race, since their manners, customs, and ceremonies resemble those of the Jews more closely than any other nation.[18]

Cadillac found parallels in the Illinois religion to the Essenes' belief in eternal bliss and the Sadducees' rejection of eternal punishment and the concept of a resurrection. Nicolas Perrot held very similar views about Judaistic survivals in native religion:

> It cannot be said that the savages profess any doctrine; and it is certain that they do not, so to speak, follow any religion. They only observe some Jewish customs, for they have certain feasts at which they make no use of a knife for cutting their cooked

meat, which they devour with their teeth. The women have also a custom, when they bring their children into the world, of spending a month without entering the husband's cabin; and during all that time they cannot even eat there with the men, or eat food which has been prepared by men's hands.[19]

The Jesuit missionaries, for their part, saw numerous Amerindian customs reminiscent of Jewish customs, without in all cases attributing these to a necessary lineal descent.[20] Some of their comparisons were purely literary, as for example the observation that the French in America "would have become savages worse than the Savages themselves" had Divine Providence not given them the Iroquois "to be their Canaanites."[21]

Whether the natives were viewed as having no religion, or a religion which contained Judeo-Christian survivals, the prospects of conversion seemed excellent. Cartier had remarked on the good disposition of the aboriginal peoples. Cobes visited Canada in 1605 and concluded that the natives were amenable to evangelization:

> Apart from that, in their manner of living they are very brutish, but they are beginning to become civilized and to take on our manners and our ways. They are easily instructed in the Christian religion and are not too opinionated in their Paganism, to the extent that if Preachers went down to them I believe that in a short time the whole country would give in to the Christian faith without being otherwise constrained, and that by this means the way would be opened in the whole of the remainder of America for the conquest of souls, which is greater than all the lands one could ever conquer.[22]

The Récollet missionaries who were the first to go into the Huron country were favourably impressed and believed a great missionary work could be accomplished. Sagard was greatly impressed by the "festival of the dead" which was held every ten years and remarked that "their zeal is more intense than ours, and that they have more love for one another, both in life and after death, than we who call ourselves better." He found a profound spiritual meaning to their festival:

> Now by means of these ceremonies and gatherings they contract new friendships and unions amongst themselves, saying that, just as the bones of their deceased relatives and friends are gathered together and united in one place, so also they themselves ought during their lives to live all together in the same unity and harmony, like good kinsmen and friends, without the possibility of ever being separated or drawn apart on account of any ill deed or misfortune; and so in fact they do live.[23]

Such a sense of spiritual union and manifestation of spiritual sensitivity augured well, he believed, for the Récollets.

It was only natural for the early missionaries to be optimistic about the rapid conversion of the natives, for if they were not they would be undermining the very *raison d'être* for their presence in the New World. Biard emphasized catechetical drill and rote mimicry of ritual by the children as a good way to begin converting savage minds:

> It comforts us to see these little savages, though not yet Christians, yet willing, when they are here, to carry the candles, bells, holy water, and other things in processions, and the funerals which occur here. Thus they become accustomed to act as Christians, and will become so in His time.[24]

The Récollets founded what they called a "seminary" near Quebec. Although it offered no theological training, they raised and tried to educate native children who, Champlain said, were "offered daliy by their parents to be instructed and brought up in the Christian language."[25] As early as 1635, Marie de l'Incarnation expressed her willingness and desire to suffer for these peoples "provided he (God) convert these poor people, and that they come to know him; for it is certain that were they to know him they would immediately be engulfed in his love."[26] The arrival of a Jesuit *Relation* indicating that the Hurons had "held a council, at which it was permitted to whosoever will to become Christian" increased the enthusiasm of the evangelical labourers. Marie de l'Incarnation wrote one of her brothers that her ambition was on the verge of fulfillment when she arrived safely at Quebec:

> What we saw upon arriving in this new world made us forget all our labours: for to hear the divine Majesty praised in four different tongues, to see baptized a great number of Savages, to hear the Savages themselves preach the law of Jesus-Christ to their compatriots, and teach them to bless and to love our God, to see them offer thanks to heaven for having sent us into their barbarous country to instruct their daughters, and teach them the way of heaven. . . .[27]

This enthusiasm was encouraged by the Jesuit report that almost two hundred and fifty converts had been won among the Hurons, and an equal number among the Montagnais that year.[28] By 1640, Marie de l'Incarnation admitted there was organized resistance to the Jesuit missionary efforts in Huronia, but she remained convinced that "the Devil works in vain, Jesus Christ will always be Master: may he be praised eternally."[29] The Ursuline mystic hoped to be able to build a convent closer to the native encampments in order to be able to receive more girls to educate and be more directly involved in the evangelical labours than was possible at their crowded monastery in the upper town of Quebec. Even when epidemics carried off hundreds of Amerindians, when opposition to the priests increased among the Huron tribes, and when it became evident that most of the converts were moribund, she retained her optimism, writing in 1641 about "the goodwill among all the neighbouring nations, all of which want to embrace our holy faith."[30] Zealous optimism was obviously as necessary as perseverance and patience.

This optimism was closely related to prevalent sixteenth and seventeenth-century apocalyptical views. Catholic eschatological undercurrents associated the discovery of the New World with the imminent end of the world.[31] The prophetic system elaborated by Joachim of Fiore had persisted up to the European discoveries of the Americas and subsequent European missionary activities.[32] These themes of the New World and the end of the world, at once revivalist and apocalyptical, were blended harmoniously in the great task of evangelizing the unconverted millions who knew nothing of the faith, founding a new church with the purity of the Apostolic church, and so hastening the Parousia.

The missionary work owed its impetus in good measure to a wave of religious revivalism and mysticism that swept France at the beginning of the seventeenth century. In 1627, Henri de Lévis, Duc de Ventadour who was the Viceroy of Canada, experienced a spiritual crisis which resulted in his proposing an association of the devout Catholic élite of France to promote the ideas of the Catholic Reformation, to combat "the evils of the age," and to sustain the new religious orders, renewed charity, foreign missions and devotional cults. In 1630 the Company of the Holy Sacrament was secretly organized, including in its membership many pious noblemen and wealthy bourgeois; by 1659 the secret society had cells throughout France and it called a congress to consolidate and co-ordinate its activities. The Company of the Holy Sacrament had a number of direct ties with Canada, notably through the Société de Notre-Dame de Montréal, the Jesuit missions, the Ursulines, and the Vicar Apostolic and his secular clergy at Quebec.[33] Mother Marie de l'Incarnation was typical of those who felt a mystical call to serve in Canada. Four years before coming to Quebec she wrote to a spiritual advisor:

> It happened that since my Religious profession, he held my spirit in a sweet contemplation of the ravishing beauties of his Law, and especially the connexion between the old Law and the

evangelical Law. In this vision my memory was continually filled with passages of holy Scripture . . . . Now this put into my soul an extreme desire for the Apostolic life, and without regard to my stupidity, it seemed to me that what God was pouring into my heart was able to convert all who do not know him . . . . I had not heard speak of the [Canadian] Mission, yet my spirit was in its desires in those strange lands. It is more than ten years now, as I told you in my last letter, that I envisage and wish for this great thing . . . .[34]

In another letter she told of a vision she had had in 1633 beckoning her to missionary labours in a foreign land, which she later recognized to be New France.[35]

This was not an isolated case. Mme de la Peltrie's desire to found a monastery in Canada for the education of Amerindian girls was told in no less mystical terms. However, the account of how she eventually surmounted the difficulties and opposition in France clearly indicates that members of the secret Company of the Holy Sacrament had successfully intervened. The life of Mother Marie de Saint-Joseph could be cited as another example of extraordinary piety and mysticism.[36]

The presence of devout women in the disorganized colony, which was still little more than a commercial counter and a missionary outpost in the 1640s, prompted the secretary of the Company of New France (Hundred Associates) to recall the special mission entrusted to the Hospital Nuns by the Holy Ghost:

To pass to New France to make the savages Christian or to remove them from barbarian habit to a proper and civil life are designs really filled with zeal and charity, but to go to reduce their infirmities, to participate in their ills and to sacrifice each day one's life in a calling which has for its object horror and infection, wounds and ulcers, those are things which surpass the natural and which would not be found in your holy persons if God did not inspire grace and grant you very special strength.[37]

These sentiments were entirely in keeping with Le Jeune's decription of the special qualities required in the Canadian missions.

The conversion of the Amerindians was associated with the foundation of the New Israel, the establishment of the millenial kingdom, and the ushering in of the "Third Age of the Holy Ghost."[38] The New World would become the site of the truly spiritual church sought by the mystics, where the primitive purity of Christianity as opposed to the corrupted church of European civilization and papal degeneracy could be preserved. Le Jeune wrote in 1635:

> . . . . but it is also true that it seems as if God shed the dew of his grace much more abundantly upon this New France than upon the old, and that the internal consolations and the Divine infusions are much stronger here, and hearts more on fire. The Lord knoweth who are his.[39]

Marie de l'Incarnation described the faithful native converts in 1640 as "in the fervour of the first Christians of the Church." They were "submissive as children to those who instruct them" and one could not find "souls purer or more zealous in observing God's law."[40] To another correspondent she wrote: "Add to this spirit of simplicity that of fervour, for we see in our primitive Church, the zeal and ardour of the primitive Church converted by the Apostles."[41] The following year she wrote about "our new church" having "devout Savages."

These were expressions of French self-dissatisfaction and a longing for a return to what was portrayed as the primitive purity of the Apostolic Age. The first reports of America depicted a New World of innocence, simplicity, fertility and abundance. Here was a happy convergence of two streams of thought; the religious and humanist visions of a better world were invoked. The *dévots* despaired of the corruption in France, the Court, and even in some of the religious foundations, and grasped what seemed to be the opportunity for re-establishing the primitive church of the apostles in the New World as yet uncorrupted by European vices.

The Huron church had been conceived by the Récollets as the nucleus of an exemplary indigenous church. The Jesuits found it easy to adopt similar objectives for the Huron mission when they succeeded and replaced the Récollets. Although they were regarded as "rigourists" in comparison to the other orders in Canada, paradoxically they led the movement for accommodation and adaptation in contacts with non-Christian peoples.[42] The Franciscans in South America had at first attempted to destroy the pagan religions, to ignore indigenous culture, and to avoid learning the native languages. The Jesuits, on the other hand, relearned the missionary principle enunciated in A.D. 601 by Pope Gregory I who instructed Augustine and Melletus to use accommodation in converting the British. The Jesuits made concessions to existing customs and sought to link indigenous beliefs and morals to Christian principles; in short, they adopted a position of relativism in order to deal with the diversity of conditions they encountered in their missionary labours.

This relativism did not always earn them the blessing of the Catholic hierarchy or the support of the theologians. Indeed, much opposition came from the Inquisition and from the Dominican and Franciscan orders. In the Orient the controversy raged over the so-called "Chinese rites," for the Jesuits wore the robes of the Chinese scholar during Mass, said Mass in Chinese and postponed full instruction of new converts in such culturally abhorrent facts as the crucifixion, while permitting Chinese converts to join in family rites honouring the dead. This controversy had direct implications for New France because the Jesuits appear to have entertained the same concept of the relativity of culture in dealing with the Hurons. Father Paul Le Jeune thought that the same techniques used with Brahmins and Mandarins could be used with primitive and "natural savages." From a concept of the relativity of culture, the Jesuits logically argued probabilism, the view that moral laws did not bind absolutely, but varied with circumstances and knowledge. Le Jeune wrote that "the world is full of variety and inconsistency and one will never find permanence." The Jesuits, in contrast to the first Récollet missionaries in Canada who had preceded them, attempted to reshape and reorient existing native practices and beliefs with a view to facilitating conversion and to ensuring subsequent fidelity. Contrary to the accusation that they expected less than others of their converts, it can be said that they accepted more tha ndid other missionaries. The concept of natural law, the accumulated wisdom of humanity which best allows mankind to develop his human potential,[43] reinforced these views because the aboriginal cultures did not have the same vision of the natural laws governing mankind. These philosophical approaches were entertained precisely because the missionaries were aware of many obstacles to Amerindians' reception of Catholicism.

A first and most obvious obstacle to evangelization of the Amerindians was the language barrier. The abbé Jessé Fléché who went to Acadia in 1610 immediately undertook the evangelization of the Micmacs and within the short period of a year had baptized over a hundred tribesmen, including the chief, Membertou, and twenty members of his family. The astonishing fact, according to a Jesuit report made the following year, was that Fléché knew nothing of the native tongue and had had to rely on the efforts of Charles de Biencourt to communicate with the natives. Biard wrote in 1611:

> The evil is that he was unable to instruct them as he would have liked, due to not knowing the language and not having the necessary things at hand . . . . It has not been possible up until now to translate into the language of the country the common creed or symbol, the Lord's prayer, the commandments of God, the sacraments and other things totally necessary to make a Christian.[44]

In spite of the language barrier this secular priest seems to have impressed the Micmacs during his brief stay among them for they always referred to him as "the Patriarch."

Lescarbot repeated the early Jesuit observation and opinion that the native languages were inadequate for expressing their religious message. He intimated that long discourses on religious and theological subjects were quite useless in Acadia because the hearers were unable to assimilate European concepts:

> For they have no words which can represent the mysteries of our religion, and it would be impossible to translate even the Lord's prayer into their language save by paraphrase. For of themselves they do not know what is sanctification, or the kingdom of Heaven, or supersubstantial bread (which we call daily), or to lead into temptation. The words glory, virtue, reason, beatitude, Trinity, Holy Spirit, angels, archangels, resurrection, paradise, hell, Church, baptism, faith, hope, charity, and an infinity of others are not in use among them. So that at the beginning there will be no need of great Doctors. For of necessity they must learn the language of the tribes whom they wish to reduce to the Christian faith; and to pray in our vulgar tongue, without attempting to impose on them the heavy burden of tongues unknown. This being a matter of custom and of human ordinance, and not of any divine law, it will be the part of prudence in the pastors to teach them carefully and not in ways fantastical, and to seek out the shortest path to their conversion. God grant the means to those that have the will![45]

Lescarbot's views were similar to those of the Huguenots, although they were also shared by the Jesuit missionaries who were ready to make accommodations to indigenous cultures in the pursuit of their missionary objectives.

There is no indication to modern linguists that the Amerindian languages were deficient; indeed, it appears that they have a wealth of vocabulary for expressing the abstract and symbolic. Le Clercq commended the Micmac language as being "very beautiful and very rich in its expressions," adding that it had a greater range of expression than European languages and that there were distinct styles for solemn and formal occasions.[46] The Jesuits asserted on the basis of their experience among both Algonkian and Iroquoian linguistic groups that the languages were definite in meaning, beautiful and regular in expression, "not at all barbarous," and full of force.[47]

As the Amerindian languages seem to have been quite adequate, it is possible that the deficiency was in the cultural approach and the missionaries' methods. The language did not always have precise equivalents, to be sure, because the world expressed by the French language was a European world whereas the Algonkian and Iroquoian languages gave expression to the New World. As the aborigines culture was non-literate, the missionaries realized that their first task was to compile dictionaries and grammars before they could translate the necessary religious books.[48] Biard was distressed by the fact that the Algonkian-speaking coastal tribes had acquired a "vulgar, vile, and shameless" vocabulary in French and Basque from the fishermen and, furthermore, that they not infrequently ridiculed the missionaries who strove to acquire the Micmac tongue. They had even taught them "indecent words" which the guileless evangelists "went about innocently preaching for beautiful sentences from the gospels."

Apart from these deliberate hindrances, there were the usual pitfalls of translating across widely divergent cultural systems. It seems that Brébeuf, for example, used the Huron word for the spirit which comes into being at one's death in his translation of the French Catholic concept of an immortal soul and of the Holy Ghost. This caused much confusion in Huron minds for the spirit born at one's death was believed to reside in the bones of the deceased. On the other hand, his inaccuracy might have enabled the Hurons to understand better the Catholic concept of relics. The word Brébeuf adopted for priest could be applied to men or women, yet he obviously intended to restrict the sacerdotal office to males. The Trinitarian formula became "In the name of our Father, and of His Son, and of their Holy Ghost."[49]

Furthermore, the aborigines, seeing some danger in divulging their religious vocabulary to the ambassadors of the "new religion," refused to offer much co-operation in many essential linguistic tasks. Gravier reported in 1700 that the Illinois tribes were "so secret regarding all the mysteries of their Religion that the Missionary can discover nothing about them."[50] What the pagan natives refused, the neophytes later supplied, although the refusal of some *coureurs-de-bois* to assist the missionaries in translations suggests there was pressure in the native encampments to offer no assistance to the Black Robes in their evangelization efforts.

Since few of the Amerindians learned French, and in the native villages and encampments both fur traders and missionaries used the native languages, it was necessary for all who had any sustained contact with the natives to learn their languages. Governor Frontenac could express his concern that the natives did not understand the King's language, although he himself apparently did not know any Amerindian languages, but the Ursulines and Sisters Hospitallers found it essential to acquire some linguistic skills. Mother Marie de l'Incarnation indicated how difficult, yet necessary, she found this task:

> We had to start studying the language of the Savages. The great desire I had to teach them made me the first to launch into it. Reverend Father Le Jeune, who was leaving the charge of superior of the missions, was instructed by Rev. Father Vimont, who had succeeded him, to help us spiritually and in this study of the language; which he did with very great charity for which we shall always be very greatly obliged to him. As it was more than twenty years since I had reasoned on any matter relating to learning or speculation, at first this study of a language very different from ours gave me terrible headaches, and it seemed to me that learning words by heart and verbs — because we studied according to rules — made rocks roll in my head, and what observations on a barbaric tongue followed![51]

Mother Marie de l'Incarnation resorted to special prayers and meditations and soon found she had sufficient fluency "to be able to instruct our dear neophytes in all that is required for their salvation."

By most standards, many of the missionaries were extremely gifted and accomplished linguists. One of them explained their task in these terms:

> Those who know what languages are will rightly consider that to learn one without books and almost without an interpreter, among wandering people, and in the midst of several other occupations, is not the work of a day.[52]

They learned not one language but several languages and dialects in the course of their evangelical labours and became valuable translators, ambassadors, negotiators and interpreters for the secular power in the colony. However, some had more difficulty with the languages, and Anne de Noue was reported as being unable to learn either Huron or Montagnais to enable him to pursue his ministry in the mission field, but his intelligence and skills enabled him to fill a useful place at Quebec and Trois-Rivières. Noel Chabanel was also unable to learn the Huron language. The natives did not always consider the missionaries to be expert linguists. Du Creux recounts that the Hurons "thought it was a joke to ask Le Jeune to speak, and when he made a stammering attempt at their language, laughter and derision greeted his childish efforts."[53]

A second problem for the missionaries who wished to establish the parochial organizations of the church, with a resident clergy supported by tithes and Mass fees, and schools for the education of the children, was the nomadism of the Algonkian tribes. It seemed an insurmountable obstacle. The missionaries believed that the tribes would have to be made sedentary to ensure regular attendance at divine service, observance of the fasts and feasts prescribed by the church calendar, observance of the sacraments, and attendance at religious instruction. Even those bands which were semi-sedentary were sufficiently unsettled during the hunting season and harvesting periods to disrupt seriously the continuity of mission work.

There was great hope that the Hurons would form the foundation of a native church because they were sedentary. The Récollets were the first to seize upon this quality of the Huron tribes for they could also become the great suppliers and middlemen in the fur trade. Sagard, in commenting on his Huron hosts, remarked:

> . . . . we exerted ourselves to receive and treat them so kindly and courteously that we won them over, and they seemed to vie in courtesy in receiving Frenchmen in their lodge when the needs of business put the latter at the mercy of these savages. Our experiences with them showed that they were useful to those who had to trade with them, while we hoped by this means to make our way towards our main purpose, their conversion, the only motive for so long and distressing a journey.[54]

The turning point in Jesuit missionary activity came in 1639 when they decided on the urging of Jérome Lalemant and Paul Ragueneau to establish a permanent centre in the Huron territory. This would become not only the mission headquarters for the region but was also planned as a model Amerindian Catholic community, a commercial and administrative centre, an experimental farm, a residence for the spiritual and physical refreshment of the missionaries, and perhaps even a fortress.[55] Huronia was a comparatively densely populated, compact area, culturally fairly homogeneous, and economically secure because of its swidden (slash-and-burn) cultivation, rich fishing grounds, long-standing trade with the hunting tribes of the north, and advantageous location for the French fur trade.[56] Nevertheless, it took a full-scale Iroquois invasion only a few months to destroy this great dream.

Although the collapse of the Huron missions forced the French to pay more attention to the West and the North it did not distract them from their determination to expand into the fertile and more moderate regions of the South to convert the tribes there. The Jesuits again considered the possibility of trying to convert the enemy Iroquois to lessen the threat to the missions and the fur trade. A split in the traditional cohesion of the Five Nations in 1654 seemed to offer the opportunity for an attempt. In 1655 Father Le Moyne went to New

Netherland, while several colleagues went to the Onondaga villages to gather first-hand information on Dutch relations with these tribes.[57] The French succeeded in consolidating friendly relations with the Onondagas and Senecas, but the Mohawks secured Dutch assistance on a scale which convinced the tribes allied to the French that they should make common cause with the Mohawks. Consequently, the Jesuits gave up their dream of converting the Iroquois by March, 1658, although their missionary activity continued to draw converts to the French settlements and to threaten the Dutch-Iroguois alliance.[58]

A third obstacle to evangelization was the well-developed native religion integrated with everyday life and tribal activities. All the human, personal, familial, clan and tribal decisions, crises and developmental stages were integrally related to native religion. Religion permeated the entire culture and culture had no meaning or sense of direction without that religion. In this respect European and Amerindian resembled each other for neither conceived his culture apart from his religion, or his religion apart from culture. Conversion was therefore more than a change of religion or a shedding of superstitions, beliefs and practices — it required a completely new life, the patterns and relationships of which had to be worked out anew without benefit of past experience or, for the neophytes, without benefit of community support. The missionaries were quick to realize that they alone could not meet this need for support and mutual assistance. Therefore, they encouraged *dogiques* or lay elders to assume responsibilities for catechizing and "keeping the young in line" in the Christianized communities. They also encouraged travelling native evangelists, unordained and unlicensed, including women and girls on occasion, to reach to new bands and to isolated encampments with the evangelical message.

That native religion was an obstacle to Catholic missionary work was made particularly clear among the Deer tribe of Hurons. During an epidemic a counter-innovative technique was developed by the medicine-men and elders. A version of baptism was initiated as a part of a healing cult said to be inspired by a deity who revealed himself as "the real Jesus."[59] There was also a story of a Christian woman who, having been buried at Sainte-Marie, rose from the dead to tell her compatriots that in heaven the French tortured the Huron converts, whereas those who refused to accept Catholicism "go after this life to a place of delights." This tale, to the consternation of the Jesuits, was widely believed and became "an article of faith for all the infidels, and even some of the Christians half believed it." On another occasion, paintings of "a thousand grotesque figures, canoes, paddles, animals" on a sheepskin and of "men singing and dancing" on a white sheet, in imitation of Catholic holy pictures, were used to heal a sick girl. Such anti-Christian practices represented an ideological resistance to Catholicism.[60]

Most troublesome to the missionaries was the Amerindian attachment to dreams. It was troublesome precisely because the native religion used an expression of supernatural direction which the Catholic church wished to use itself. Marie de l'Incarnation, like so many of the mystics who became involved in early seventeenth-century pious enterprises, had first received her religious vocation for Canada in a series of dreams and trances of "spiritual union with God." The central role played by dreams in aboriginal spiritual life, which was integrated with all aspects of their material existence, was aptly summarized by the Récollet missionary, Louis Hennepin:

> Their Dreams are to them instead of Prophecy, Inspiration, Laws, Commandments, and Rules, in all their Enterprizes, in War, Peace, Commerce, and Hunting: They regard them as Oracles. The Opinion they have of their Dreams draws them into a kind of necessity to be ruled by them; for they think 'tis an Universal Spirit, that inspires them by Dreams, and adviseth them what to do: And they carry this so far, that if their Dream orders them to kill a Person, or commit any other wicked Action, they presently execute it, and make satisfaction for it afterwards, as we shall shew anon. The Parents dream for their Children, the Captains for their Village. There are some among them, that take upon them to interpret Dreams, and explain them after their own fancy or inclination; and if their Interpretations don't prove true, they are not lookt upon as Cheats ere the more for that.[61]

These dreams, which were common to all the Amerindian cultures, have been characterized as either symptomatic dreams or visitation dreams. The symptomatic dreams expressed a wish of the dreamer's soul or inner being, whereas the visitation dream expressed the wish of a supernatural being who appeared in the dream or vision.[62] Both types of dreams, as shall be seen presently, presented some danger for and opposition to the missionaries.

The Huron dream theory was described by Father Paul Ragueneau in 1649 as basically psychoanalytic or symptomatic:

> In addition to the desires which we generally have that are free, or at least voluntary in us . . . the Hurons believe that our souls have other desires, which are, as it were, inborn and concealed. These, they say, come from the depths of the soul, not through any knowledge, but by means of a certain blind transporting of the soul to certain objects . . . . Now they believe

that our soul makes these natural desires known by means of dreams, which are its language. Accordingly, when these desires are accomplished, it is satisfied; but, on the contrary, if it be not granted what it desires, it becomes angry, and not only does not give its body the good and the happiness that it wished to procure for it, but often it also revolts against the body, causing various diseases, and even death . . . .[63]

Father Jouvency, in recording the Iroquois concept of the origin of disease or infirmity, reported they believed it resulted from such things as injury, witchcraft, or "by the mind of the patient himself, which desires something, and will vex the body of the sick man until it possesses the thing required." In the *Relation* of 1656-57 it was reported that:

> They make their most serious illnesses ridiculous by the gross superstition with which they seek to cure them. They are convinced that they are afflicted with diseases only because the soul is in want of something for which it craves; and that it is only necessary to give it what it desires, in order to detain it peacefully in the body.[64]

The importance of the dream in Amerindian societies was universally commented on by the missionaries. But none was more disturbed by the belief than Father Jacques Frémin who took the Senecas to be the most religious and the most superstitious of all the tribes:

> The Iroquois have, properly speaking, only a single Divinity — the dream. To it they render their submission, and follow all its orders with the utmost exactness. The Tsonnontouens are more attached to this superstition than any of the others; their Religion in this respect becomes even a matter of scruple; whatever it be that they think they have done in their dreams, they believe themselves absolutely obliged to execute at the earliest moment. The other nations content themselves with observing those of their dreams which are the most important; but this people, which has the reputation of living more religiously than its neighbours, would think itself guilty of a great crime if it failed in its observance of a single dream. The people think only of that, they talk about nothing else, and all their cabins are filled with their dreams.[65]

The missionaries lived in fear of being murdered "in cold blood if they have dreamed of doing so." As the Senecas had adopted many Huron resistors to evangelism into their tribe they were regarded as particularly dangerous.

Father Bruyas did not believe the Oneida were any less difficult to convert or less dangerous to work among. Although in the short period of four months he had made fifty-two conversions he displayed more caution than optimism:

> These are, for the most part, Children; for with Adults one must proceed with great discernment, for fear of making more Apostates than Christians. They regard a dream as a Divinity, which they adore; and they have, in the instability of their marriages, an open door, as it were, to the riot of their lusts. These are two great obstacles to the Faith, which make it more difficult for me to admit them into the Church.[66]

The visitation dream could be an even greater threat than the symptomatic dream. In the winter of 1640, during an epidemic of smallpox among the Hurons, a young fisherman had a dream in which the spirit appeared to him to advise the tribe in its distress. Father Jérome Lalemant reported the "demon" had issued the following warning:

> I am the master of the earth, whom you Hurons honor under the name of Iouskeha. I am the one whom the French wrongly call Jesus, but they do not know me. I have pity on your country, which I have taken under my protection; I come to teach you both the reasons and the remedies for your fortune. It is the strangers who alone are the cause of it; they now travel two by two through the country, with the design of spreading the disease everywhere. They will not stop with that; after this smallpox which now depopulates your cabins, there will follow certain colics which in less than three days will carry off all those whom this disease may not have removed. You can prevent this misfortune; drive out from your village the two black gowns who are there.[67]

It was indeed with great difficulty that the Jesuits were able to remain among the Hurons after this particularly clear revelation of Iouskeha. This would not have been the case unless the tribesmen gave great credence to omens, to messages from the spirit world, to revelations of the soul's desire, and to supernatural guidance in tribal action as well as in individual behaviour.

Particularly offensive to the Jesuit missionaries were dreams involving overt sexuality because these were usually acted out in therapeutic orgies. De Quen reported such an incident among the Onondaga in 1656, and Le Jeune among the Huron in 1639. Le Jeune also described a dream guessing game:

> Another will intimate that he desires an Andacwandat feast —
> that is to say, many fornications and adulteries. His Riddle
> being guessed, there is no lack of persons to satisfy his desire.[68]

It should be noted that this was abnormal behaviour and the Iroquoian peoples were generally modest, rather shy in heterosexual contacts and upheld the ideal of marital fidelity.

When the missionaries countered such opposition by invoking signs from heaven indicating the intervention of God or the intercession of the saints, by calling on the accumulated evidence of revelation and divine guidance, or by the consolation that God Almighty ruled over the affairs of men and of nations, they were setting up their god against the Amerindian spirits and inviting a contest of strength between them. In 1673 at Folle-Avoine on the Menominee river, Father Louis André invited such a contest when he replaced sacrifices offered to the sun in order to assure good fishing by a crucifix. The fact that the following morning a very great number of sturgeon entered the river suddenly made the natives pay heed to him.[69] The following year Father Pierre Millet reported that an Iroquois chieftain exhorted his compatriots to hold prayer in esteem "as Monsieur the governor had recommended them to do at Catarakoui," but far more effective was the fact that he had correctly predicted an eclipse of the moon a few days previously.[70] A letter composed by Mother Marie de l'Incarnation indicated that although the French wished to break the aborginal peoples' belief in demons, the French themselves did not deny the existence or power of these demons. She reported:

> Reverend Father Adam tells me that the Manitou was so enraged at the progress of the Faith in the places where he is preaching, that on St. Barnabas day he made the earth quake, so that the dwelling of the Reverend Fathers, they and their people were terribly shaken. This quake was felt over an area of five leagues, the earth heaving as if it were running after the Savages . . . .[71]

Unusual events were attributed either to the divinity or to the demons, depending on one's own position.

Le Jeune attempted to explain his concept of supernatural intervention to the Hurons in 1636. He told them that neither the French nor any other people could bring rain or fine weather, but that the Creator alone was master of these elements and therefore "recourse must be had only to him." However, when the Récollets had first gone into the Huron country the natives had asked them to pray God to stop a long and devastating rain. Sagard recorded the outcome of this request:

> And God looked with favour on our prayers, after we had
> spent the following night in petitioning Him for His promises,
> and heard us and caused the rain to cease so completely that
> we had perfectly fine weather; whereat they were so amazed and
> delighted that they proclaimed it a miracle, and we rendered
> thanks to God for it.[72]

The story of this extraordinary event would probably have been recounted in the Huron villages, so it was not surprising that the tribesmen believed the missionaries were capable of controlling the weather.

As for the allegation that the planting of a cross was the cause of
the drought then destroying their crops, Le Jeune observed that "it
had often rained and thundered since we had erected it." After these
rejections of supernatural interventions in the course of nature, as
conceived by the Hurons, he proceeded to expound to them how he
conceived supernatural intervention in natural phenomena. He suggested, first of all, that "perhaps God was angry because they had
spoken ill of him and had had recourse to wicked Arendiowane" who
apparently had no power to bring the drought to an end. Alternatively,
he suggested that they "perhaps had themselves caused the drought by
their intercourse and pacts with the devil."[73] Neither of the explanations Le Jeune considered plausible would have disabused the Hurons
of the conviction that the drought was directly related to the world of
the supernatural.

Supernatural intervention was invoked by the partisans of the new
religion as well as by those of the old religion. The missionaries
taught those who would give them a hearing, among other things, the
wonder-working power of the sacraments, novenas, and relics; they
sought to instill in their pagan hearers a reverence for the cross, religious images and various pious practices and symbols. In the adversities
which often accompanied the coming of the missionaries to the villages, the tribesmen concluded, not without some logic, that the supernatural invoked for good could also be invoked to produce harmful
effects. Was not this what Iouskeha had proclaimed to the Hurons?
These religious symbols came to be greatly distrusted. In 1635 the
Hurons insisted that a cross on top of the Jesuit mission house be removed as they believed it had caused the summer's drought:

> Then the Indians gathered from the surrounding villages and
> insisted that the Fathers should remove the cross; they told
> them that should the drought wither the crops there was dan-
> ger that the infuriated Hurons would attack them as sorcerers
> and poisoners and beat them to death.[74]

The converted tribesmen forced Iroquois captives, who feared or hated
the cross, to genuflect before it upon arrival at the reservation.[75] The

Pottawatomie tribesmen were reported during several feasts they held in 1674 "in honour of the devil" to have used the wood of a mission cross to kindle their fires.[76] Even the sign of the cross aroused intense feelings of hostility among the pagans.

Jean Pierron used religious images in mission work as a means of arousing the curiosity of indifferent or hostile tribesmen. Some depictions of the Last Judgment showed pagan resistors being cruelly tormented in hell. Such use of religious art may have come from a French belief that barbarous peoples had to be inculcated with a wholesome fear of God. On the other hand, it tended to reinforce native belief in the malevolent effects of the introduction of the new religion. Thus in 1630, Huron villagers had cause for further alarm as an epidemic spread rapidly through the lodges killing many of the natives. The rumour spread that the two life-size images, one of Jesus and the other of the Virgin Mary, that the Jesuits had displayed in their chapel were the cause of the pestilence. The annual *Relation* reported that:

> This unfounded suspicion, which should have been dismissed with a laugh, spread so rapidly in a few days that throughout the length and breadth of the land it was soon reported that the French priests were the cause of the trouble; and although we may conjecture that those from whom this ridiculous falsehood emanated were not so foolish as to persuade themselves to accept what they wished others to believe, still they told their lie so cunningly that the majority who heard the report had no doubt that the thing was true. For the most part they gradually refused to associate with the Fathers, and the women and children, otherwise of no account but ready to believe anything, execrated them as public malefactors. In all the gatherings and meetings the talk was against the Fathers, who, it was said, had come to the Huron country on an evil day and who were destined to be the ruin of the whole race.[77]

If the pagan resistors had been aware of the Jesuit allegation that women and children were most active in opposing truth, they might have retorted that these were the very members of their homogeneous clans that the missionaries sought to use to spread the new religion.

In general the use of religious images caused much controversy among the Amerindians. Although the Montagnais are known to have used images in their healing rites, there is no indication that the Hurons ever used them. Catholic images were probably regarded in much the same way as amulets, but their magical powers remained unproven in comparison to their well-known traditional charms. They did not forget that the missionaries suggested that pagan mocking of the efficacy of Catholic images brought premature death.

The Amerindians' charge against the missionaries gradually became one of sorcery and witchcraft, more through obsessive fear than through hatred. Mother Marie de l'Incarnation summarized the situation for a correspondent in France:

> Father Chastelain gathers no less fruit among the Hurons. He writes me that he and those who accompany him were within inches of death. They were on the dock as criminals in a council of the savages. The fires were lit closer to each other than usual, and they seemed to be so only for them, for they were esteemed convicted of witchcraft, and of having poisoned the air which caused the pestilence throughout the country. What put the Fathers in extreme peril was that the Savages were as it were convinced that these misfortunes would cease with their death.[78]

By 1640 the opposition had become so organized and persistent that it was called persecution. Three letters from the Ursuline nun told of the missionaries being "outrageously beaten and seriously wounded," of the near-martyrdom of Ragueneau, and of the conspiracy of the demons to have "great assembles" called, the avowed purpose of which was the extermination of the Jesuit missionaries.[79] Marie de l'Incarnation reported that the oldest and most prominent woman of the nation had harangued the consultative assembly of the four tribes saying:

> It is the black Robes who make us die by their spells; listen to me, I prove it by the reasons you are going to recognize as true. They lodged in a certain village where everyone was well, as soon as they established themselves there, everyone died except for three of four persons. They changed location and the same thing happened. They went to visit the cabins of the other villages, and only those where they did not enter were exempted from mortality and sickness. Do you not see that when they move their lips, what they call prayers, those are so many spells that come forth from their mouths? It is the same when they read in their books. Besides, in their cabins they have large pieces of wood (they are guns) with which they make noise and spread their magic everywhere. If they are not promptly put to death, they will complete their ruin of the country, so that there will remain neither small nor great.[80]

The Ursuline correspondent concluded that the outcome of this persecution was unknown at the time "because the accusations brought against them are presented in a light that makes them appear to be true." The missionaries were regarded as sorcerers because wherever they travelled in their apostolic work they carried the epidemic "to purify the faith of those they have converted." This charge would electrify French readers because of the prominence witchcraft trials had reveivd in France in the early decades of the seventeenth century.

Chaumonot and his companion left the Huron country during this time of troubles to visit new tribes, only to find that the rumours of sorcery and witchcraft had preceded them and ruined any hope of founding a mission among these peoples:

> As for the adults, not only have they not been willing to listen to the good news, but they even prevented us from entering their villages, threatening to kill and eat us, as they do with their most cruel enemies. The reason of this great aversion arose from the calumnies disseminated by some evil inhabitants of the country from which we came. In consequence of these calumnies, they were convinced that we were sorcerers, imposters come to take possession of their country, after having made them perish by our spells, which were shut up in our inkstands, in our books, etc., — inasmuch that we dared not, without hiding ourselves, open a book or write anything.[81]

The evil report travelled to the Iroquois tribes too. Marie de l'Incarnation said that it was commonly believed in Quebec and Trois-Rivières that the Iroquois had broken the peace of 1645 because of the aversion that some Huron captives had aroused in them to Catholicism, saying that it had brought manifold disasters upon the Huron tribes, including "the infection of contagious diseases, . . . which had rendered their hunting and fishing more sterile."[82]

The extent to which this fear of the new religion seized the imaginations of the Iroquois was expressed in a report of 1647:

> It is further said that they have seen issuing from the lips of a Christian, whom they were burning, a strange brightness which has terrified them; so, indeed, they have knowledge of our doctrine, but they regard it with horror, as of old did the Pagans in the early age of Christianity.[83]

This obsessive fear was not only for the external symbols of the new religion and its practices, but also for the Eucharist itself (some of the pagans asking to see the corpse of Christ which the priests brought to life at Mass), and eventually to purely secular objects such as weathervanes or clocks.

Both the French and Amerindians believed in spirit possession, about which more shall be said later in connection with alcoholism, but the French tended to regard it as undersirable and resorted to exorcism to control it, whereas the Amerindians valued it highly and sought this religious experience as ardently as did Montanists in early Christian times. Just as the Huron elders had used the threat of torturing and bringing to trial individuals who defied established authority with witchcraft and sorcery, so they threatened those who converted to Catholicism.[84] Conversion was as much a deviation from accepted forms of behaviour and as much a threat to group cohesion and established authority among the Hurons as Huguenotism was a threat to national unity and prosperity to the Catholics in France.

Another source of opposition to Catholic evangelization was the implication of religious conversion for traditional aboriginal leadership, hegemony and independence. If the Catholic missionaries gained ascendancy the *shaman* and *sagamos* necessarily lost status and power. The Huron experience offers the best example of this development. By 1648 Paul Ragueneau could report a network of ten mission stations in Huronia with Ossossané the "most fruitful of all, as regards both numbers of Christians and their zeal." This predominantly pro-French Bear community was organized into a model Catholic village under converted chieftains who refused to tolerate pagan festivals and observances and appointed a Jesuit as the Chief headman with authority to act as censor of public morals.[85] A growing division made itself felt throughout the Huron confederacy as the Deer and Rock tribes resisted conversion and the Bear and Cord tribes were more receptive although still internally divided. One missionary said it was difficult to be a good Christian and a good Huron at the same time; one convert said "I am more attached to them [the church] than to my country and to all my relatives."[86] The plot of the pagans to drive out the missionaries and their converts failed as the Christianized leaders were able to regain the upper hand and "carried even the majority of the infidels with them; so that it was publicly decided that reparations should be made to us in the name of the whole country."[87] The Jesuits seemed to have won an important, if temporary, victory in their attempt to set up a Christian Huron state somewhat after the model of their Paraguayan experiment.[88]

The threat posed to the prestige and credibility of the medicine men and jugglers by the missionaries was present in the encounters with all the tribes where the Jesuits, Récollets, Sulpicians or other secular clergy penetrated. Hennepin described the jugglers' opposition when a woman attributed the healing of her child to the fact that he had received baptism. These jugglers spread the rumour that the priest ate serpents and poison and that he swallowed thunderbolts:

> The savages were astonish'd at the strange Stories these Rascals made upon me on the occasion of baptizing the Child; nay, these imposters added, that we had Tails like Beasts, that the European Women had but one Pap in the middle of the Breast, and bear five or six Children at a time, and a great deal more of such stuff to make us odious; and this they did because they thought that what I did would lessen their Credit, and thereby they should be depriv'd of many a good Treat.[89]

The conflict became more acute when the missionaries used their medical knowledge to heal the sick and their scientific knowledge to explain some natural phenomenon. The missionaries' opposition to divorce, to the frequent changing of spouses (although most northern tribes were monogamous in the sense of having only one wife at a time), and their attempts to enforce the Catholic moral code were added hindrances to rapid or easy conversion.

The Huron experience was sufficiently linked to political and economic factors to raise a genuine query about the sincerity and genuineness of conversions. The much debated question had been raised from the very onset of evangelization in New France. It was first raised about the ministry of the abbé Jessé Fléché in Acadia and the Jesuits resolved not to emulate his policy of baptizing large numbers of well-disposed but ignorant and unprepared natives. This was largely a question of the number and rapidity of conversions. The missionaries resisted the temptation to baptize large numbers of children in the hope they would grow up in the new religion; they decided to baptize only fully convinced, well-instructed and experienced adults. One Jesuit wrote:

> Were we not convinced by experience that it is dangerous to administer baptism to little children who are not sick, we would baptize a very large number of them, with their parents' consent; but we do not venture to risk administering the sacrament, lest they might, later on, profane it by the infidelity in which they usually live when they grow older. Therefore we baptize only the children of Christians and of catechumens, and all who are in danger of death.[90]

Although the Jesuit *Relations* gave encouraging statistics on the number of conversions in order to encourage the financial support they sought in France and retain the favour and protection of the authorities, these statistics when examined more closely indicated more gains for the church rtiumphant than for the church militant. It was quality rather than quantity that made for a good foundation for a nascent church.

Hennepin summarized the Récollet experience up to 1680 by saying that "these miserable dark Creatures" listened willingly to the Gospel as if it were a sweet song, that they would accept baptism ten times a day for a glass of brandy or a pipe of tobacco, and that they even gave their children for baptism and instruction "but all without any Religious Motive."[91] He based his conclusion on the experiences he and his companions had among the Cayugas at Fort Frontenac and on early Récollet missions among the Hurons and Montagnais. The baptized adults often "fell again into ordinary indifference for Salvation" and the children grew up to follow the examples of the unconverted tribesmen so that it was "no better than a plain profanation of Baptism to administer it to them."

Doubts about the quality of conversion persisted. Were Amerindian converts unreliable practitioners, sometimes demonstrating excessive zeal and at times relapsing into their former habits? There was some suspicion that even when apparently converted and civilized, the aborigines were not to be trusted or accepted as equals because the transformation might only be "skin deep" and they might "revert to savagery." This view of the "praying Indians" on the New England frontier seems to have been prevalent among the English. The Hugeunots had been no more certain, in fact, of their converts in Brazil. Jean de Léry confided: "Look at the inconstancy of this poor people, a fine example of the corrupt nature of man."[92] In New France there were similar fears expressed by experienced missionaries. Chrestien Le Clercq, a Récollet who worked among the Micmacs from 1675 to 1679, became so discouraged that, while describing the external attachment of his converts to Catholic practices, he despaired of their perseverance:

> But it can be said that the number is very small of those who live according to the rules of Christianity, and who do not fall back into the irregularities of a brutal and wild life, which they do either because of the natural insensibility of these people to matters concerning their salvation, or by reason of drunkenness, of their delusions, of their superstitions, and other considerable defects to which they are greatly addicted.[93]

Le Clercq thought that the Jesuits were no more successful than the Franciscans in their missions at Cape Breton, Miscou and Nipisguit in founding "any solidly established Christianity."

The question was also raised about the relationship between conversion and economic inducements. In several cases missionary work was begun among new tribes when the missionaries presented themselves before the councils, were adopted into the tribe, and promised to promote trade with the French in return for the right to preach the new religion freely. Hennepin wrote of the tribes of the far interior:

The Savages often accept the Offers of the Missionaries, and assure them they are well satisfied with their Persons: but to win the Barbarians, 'tis requisite that the Missionaries give them Hatchets, Knives, or other European Merchandizes, which the Savages, especially those who never yet had any Commerce with the Europeans, set a high value upon.[94]

Converted Amerindians were accorded special treatment on numerous occasions. One of the specific complaints of the Huron pagan resistors was that the fur trade flotillas were disproportionately manned by converts. Converts received medals, were subject to hospitality at religious establishments in the towns, and were the first persons contacted by the missionaries and civil officials when seeking advice or bringing counsel. There were complaints about the "wheat and eel" Christians who took up space at the Hotel-Dieu which was required for patients.[95] Besides the usual distribution of medals, rings, and beads to those receiving religious instruction, the sale of guns and ammunition was limited at first to converted tribesmen. State officials began to raise questions about the numbers and genuineness of conversions as a means of bringing pressure to bear on certain religious orders and communities. La Salle suggested, for example, that the Jesuit missionaries were more interested in the "conversion of beaver," and Frontenac said their missions were "mockeries." There were cases, not always proven to the satisfaction of the detractors of the missions, of pagans converting merely to avoid the onerous costs of offering pagan feasts and to shun tribal responsibilities.

The charge that the Jesuits baptized hundreds of insufficiently instructed natives had been widely circulated in France in 1659 by the Jansenists who translated and published a letter from the Spanish Bishop of New Spain to Pope Innocent X. The letter had absolutely no bearing on New France but, nevertheless, created a great stir in France and served to arouse doubts about the efficacy of Jesuit missionary work. Antoine Arnauld later wrote a history of the notorious controversy.[96] Louis Hennepin, the Belgian Récollet, affirmed at the close of the seventeenth century that the Jesuit missions were a failure and that the Récollets would have done better had the authorities supported them. He advanced the argument that the Récollets would have been more acceptable to the aborigines than the Jesuits because they went barefooted like the Amerindians and because they held their property in common as did the native peoples.[97] These arguments, although ill-founded, illustrate the type of criticism that was being directed against evangelization efforts. A Sulpician chronicler suggested that "these barbarous nations which appeared for so many years completely incapable of being grounded in our Religion" were, through the efforts of Sulpician missionaries, becoming "instructed and tamed."[98] Allouez gave an overall comparative assessment of the genuineness of Amerindian conversions in 1672:

> The name "Savage" gives rise to so very disparaging an idea of those who bear it, that many people in Europe have thought that it is impossible to make true Christians of them. But such persons do not reflect that God died for the barbarian as well as for the Jew, and that his spirit breathes where it wills . . . . What has been said and what will be said will be sufficient to show that not only are there true Christians among these savage peoples, but also that there are many more in proportion than in our civilized Europe.[99]

The Jesuits repeatedly praised their converts for their charity, their conscientiousness, the excellence of their confessions, their earnestness and their activism in spreading the faith. They praised the well-known aboriginal qualities of docility, generosity, humility and resignation which conformed so well to the Catholic ethic.

Indeed, the excessive fervour of some converts, called "Marians" in mockery by the pagans, gave rise to misgivings and unease. At Tadoussac in 1645 the Jesuits had to intervene to terminate scenes of spontaneous public penance accompanied by bloody self-flagellation. In 1672 the converts at Lorette village were reported to have desired "to mingle their blood with their tears" during the Good Friday observances. Claude Chauchetière reported excesses of zeal in the early 1680s as near-hysterical women threw themselves, or dipped their infants, into icy streams in mid-winter. He added:

> Savages, both men and women, covered themselves with blood by disciplinary stripes with iron, with rods, with thorns, with nettles; they fasted rigourously, passing the entire day without eating, — and what the savages eat during half the year is not sufficient to keep a man alive. These fasting women toiled strenuously all day in summer, working in the fields; in winter, cutting wood. These austerities were almost continual. They mingled ashes in their portion of Sagamité; they put glowing coals between their toes, where the fire burned a hole in the flesh; they went bare-legged to make a long procession in the snows; they all disfigured themselves by cutting off their hair, in order not to be sought in marriage. These things, and all the harm that they could do to the body, which they call their greatest enemy, reduced them so low that it was not possible for ill-fed men to persevere further. Most of these things took place in the woods, where the savages were hunting, or under enthusiastic excess of indignation against themeselves.[100]

It could be argued that they were in the company of the colonial bishop, who as an exercise in self-mortification and humiliation sucked in the pus from wounds he dressed, and of the Hospital nun, who as an exercise in self-denial and complete submission swallowed caterpillars. They were imitating the fanatical behaviour of their evangelists, such as Brébeuf, who added to his ardous labours, innumerable sufferings, and fatiguing travels "many voluntary mortifications: disciplines every day, and often twice each day; very frequent fasts; haircloths, and belts with iron points; vigils which advanced far into the night."[101] Less demonstrative, but no less austere in their mortifications and assiduous in their vigils, were a number of mystics such as Joseph Chihouatenhoua, René Tsondihouanne, Ignace Onakonchiarroenk, Cecile Gannadaris, Catherine Tegakouita and numerous others.[102]

Actually, mysticism provided a cultural bridge between Amerindian religions and Catholicism. In Amerindian religions each individual was expected to make his own contacts and relationships with the supernatural, to acquire a spirit guardian, and to determine by visions the life and success he might expect. Mysticism was a reaction to the dominant collectivist spirituality of Catholicism and it fostered an individual awareness of and identification with the supernatural. As fasting and mutilation were often part of the quest for spirit guidance in Amerindian religions, so they were in mystical Catholicism. The mystic experience in both cultures gave the individual a spiritual freedom and latitude which in the Catholic framework in particular was unusual. For the Amerindians the supernatural forces were part of nature, but in Catholicism the supernatural forces were above and outside nature, with the institutional church having in a substantial measure replaced the role nature played in the aboriginal beliefs. A cultural difference that mysticism was less successful in bridging was the temporal orientation to the future rather than to the present, as in Amerindian religions. But it facilitated this radical change by concentrating on the present sense of spiritual direction, satisfaction and sanctification within an eternal plan.

Was excessive zeal ever related to undue pressure and the use of force to obtain conversions? New France's history appears quite different from the Spanish American experience, although there are fleeting references to the excessive zeal of some dogiques and to the use of the secular arm to bring recalcitrant tribes to be more favourable to receiving missionaries in their villages. Bertrand recorded in 1610 the conversion of the Micmac chieftain who "promises to have the others baptized, otherwise, he will wage war against them."[103] Marie de l'Incarnation informed her son in 1660 that it had been decided to wage a "holy war," a "crusade," a war of extermination against the Iroquois tribes in order to further the evangelization of the country. She anticipated her son's reaction to such a proposition with these comments:

> You are astonished by this resolution, and you say that it is repugnant to the spirit of the Gospel and the Apostles who risked their lives to save the infidels, even those who caused them sufferings. Monseigneur our Prelate was of your opinion, he even had Monsieur de Bernières learn their language to go to instruct them; you know how often our Reverend Fathers went there for the same purpose; just recently they wanted to go to make a last effort, but they were restrained as by violence, the peril being too evident and inevitable. After so much useless effort and so many experiences of the perfidy of these infidels, Monseigneur changed his views, and he fell into agreement with all the wise persons of hte country, either that he have them exterminated, if it can be done, or that all Christians and the Christianity of Canada perish. When there is no longer any Christianity or any Missionaries what hope will there be of their salvation? Only God be a very extraordinary miracle can put them on their way to heaven.[104]

The rationalization, as in the Spanish case, was that force was necessary to render the Amerindians amenable to conversion. Denonville, in reporting on his Seneca campaign of 1686, said that the captives he had distributed throughout the reserves of sedentary converts were "all the men, women and children [who] were baptized testifying joy on the occasion." But he added the cautionary note that "It remains to see if it was in good faith."[105]

Apart from using force to win converts, force was also used to keep the new Catholics in the proper and strict observance of their duties. The tradition of the church was long and well-established in this matter but Amerindian independence and freedom (in a context in which the French were dependent upon them for the success of their enterprises, including the missions) did not encourage frequent resort to the secular arm to keep up religious practice. On the reservations a theocratic rule was enforced by the missionaries and the *dogiques*. The "whip of discipline" was a familiar instrument to both French missionaries and native zealots, and was eventually imposed on converts in an attempt to eradicate drunkenness. The missionary to the Mohawks in 1669-70 reported that he attacked drunkenness and debauchery by exciting "fear of God's Judgment" and also "by the dread of the arms of a Great King, whose name alone is able to hold them to their allegiance."[106]

Another difficulty which stood in the way of conversion was the aboriginal incomprehension of the values and concepts of the missionaries. The missionary was an enigma, his doctrine was a mystery, and his ethic was a riddle. The missionaries expected the tribesmen to respect them for their sacrifices and sufferings in bringing them the Gospel under such unattractive conditions, especially compared to the life they had led in the élitist colleges of France where most of them had previously taught. One of the missionaries, obviously depressed by what he interpreted as native ingratitude, wrote:

> If you love the French people as you say you do, then love them, and they will teach you the way to heaven. This is what makes them leave their country, their friends and their comforts to instruct you and especially to teach your children a knowledge so great and so very necessary.[107]

Missionaries expected to be respected for their vows of chastity and poverty, but the Amerindians felt differently about their self-denial and celibacy. Sagard indicated that the Hurons regarded heterosexuality as normal, homosexuality as deviant, and celibacy as abnormal. He confided that the Récollet missionary had been greatly harassed because of the Huron moral assumptions:

> One of the great and most bothersome importunities which they caused us at the beginning of our stay in the country was their continual pursuit of pleas to marry us, or at least that we should join ourselves to them, and they could not understand our manner fo Religious life ....[108]

The nomadic Algonkian tribes, who feasted in times of good hunting and were forced to fast when game was scarce, had difficulty in grasping calendar-oriented fasting. Their concepts of property and its sharing left them much less impressed by clerical vows of apostolic poverty than Europeans were inclined to be. Even the missionary attitude in the face of death was often incomprehensible to native minds. How could a Black Robe rejoice at the baptism of a person who died soon after? The missionary rejoiced at the spiritual rebirth of his agonizing convert, but the tribesmen saw only the physical death of their compatriot, and wondered at the foreigner's satisfaction.

There was the danger, on the other hand, that the Amerindians might be impressed by Protestant piety, or that they might be confirmed in their skepticism, as Sagard suggested, as they observed the internal quarrels between Catholic and Huguenot seamen, fishermen, traders and especially ministers of religion.[109] No consideration of Catholic missionary work in North America can ignore the Huguenot role. Although the "Religion Prétendue Réformée" never launched a serious missionary movement in the New World, being too hard pressed to maintain its precarious position in metropolitan France, it did serve as an inducement to Catholics to hasten their own efforts, to establish themselves in every quarter, and to remove all occasions for unfavourable comment on their activities. Robert Pontgravé, son of François Pontgravé who was financially associated with the De Monts' venture and described by Lescarbot as "not French but a Turk, not a Turk but an athiest," spoke against Catholic missions, telling the natives that Poutrincourt was hoodwinking them by religious means and that "he would have them die in order to obtain their beaver."[110] There was also a campaign directed against the Jesuit order, for in 1627 Charles Lalemant warned that a particularly offensive pamphlet was circulating in New France. It was probably written by the Huguenot minister Pierre Dumoulin, pastor of Charenton, and was directed against the Society and the royal confessor associated with the Canadian missions.

> So after having striven by my exhortations and our conversation to correct the impressions concerning our Society that exist in this country, can Your Reverence believe that we have found here the "Anti-Coton", which was circulated from chamber to chamber, and which was finally burned, about four months after our arrival.[111]

The Jesuit reputation for political intrigues was also kept before the public by enemies described as "English, Dutch and other heretical Europeans," the latter probably being a reference to the number of Walloon Protestants and Huguenot exiles in the English colonies to the south of New France.[112]

The missionary d'Avaugour summarized the continual threat of the converts' desertion to the heretics in these terms:

> For nothing else than religion retains the savages in their fidelity to the French; that, being lost, they will flock to the neighbouring heretics, from whom they make a much more greater profit than from the French, and much more easily dispose of their goods. The motive of eternal salvation is the only one to prevent them from dealing with those with whom, they know, there is no hope in that direction. This link once broken, care for salvation and religion once relaxed by drunkenness and its accompanying plagues, and all is over with the colony of the French in Canada.[113]

However these verbal attacks on the missionaries' efforts had little real effect. Only the organization of large-scale competitive missionary enterprises, such as developed in the nineteenth century, could seriously undermine or ruin the Jesuit undertaking. Lescarbot, to cite but one observer at a period when Huguenots were an important element in New France's development, did not believe the evangelism of the Protestants posed any threat to the missions of the Catholics:

> Some foolish and over-scrupulous folk will say that it is better to leave them [Amerindians] in their present condition than to give them an evil dye. But I shall reply that the Apostle Saint Paul rejoiced that, though by envy and contention and not sincerely, every way, whether in pretence or in truth, Christ was preached. It is difficult, not to say impossible, for mortals to lead all men into the same opinion, and especially where matters are concerned which can be subject to interpretation.[114]

Of course, there was no indication that Huguenot missionary work among the Amerindians was seriously contemplated.

The Protestants, for their part, tended to overestimate the success of the Catholic missions. The Huguenots in New England launched a bitter attack on Jesuit missionary methods in 1690.[115] Cotton Mather, in admitting what he believed to be a more successful approach, could only suggest that the conversions were superficial. He wrote:

> It is to be confessed, that the Roman Catholics have a clergy so very numerous, and so little encumbered, and are masters of such prodigious ecclesiastical revenues, as renders it very easy for them to exceed the Protestants in their endeavours to Christianize the Pagan salvages. Nor would I reproach, but rather applaud their industry in this matter wishing that we were all touched with an emulation of it.[116]

His comments showed the common Protestant belief that the Catholics disposed of vast sums of money and an almost unlimited personnel in the pursuit of their missions; they also acknowledged the advantages enjoyed by celibate evangelists unencumbered by family responsibilities.

The Amerindians gave every indication of being greatly impressed by the beautiful ritual of the Mass, the solemn processions, and such devotional practices as the adoration of the Blessed Sacrament. A missionary wrote with obvious satisfaction:

> I say nothing of the esteem manifested by this new Church for all The outward signs of our holy Religion. Crosses, medals, and other similar Articles are Their most precious jewels. So fondly do they preserve These that they wear them around their necks, even at preaching in New Holland, where The heretics have

never been able to tear away from Them a single bead of Their Rosaries.[117]

The converts celebrated the great festivals with enthusiasm and entered into the dramatic events of Holy Week with uncommon self-denial, mortifications and flagellation. Nevertheless, there was always the threat, at least in the minds of the Catholic missionaries, during the first three decades of the seventeenth century that the participatory worship, the singing of the "songs of Marot," the extempore prayers of the Huguenots, who were well-represented among the visiting seamen and traders, would attract the Amerindians.[118] Nothing was so hateful to the Récollets as to see the Amerindians standing on the wharves at Quebec attentively watching the Huguenots at worship on the decks of their anchored vessels.

Another remarkable feature of evangelization was the lack of religious vocations among the Amerindians. There were never any native brothers or priests. In 1657 a Huron girl, Geneviève-Agnès Skanudharoua, who at the tender age of fifteen left the Ursulines to become a novice at the Hotel-Dieu of Quebec, spent eight months in the order of Hospitalièrs before succumbing to a fatal lung disease. She was permitted to take her final vows a few hours before she died. An Algonkin girl, Marie-Thérèse Gannensagouas, entered the secular company of the Sisters of the Congregation and an Iroquois convert from the reservation at Lac des Deux Montagnes, Marie-Barbe Atontinon, was received into the same community and spent twelve years in the uncloistered order until her death. There were also a couple of half-breed Acadian girls who entered convents in France. However, these few religious vocations were virtually without influence so far as the work of evangelization was concerned.[119]

The institution of *dogiques,* on the other hand, was extremely useful in providing a liaison between Europeans and Amerindians. The *dogiques* were native catechizers confirmed in the new religion who performed many of the missionaries' services during their absence, and who assisted the priests in their evangelization of the tribesmen. The *Relation* of 1643-44 described their functions in these terms:

> They perform the office of Dogique, in the absence of our Fathers. In their wars and on their hunts, even when they are in large bands, they offer public prayers, and hold divine service, as strictly as if they were in their Church; they instruct and baptize, with much satisfaction and edification, in times of danger; the reputation of their virtue pervades the foreign Tribes with whom they trade; they preach there the holiness of the Christian law; they inspire everywhere the desire of

enjoying the blessing that they possess and imperceptibly open the door for us to many great nations who could not hear our name without a shudder, and who had looked upon us in the past only as persons who brought misfortune upon them.[120]

It seems there were female catechizers too — a remarkble innovation in the Catholic church. The Jesuits used numerous Amerindian women as volunteer missionary helpers in spreading their message. The commendation offered one such assistant, who had been instructed by the Hospital Nuns at Quebec, merits citing:

> She formed little gatherings, instructed, catechized, encouraged, and taught them, and induced her companions to pray. In a word, God enabled her to perform, in that land of horror and darkness, the office of a *dogique* or a preacher.[121]

Her case was all the more remarkable because she was a blind Algonkin girl living in Iroquois captivity; blind captives were rarely adopted and given the liberty she enjoyed. Father Pierron wrote about an "elderly Christian woman" who preached to any who would give ear, using religious pictures depicting Biblical stories and themes to attract attention. Another woman convert was sufficiently aggressive to argue in a Dutch settlement the merits of medals, crucifixes and holy images. In comparison, however, the Protestant New Englanders reported more success in religious vocations. In 1671 Thomas Mayhew reported ten native teachers and preachers in Martha's Vineyard and Nantucket alone, and by 1705 thirty-five were engaged in full-time missionary work among the Amerindians of New England.[122] The reason for the lack of an Amerindian clergy in francophone North America was the exceedingly rigorous academic and cultural requirements exacted.

The strongest indictment the Huguenots sought to bring against Catholic evangelization was its incorporation of pagan and pre-Christian elements. Since most cultural descriptions were couched in comparative terms, there was some danger that the Huguenots might add to the already numerous examples supporting the charge if they were able to draw parallels between Amerindian idolatry and superstition and Catholic belief and practices. Guillaume du Choul, Polydore Vergil, Pierre Viret and Pierre Mussard had already elaborated on pagan survivals in Catholicism.[123] The Huguenots had to be prevented from learning that the Jesuits used the symbols and practices already known and understood by the tribesmen to express the beliefs of Catholicism. One can imagine the attacks in Huguenot publications had it been commonly known, for example, that Jean Pierron had invented a game called "Point au point" to teach the mysteries of the faith to the Iroquois. The Catholics therefore tried to exclude all Protestants from the colony.

Finally, the encounter of French missionary and Counter-Reformation Catholicism with the Amerindian religions and superstitions resulted in some re-evaluation of Catholic traditions and practices. In general, the Catholic French were more than ever convinced of the truth of their revealed religion. Contact with pagan tribes had confirmed their own assumptions of superiority. On the other hand, the skeptics among them found more reasons for doubing many commonly held traditional beliefs. The Jesuits in particular were confirmed in a relativist approach to divergent cultures. Two specific problems will illustrate how the French reacted to new problems posed by the New World. Firstly, how could Europeans account for the diversity of Amerindian religions and beliefs? Two main responses were known and used in the sixteenth and seventeenth centuries. One response was to stress the effects of original sin, the disruptive effects of Cain's sin, the Tower of Babel and the deluge, the migrations and the breakdown of communication among the bearers of the Adamic tradition. The second response, developed by Jean Bodin, was environmentalist and stressed the relation of culture to geography, climate and topographical features.

A second problem that indicates how Catholics reacted to new challenges was the attempt to account for similarities between Amerindian religions and Catholicism. Two responses were again common at the time. There were those who asserted that the devil had introduced religious parallelisms to keep the aborigines subject to himself. Others maintained that similarities represented a corruption, a degradation and a degeneration of earlier truth once known to the pagans. The Huguenot explanation, which had to be silenced at all costs, was that Catholicism was founded on such paganism, had retained some and transformed much of it. The Amerindian response, reported back to France in 1616, saw differences and similarities in a general cultural framework rather than a more narrowly religious one:

> For all your arguments, and you can bring a thousand of them if you wish, are annihilated by this single shaft which they always have at hand, Aoti Chaboya, (they say) "That is the Savage way of doing it. You can have your way and we will have ours; every one values his own wares."[124]

Contact with aboriginal peoples could give rise to certain antireligious sentiments, or could support already existing deist tendencies.[125] An apparently innocent observation, universally attested, that Amerindian women seemed to have easy childbirths and resumed their normal duties within hours of giving birth could bring into question doctrines of original sin and woman's condemnation to bring forth her children in suffering. Yet the missionaries were unanimous in their reports on this matter. Likewise, a consequence of Adam's fall and consciousness of sin was the desire for covering. However, travellers reported among southern Amerindians a lack of shame of nakedness and their apparent modesty apart from this trait. The missionary Abbeville satisfied himself, if not his readers, with the searing comment:

> By comparison there is much less danger in seeing the nakedness of Indian women than the curiosity of the lustful allurements of the worldly Ladies of France. For these Indian women are modest and seemly in their nakedness.[126]

In other words, nakedness was depicted as a sign of depravity in some literary works and as a sign of innocence in others. There was some nudity in New France but the references to it concerned Neutral and Ottawa men who discarded their clothing in the heat of summer.

The widespread belief in immortality, reported especially by Champlain, Sagard and Charles Lalemant, undermined the absolute necessity of revealed religion to arrive at religious truth. Lescarbot noted that the Micmacs were skilled sculptors and painters but they never adored any of their stone or wooden images; the comment might have been a veiled Protestant remark. In another place he remarked that "if they do not know God, at least they do not blaspheme him at all, as do most Christians."[127]

If the Amerindians did not readily accept the gospel brought by the missionaries, the explanation that simple barbarians did not possess a sufficiently developed vocabulary to grasp spiritual truths, or a reasonably evolved moral code to understand Christian ethics, might be accepted by dévot readers. The skeptics and heretics, however, were not so readily convinced. While criticisms, implied or direct, were aimed at bad Catholics rather than at Catholicism itself, the lessons learned by readers were not always those intended by the authors. Du Tertre merely stated a fact when he reported that the natives in the West Indies had such a bad impression of Christians that "the greatest insult they could give a man was to call him Christian." This could only strengthen deist and heretical opinions in France in those already critical of the established church. Travel literature and missionary accounts, by accumulating evidence of aboriginal religion and virtue, undermined the simple equating of Catholic with good.

Whatever the effects culture contacts had on the French, they do not seem to have been as immediately disquieting and traumatic as the effects on Amerindian societies. Conversion could only be a disruptive factor, unless the entire population converted and the whole apparatus of French institutions and life-style were adopted. What was formerly a homogeneous and logically integrated system of beliefs and values was challenged and became disorganized. The result was sometimes personal and social demoralization reflected in the excessively high rates of social dependency among the converts. The conversion experience carried with it a mandate to assimilate the Amerindians (unless they could be kept completely isolated, as in the early Jesuit plan for Huronia) so as to bring them into a new homogeneous and logically integrated European Christian society.

1. Clarence J. Glacken, *Traces on the Rhodian Shore. Nature and Culture in Western Thought from Ancient Times to the End of the Eighteenth Century* (Berkeley: 1967), pp. 355-362, 398-405.
2. Margaret T. Hodgen, *Early Anthropology in the Sixteenth and Seventeenth Centuries* (Philadelphia: 1964), pp. 112-114, 166-170.
3. The influence can be seen, for example, in Louis de Gaya, *Cérémonies nuptiales de toutes les nations du monde* (Paris: 1681).
4. *Archives Municipales de Saint-Malo, Série H.H.,* Carton I, 1.
5. André Thévet, *Les Singularitez de la France antarctique, autrement nomée Amérique et de plusieurs Terres, et Isles descouvertes de nostre temps* (Paris: 1555), p. 51.
6. Samuel de Champlain, *Voyages et Descouvertes faites en la Nouvelle France, depuis l'année 1615 jusques à la fin de l'année* 1618 (Paris: 1620), p. 1.
7. Antoine Biet, *Voyage de la France Equinoxiale en l'Isle de Cayenne* (Paris: 1664), p. 361.
8. Claude d'Abbeville, *Histoire de la Mission des Pères Capucins en l'Isle de Maragnan et terres circonvoisines* (Paris: 1614), p. 328; Paul Le Jeune, *Relation de ce qui s'est passé en la Nouvelle-France en l'année 1633* (Paris: 1634), p. 76.
9. R. G. Thwaites, ed., *The Jesuit Relations and Allied Documents* (New York: 1959), Vol. IV, pp. 191-193.
10. Paul Le Jeune, *Briève Relation du Voyage de la Nouvelle France* (Paris: 1632), p. 28.
11. Thomas LeFebvre, *Discours Sommaire de la Navigation et du Commerce* (Rouen: 1650), p. 207.
12. J. Tailhan, ed., *Mémoire sur les Moeurs, Coustumes et Relligion des Sauvages de l'Amérique septentrionale par Nicolas Perrot* (Paris: 1864), pp. 3-7, 12-21, 40-41. The citation is from pp. 12-13.
13. Thwaites, *op. cit.,* Vol. II, p. 77.
14. *Ibid.,* Vol. L, p. 285.
15. *Ibid.,* Vol. I, p. 59; VI, p. 159.
16. *Ibid.,* Vol. X, pp. 129-131.
17. Chrestien Le Clercq, *Nouvelle Relation de la Gaspésie, qui contient les Moeurs & la Religion des Sauvages Gaspésiens* (Paris: 1691), pp. 268-275.
18. Milton Quaife, ed., *The Western Country in the 17th Century. The Memoirs of LaMothe Cadillac and Pierre Liette* (New York: 1962), pp. 53-58.
19. Nicolas Perrot, "Memoir on the Manners, Customs, and Religion of the Savages of North America," in Emma Helen Blair, ed., *The Indian Tribes of the Upper Mississippi Valley and Region of the Great Lakes* (Cleveland: 1911), Vol. I, pp. 47-49.

20. Thwaites, *op. cit.*, Vol. IX, p. 308; X, p. 320; XXIX, p. 109; XXXVIII, pp. 255, 259; XLIV, pp. 235, 283; XLVIII, p. 109; LXVII, p. 343.
21. *Ibid.*, Vol. XLVI, p. 65.
22. Sieur de Cobes, *Coppie d'une Lettre Envoyée en la Nouvelle-France, ou Canada par le Sieur de Cobes, Gentilhomme Poictevin, à un sien amy* (Lyon: 1609), p. 13. On the other hand, Jacques-August de Thou published the first edition of his history in Latin in 1604, in which he summarized Thévet, de Léry and Lescarbot, and he concluded that the Amerindians could not be readily Christianized nor New France effectively colonized. Cf. Jacques-A. de Thou, *Histoire universelle de Jacques-Auguste de Thou depuis 1543 jusqu'en 1607* (Basel: 1742), Vol. X, pp. 232-233.
23. George M. Wrong, ed., *The Long Journey to the Country of the Hurons by Father Gabriel Sagard* (Toronto: 1939), pp. 213-214.
24. Thwaites, *op. cit.*, Vol. II, p. 13.
25. John G. Shea, ed., *Chrestien Le Clercq: First Establishment of the Faith in New France* (New York: 1887), Vol. I, p. 165.
26. Dom Guy Oury, *Marie de l'Incarnation, Ursuline (1599-1672). Correspondence* (Solesmes: 1971), pp. 36-37, 57.
27. *Ibid.*, September 1, 1639, p. 88.
28. Thwaites, *op. cit.*, Vol. XVI, p. 58; XVII, pp. 60-62.
29. Oury, *op. cit.*, September 3, 1640, p. 94.
30. *Ibid.*, September 4, 1641, p. 137.
31. J. H. Elliott, *The Old World and the New, 1492-1650* (Cambridge: 1970), p. 25; Marcel Bataillon, "Novo Mundo e fim do Mundo," *Revista de Historia* (Sao Paulo), No. 18 (1954), pp. 343-351; Charles L. Sanford, *The Quest for Paradise. Europe and the American Moral Impression* (Urbana: 1961), pp. 38-40. Also relevant are George Boas, *Essays on Primitivism and Related Ideas in the Middle Ages* (Baltimore: 1948); George Boas and Arthur O. Lovejoy, eds., *Documentary History of Primitivism and Related Ideas* (Baltimore: 1955); M. Eliade, *The Myth of the Eternal Return* (London: 1955); P. Vleilliaud, *La Fin du Monde* (Paris: 1952).
32. Norman Cohn, *The Pursuit of the Millenium* (London: 1957), pp. 97-107.
33. E. R. Adair, "France and the Beginnings of New France," *Canadian Historical Review* XXV, No. 3 (September, 1944), pp. 246-278; Raoul Allier, *La Cabale des Dévots, (1627-1666)* (Paris: 1902); Alphonse Auguste, *Les Sociétés secrètes catholiques du XVIIe siècle* (Paris: 1913); Alfred Rébelliau, *La Compagnie secrète du Saint Sacrement: Lettres, 1639-1662* (Paris: 1908); Maurice Souriau, *Le Mysticisme en Normandie au XVIIe Siècle* (Paris: 1923).
34. Oury, *op. cit.*, XII, pp. 26-27.
35. *Ibid.*, XVII, pp. 42-43.
36. Thwaites, *op. cit.*, Vol. V, p. 159; XXXVIII, pp. 109-119.
37. *A.H.D.Q., Lettres, Séries I,* Lamy to Mother Marie de St. Bonaventure, March, 1648.
38. Cohn, *op. cit.*, pp. 97-107; also, Henri Desroche, "Micromillénarismes et communautarisme utopique en Amérique du Nord du XVIIe au XIXe siècle," *Archives de Sociologie des Religions,* No. 4 (juillet-décembre, 1957), pp. 57-92; for the Spanish Franciscan antecedents see J. L. Phelan, *The Millenial Kingdom of the Franciscans in the New World* Berkeley: 1956).
39. Thwaites, *op. cit.*, Vol. VIII, p. 189; Joseph P. Donnelly, *Thwaites' Jesuit Relations, Errata and Addenda* (Chicago: 1967), p. 64.
40. Oury, *op. cit.*, L, p. 119.
41. *Ibid.*, XLV, p. 104; LVIII, p. 139.

42. Peter Duignan, "Early Jesuit Missionaries: A Suggestion for Further Study," *American Anthropologist* 60, No. 4 (August, 1958), pp. 725-732.
43. Jacques Maritain, *Man and the State* (Chicago: 1951), pp. 81-95. The argument is that general Catholic morality was not binding for an individual living in a non-European culture until such time as his moral sense could be awakened and it was possible for him to observe consistently the moral laws of Catholicism.
44. Lucien Campeau, ed., *La Première Mission d'Acadie (1602-1616)* (Québec: 1969), Vol. I, Doc. 63, Pierre Biard to Christopher Baltazar, June 10, 1611, pp. 139-140.
45. W. L. Grant, ed., *The History of New France by Marc Lescarbot* (Toronto: 1911), Vol. II, pp. 179-180.
46. William F. Ganong, ed., *New Relation of Gaspesia by Father Chrestien Le Clercq* (Toronto: 1910), pp. 140-141.
47. Thwaites, *op. cit.*, Vol. VI, p. 289; X, p. 119; XV, p. 155; XXXIX, p. 119; LXVII, p. 145.
48. *Ibid.*, Vol. IV, pp. 261-262; XVI, p. 256; XXIV, p. 309; LXVII, pp. 145-147; LXIX, pp. 289-290; LXXI, pp. 222-223, 254, 272-275, 290.
49. *Ibid.*, Vol. X, p. 119.
50. *Ibid.*, Vol. LXV, p. 131; LXVIII, p. 299.
51. Dom Albert Jamet, ed., *Marie de l'Incarnation, Ursuline de Tours: Fondatrice des Ursulines de la Nouvelle-France. Ecrits Spirituels et Historiques* (Paris: 1930), Vol. II, *Relation* of 1654, pp. 368-370.
52. Thwaites, *op. cit.*, Vol. IX, pp. 87-88.
53. James B. Conacher, ed., *The History of Canada or New France by Father François du Creux, S. J.* (Toronto: 1951), Vol. I, p. 160.
54. Wrong, *op. cit.*, p. 97.
55. Thwaites, *op. cit.*, Vol. XIX, pp. 123-165; XXVI, p. 201; XXXII, p. 99. *Narratives of New Netherland, 1609-1664* (New York: 1909), pp. 359,
56. Bruce G. Trigger, *The Huron, Farmers of the North* (New York: 1969), pp. 11-20; *ibid.*, "Settlement as an Aspect of Iroquoian Adaptation at the Time of Contact," *American Anthropologist* 65 (1963), pp. 86-101.
57. Thwaites, *op. cit.*, Vol. XXXVIII, p. 179, 189-191; XL, p. 24; XLI, pp. 37-39, 61, 87, 91, 201-203, 219; XLII, pp. 33, 39, 45, 49, 59, 201, 215; S. Fernow, ed., *Documents relating to the History and Settlement of the Towns along the Hudson and Mohawk Rivers* (Albany: 1881), Vol. XIII, pp. 176, 185, 186, 240; XIV, pp. 359, 373; J. F. Jameson ed., *Narratives of New Netherland, 1609-1664* (New York: 1909), pp. 359, 404.
58. Thwaites, *op. cit.*, Vol. XLIII, pp. 97-103, 169; Fernow, *op. cit.*, Vol. XIII, pp. 72-74, 531-532.
59. Thwaites, *op. cit.*, Vol. XX, pp. 27-31.
60. *Ibid.*, Vol. VIII, p. 261; XXX, p. 27, 29-31.
61. Louis Hennepin, *A New Discovery of a Vast Country in America* (London: 1698), Vol. II, p. 66.
62. Anthony F. C. Wallace, "Dreams and the Wishes of the Soul: A Type of Psycho-analytic Theory among the Seventeenth Century Iroquois," *American Anthropologist* 60, No. 2 (April, 1958), pp. 234-248.
63. Thwaites, *op. cit.*, Vol. XXXIII, p. 189.
64. *Ibid.*, Vol. XLIII, pp. 265-267.
65. *Ibid.*, Vol. LIV, p. 97.
66. *Ibid.*, Vol. LI, p. 235.
67. *Ibid.*, Vol. XX, pp. 27-29.
68. *Ibid.*, Vol. XVII, p. 179.
69. *Ibid.*, Vol. LVIII, p. 275.
70. *Ibid.*, Vol. LVIII, p. 201.
71. Oury, *op. cit.*, p. 67.

72. Wrong, *op. cit.,* p. 78.
73. Thwaites, *op. cit.,* Vol. X, p. 39.
74. Conacher, *op. cit.,* Vol. I, p. 194.
75. Thwaites, *op. cit.,* Vol. XXXIII, p. 45.
76. *Ibid.,* Vol. LVIII, p. 285.
77. Conacher, *op. cit.,* Vol. I, p. 227.
78. Oury, *op. cit.,* Letter XXX, pp. 67-68.
79. *Ibid.,* XLIV, p. 102; XLV, p. 104; L, p. 117; Thwaites, *op. cit.,* Vol. XIX, pp. 90-120.
80. Oury, *op. cit.,* Letter L, pp. 117-118.
81. Thwaites, *op. cit.,* Vol. XVIII, p. 41.
82. Oury, *op. cit.,* Vol. CX, p. 323.
83. Thwaites, *op. cit.,* Vol. XXXI, p. 123.
84. *Ibid.,* Vol. VIII, pp. 121-123; X, p. 223; XIV, pp. 37-39; XV, p. 49; XIX, pp. 85-87, 197; XX, p. 75; XXIII, p. 67; XXVIII, p. 63; XXX, pp. 21, 23; XXXIII, p. 219.
85. *Ibid.,* Vol. XXXIV, pp. 105, 217.
86. *Ibid.,* Vol. XXVIII, p. 53; XXIII, p. 137.
87. *Ibid.,* Vol. XXXIII, p. 233.
88. *Ibid.,* Vol. XII, pp. 211, 276; XV, p. 127.
89. Hennepin, *op. cit.,* Vol. II, p. 84.
90. Thwaites, *op. cit.,* Vol. LVIII, pp. 217-219.
91. Hennepin, *op. cit.,* Vol. II, p. 63.
92. Jean de Léry, *Histoire d'un Voyage fait en la Terre du Brésil, autrement dite Amérique* (La Rochelle: 1578), p. 278.
93. Chrestien Le Clercq, *Nouvelle Relation de la Gaspésie qui contient les Moeurs et la Religion des Sauvages* (Paris: 1691), p. 276.
94. Hennepin, *op. cit.,* Vol. II, p. 76.
95. C. H. Laverdière and H. R. Casgrain, eds., *Le Journal des Jésuites* (Montréal: 1892), pp. 10, 15.
96. Gilbert Chinard, *L'Amérique et le rêve exotique dans la littérature française au XVIIe et XVIIIe siècle* (Paris: 1934), pp. 152-156. The Jesuit reply to the Jansenist publication was François Annat, *Faussetez et imposture d'un Cahier qui a pour titre: Lettre de l'Illustrissime Jean de Palafox de Mendoza, évesque d'Angelopolis* (Paris: 1659).
97. Louis Hennepin, *Nouvelle Découverte d'un très grand Pays, situé dans l'Amérique entre le Nouveau Mexique et la Mer Glaciale* (Utrecht: 1697), pp. 70, 132, 331.
98. François Giry, *La Vie de M. Jean Jacques Olier, prêtre, fondateur et premier Supérieur du Séminaire de Saint-Sulpice* (Paris: 1687), pp. 98-99.
99. Thwaites, *op. cit.,* Vol. LVIII, p. 85.
100. *Ibid.,* Vol. LXIII, p. 219. See also Vol. XVIII, p. 198; LV, p. 276.
101. *Ibid.,* Vol. XXXIV, p. 183.
102. *Ibid.,* Vol. XIX, pp. 146, 150; XX, p. 82; XXXIII, p. 168; XXXVI, pp. 208, 210; XXXIX, p. 286; L, p. 108; LII, pp. 26, 244. Useful is Léon Pouliot, "Etats mystiques chez les Convertis Indiens dans la Nouvelle-France," *Société Canadienne d'Histoire de l'Eglise Catholique, Rapport 1939-1940* (1940), pp. 99-106.
103. Sieur Bertrand, *Lettre Missive touchant la conversion et baptesme du grand Sagamos de la Nouvelle France* (Paris: 1610), pp. 3-4.
104. Oury, *op. cit.,* p. 649.
105. *A.N., Colonies, Series C11A,* Vol. IX, Denonville to Minister, August 25, 1687, pp. 70-71.
106. Thwaites, *op. cit.,* Vol. XXVII, pp. 101, 119; XXIX, p. 35; XXXIV, p. 183; XXXIX, pp. 171, 261; LIII, p. 203.
107. *Ibid.,* Vol. V, p. 251.
108. Gabriel Sagard Théodat, *Histoire du Canada et Voyages que les frères*

Mineurs Recollects y ont faicts pour la Conuersion des Infidelles (Paris: 1636), p. 165.

109. *Ibid.*, p. 9.
110. Marc Lescarbot, *La Conversion des Sauvages qui ont esté baptizés en la Nouvelle France, cette année 1610* (Paris: 1610), pp. 23-34.
111. Thwaites, *op. cit.*, Vol. IV, pp. 211, 269.
112. *Ibid.*, Vol. XXXIX, p. 141.
113. *Ibid.*, Vol. LXVI, p. 173.
114. Grant, *op. cit.*, Vol. I, p. 132, my addition.
115. Ezechiel Carré, *Echantillon de la Doctrine que les Jésuites ensègnent aus Sauvages du Nouveau Monde* (Boston: 1690), pp. 1-11.
116. Cotton Mather, *Magnalia Christi Americana: or, the Ecclesiastical History of New-England, from its First Planting unto the Year of our Lord, 1698* (London: 1702), Vol. L, p. 521.
117. Thwaites, *op. cit.*, Vol. LVII, pp. 95-97.
118. *Ibid.*, Vol. I, pp. 4, 305; III, p. 81; IV, pp. 93, 219, 256-260; also, William F. Ganong, ed., *New Relation of Gaspesia by Father Chrestien Le Clercq* (Toronto: 1910), pp. 101-102.
119. *Journal des Jésuites*, p. 224; Thwaites, *op. cit.*, Vol. XLIV, pp. 261-275; Jeanne-Françoise Juchereau de la Ferté, *Histoire de l'Hôtel-Dieu de Québec* (Montauban: 1751), pp. 108-110; *P.A.C.*, MG 18/E7, "Ecrits Autographes de Marguerite Bourgeoys," p. 9, Cf. Frederick Eberschweiler, "An Indian Clergy Impossible," *Catholic World* 65 (1897), pp. 815-824; L. W. Reilly, "Why there is no Indian Priest," *American Ecclesiastical Review* IV, No. 4 (April, 1891), pp. 267-280.
120. Thwaites, *op. cit.*, Vol. XXVII, pp. 67-69.
121. *Ibid.*, Vol. XXXV, p. 249.
122. J. W. Ford, ed., *Some Correspondence between the Governors and Treasurers of the New England Company in London and the Commissioners of the United Colonies in America, the Missionaries of the Company, and Others between the Years 1657 and 1712* (London: 1897), pp. 42, 84.
123. Guillaume du Choul, *Discours de la religion des anciens Romains*, 2 vols. (Lyon: 1567); Pierre Mussard, *Les Conformités des cérémonies modernes avec les anciennes où il est prouvé que les cérémonies de l'Eglise romaine sont empruntés des payens* (Leyden: 1667); Polydore Vergile, *An Abridgment of the notable works of Polidore Vergile conteynyng . . . rites and ceremonies commonly used in the Churche, and the originall beginning of the same* (London: 1546); Pierre Viret, *Du Vray ministere et des vrais sacremens d'icelles, et des faus sacremens de l'Eglise de l'antéchrist, et des additions adjoustées par les hommes* (Genève: 1560). The most influential Protestant history that attacked the Spanish treatment of the Amerindians, the Catholic missionary approach, and the official French policy of reserving New France to Catholic missionary work was Urbain Chauveton, *Histoire nouvelle du Nouveau Monde, contenant en somme ce que les Hespagnols ont fait jusqu'à present aux Indes occidentales* (Genève: 1579).
124. Thwaites, *op. cit.*, Vol. III, p. 123.
125. I am indebted to Geoffrey Atkinson, *Les Relations de Voyages du XVIIe Siècle et l'Evolution des Idées. Contribution à l'étude de la formation de l'esprit du XVIIIe Siècle* (New York: 1971), pp. 128-162, for this line of reasoning.
126. Abbeville, *op. cit.*, p. 271.
127. Marc Lescarbot, *La Conversion des Sauvages qui ont esté baptisez en la Nouvelle France, cette année 1610* (Paris: 1610), p. 33.

CHAPTER III

SOCIAL PROBLEMS AND DIFFERENCES

The contact experience was rife with cultural implications which were not always understood at the moment, and the passage of time has not always clarified the nature of the tensions and accommodations that were the result of the meeting of French and Amerindians in North America. Apart from the French views of Amerindian nature and nurture, and the ideological impositions of evangelization, there was a complex of social problems resulting from cultural clashes.

A commonly expressed French opinion of Amerindian societies, particularly of the various nomadic Algonkian-speaking groups, was that the natives were idlers and vagabonds. Nomadic aboriginal life was compared with the movement of beggars in France, who in many cases were the unemployed and the unfortunate in search of work, better living conditions, or charity. France was subject to great periods of scarcity and famine; one of the principal objectives of the secret Company of the Holy Sacrament was to combat the disorders, real or imagined, created by the lower-class malcontents. The missionaries deplored the lack of sedentary settlements in the Acadian, Gaspesian and Tadoussac regions where permanent mission stations could be located, and equated Algonkian nomadism to some extent with the unsettling movement of populations in France. Even the divison of labour between men and women in native societies displeased the French monarch who was certain he detected in this a serious defect with grave social consequences:

> His Majesty knows that the males among these peoples wish to devote themselves not to the tilling of the soil but only to the chase of animals, whose pelts they sell to the Europeans in exchange for cloth or trinkets, but His Majesty knows also that the Indian females are very hard-working especially for the growing maize which is their food.[1]

Colbert, as Minister of the Marine with responsibility for the colonies, was not long in suggesting to colonial officials the need for and means of stamping out nefarious aboriginal idleness.

The Amerindians, on the other hand, were surprised to learn that famines, begging, poverty and discontent were common in contemporary France. Some had naively expected that France was a land where the ideals preached by the missionaries were the everyday qualities of life. But the description of life given by those natives who had visited France, and who had survived to return and recount their adventures to their compatriots, indicated a land enjoying an abundance of food, many large towns, and a large population, yet with many poor and unfortunates reduced to charity for survival. On the contrary, the Récollet missionaries, upon arriving in the country of the Hurons, commented favourably on the absence of beggars and on the sharing habits of the natives:

> . . . . those of their Nation, who offer reciprocal Hospitality, and help each other so much that they provide for the needs of all so that there is no poor beggar at all in their towns, bourgs and villages, as I said elsewhere, so that they found it very bad hearing that there were in France a great number of needy & beggars, and thought that it was due to a lack of charity, and blamed us greatly, saying that if we had some intelligence we woul dset some order in the matter, the remedies being simple.[2]

To Frenchmen who thought that they had a well-ordered and disciplined society, a reasonable way of life, and a civilized community, it came as quite a shock to be reproved by unsophisticated aborigines whom they sometimes regarded as deprived of right reason and right religion, for their injustice, their improvidence, and their inequality.

There is evidence that the first contacts added a new element of violence and disturbance to Amerindian societies which, because of inter-tribal wars and the blood feud, could hardly have been termed a pacific civilization. Nicolas Denys believed that the contact of fishermen with the Atlantic coastal tribes resulted in increased violence, drunkenness and immorality. He was pessimistic of the outcome of sustained contact between the two cultures to the point of deploring even the practice of bringing tribesmen to France. He wrote:

> And the Indians whom the fisherman have taken to France have contributed still more to it through consorting there with blasphemers, in pot-houses and vile places, to which they have been taken.[3]

Amerindian hospitality and sharing of goods were regarded as the most praiseworthy qualties of aboriginal life by the fur traders and *coureurs-de-bois* who were so often the beneficiaries and whose survival and success depended on the goodwill of the natives. Nicolas Perrot, who knew the tribes of the Great Lakes region well, reported that when strangers who had sojourned among them departed they were laden with the necessary goods for the voyage, or "if he is inclined to prefer peltries to other goods, these are given to him." He emphasized that this liberality was exercised as abundantly towards those "who give them nothing" as to "those who carry to them." Unfortunately, in his opinion, contact with Europeans was eroding these fine qualities:

> This sort of reception is ordinary among the savages; in point of hospitality, it is only the Abenakis, and those who live with the French people, who have become somewhat less liberal, on account of the advice that our people have given them by placing before them the obligations resting on them to preserve what they have. At the present time, it is evident that these savages are fully as selfish and avaricious as formerly they were hospitable . . . . Those of the savages who have not been too much humoured [by the French] ar eattached to the ancient custom of their ancestors, and among themselves are very compassionate.[4]

D'Avity reported that the aborigines were "in no wise ungrateful, but give each other everything without ever daring to refuse their companions; or to eat without sharing with them what they have."[5]

It was a communalism that appealed to those inclined to Christian utopianism. The Récollets were very moved by the Huron demonstrations of hospitality and kindness towards them, and their willingness to share their lodges, their food, and their feasts. The priests regretted that they were unable to share some of their possessions with their hosts, and feared they might be misunderstood and deemed ungrateful and avaricious. Dièreville praised the Micmacs for their unbounded hospitality and sharing of goods:

> They assist one another to the full extent of their power; if one has food, he never fails to share it with those who have none & who are suffering from lack of it. An Indian would die of hunger rather than eat alone a Teal which he had killed, even though it might be the means of restoring his strength; he would take it to the Wigwam, where he knew others, like himself, were in need of it, & each one would have his share.[6]

This contrasted favourably with growing evidence of French greed and competitiveness.

Sagard told of being adopted by a Huron family, the solicitous care his "brother" and "mother" took of him, and the general curiosity and kindness of the entire village where he first settled. He was most impressed by the fact that they had given him "as much space as could be occupied by a small household" and he later discovered that "they turned one out for my sake the day after my arrival." The welcome reserved for him amazed him:

> The parents of my savage gave me a very kind reception in their own way, and with extraordinary caresses showed me how pleased and glad they were at my coming. They treated me as kindly as they did their own child, and gave me abundant cause to praise God, when I saw how benevolent and faithful these poor people are, although without the knowledge of Him.[7]

He noted the co-operative spirit that pervaded the village, even to the point that the whole village turned out to build a lodge for a man who needed one.

> This is an excellent institution, and much to be admired among savage people whom we think to be, and who in fact are, less civilized than ourselves. But as regards us, who were strangers to them and new-comers, it was a great thing that they should show themselves so full of human kindness as to put up a building for us with good feelings so general and universal . . . .[8]

Sagard attempted to give a balanced picture of Huron life and, as he said, along with the praiseworthy he was obliged to give "many uncivilized and extravagant details." He warned against assuming "they have no faults" because "all men are subject to imperfection," especially untutored savages without "decorum and polite behaviour" except such as "taught by nature pure and simple."[9] Because they lacked refinement and discipline one could discern "but little of the light of reason and the purity of a purified nature."

Their hospitality was spontaneous and generous for whenever Sagard went to visit from lodge to lodge the natives were quite pleased "deeming it an honour and a favour, and complaining that they did not see us there often enough." His hosts invariably made room for him to sit on a mat, offered him food, and passed the calumet to smoke, which he always refused because, as he said, "I had never wished to become habituated to tobacco."[10] French standards of hospitality and communalism were sadly deficient in comparison to Huron practices. Sagard concluded that they "held it proper to help wayfarers" without looking for remuneration or gain, and that they received "with politeness," expecting no reward, "anyone who is not an enemy."

If the social values of the French and the various Algonkian peoples are compared a wide divergence becomes apparent. The Algonkians shared material resources although each man was expected to provide for himself and his dependents both food and the other necessities of life. Outside the family, leadership and authority were largely lacking; although individuals could acquire more prestige on the basis of skill in hunting, warfare, or healing. The area occupied by a tribe or band was owned collectively and was available for anyone to use. The French commented on the initiative and enterprise of the tribes in such minimal economic organization. The Algonkins, Abenakis, Eskimos and "abundance more Savages that have convers'd with the Europeans" were described as being "as sharp and politick" as Frenchmen; Hennepin added they were not "Brutes and irrational" but they understood "their own Interest thorowly, and order their Affairs very discreetly."[11] The Iroquois' admiration for the Récollet community of goods and observance of apostolic poverty was an exceptional case of cultural convergence. As Hennepin observed: "It is certain, that the Iroquese had a most tender Respect for the Franciscan Monks, having observ'd them to live all in common, without reserving any particular Possessions."[12] Clearly, these circumstances encouraged individual efficiency and practicality.

Intimately related to such an economic arrangement was the fact that even skill in hunting or in warfare did not grant power or command over others, or imply the obligation to be obeyed by others. This lack of leadership greatly puzzled the French, just as the French insistence on commands, class, hierarchies and estates puzzled the natives. The Jesuits did not know how to gain the ascendancy over peoples holding such a concept of power:

> There is nothing so difficult as to control the tribes of America. All these barbarians have the law of wild asses, — they are born, live, and die in a liberty without restraint; they do not know what is meant by bridle or bit.[13]

They were quite mistaken to imagine that the natives knew no restraints, no punishments and no taboos, and, in fact, their own correspondence afforded proof to the contrary. A child who violated an important taboo was impressed with the possible consequences for the community. In the absence of political authority as conceived by the French, the individual was compelled to protect himself, to seek supernatural power, and to rely as best he could on his own resources. Hennepin reported that the natives of the Mississippi regions were more politically organized than their northern neighbours:

> Their Chiefs have a more absolute Authority than those of the other Savages, which Power is very narrow; and those that live

the nearest to the Mouth of the River, have such a deference for their Chief, that they dare not pass between him and a Flambeau, which is always carri'd before him in all Ceremonies. These Chiefs have Servants and Officers to wait upon them; They distribute Rewards and Presents as they think fit. In short, they have amongst them a Form of Political Government; and I must own they make a tolerable use of their Reason.[14]

A deeper understanding of some of the democratic principles operating in Iroquoian societies would have astonished him even more.

The importance of the dream as a source of supernatural authority and sanction for behaviour has already been discussed in the context of Amerindian religions. It must, in addition, be seen in the framework of the whole society, as part of a well-integrated life-style. The leader, whom the French thought did not exist in Algonkian society, was the man who through a visionary dream had acquired supernatural power directed towards practical everyday skills, resourcefulness in hunting, success in warfare, or discernment in healing the sick. The same qualities of leadership existed in Iroquoian societies. The individual was, by aboriginal ideals, attuned to the power and mystery of nature, sensitive to the emotional and aesthetic aspects of life, and extremely concerned about his personal, as well as tribal, spiritual and moral welfare.

What similarities, differences and accommodations in value systems became evident in culture contact? It is clear that the Amerindians placed great value on individualism, self-reliance, personal identity and independence. French political, economic and religious institutionalism was group-centred rather than individualistically oriented. Tendencies towards subservience and social identification found among the French were very limited among the Amerindians. Perrot was very critical of this quality in the natives:

> The savage does not know what it is to obey. It is more often necessary to entreat him than to command him; he nevertheless yields to all demands made upon him — especially when he fancies that there is either glory or profit to be expected therefrom, and then he comes foreward of his own accord and offers his aid.[15]

The fur traders and interpreters who lived among the natives were accused by their compatriots and coreligionists of the same egocentricity.

Native ability to grapple with problems in a resourceful manner, but with a minimum of abstract speculation, was necessary to the

French for survival in the New World. The French soon adopted native modes of travelling, dressing, hunting, fighting and even eating. They learned much about new foods, new medicines, new ways of building shelters, and generally surviving in the woods. This utilitarianism soon became one of the qualities distinguishing a Canadian from a metropolitan Frenchman. Not a little was owed to the aborigines who had learned over the centuries to live in harmony with the physical world that was so new to Frenchmen. Nicolas Perrot maintained that this dependency upon the natives became known to the tribesmen and was one of the causes of the great insolence of the Hurons, Ottawas, Fox and Sioux to French traders in the late seventeenth century:

> See what the French accomplished in the first establishment of the Colony, although it was then of very little importance in the world. They have been able to preserve and maintain the glory of the nation against the savages (who were incomparably stronger and more numerous at that time than they are now), since, if I dare say it, we were the masters. Did we not oblige them to recognize this by valuable presents, which were acknowledged only by very ordinary ones? and did we even inform Them, in offering these, that it was done only through compassion for their miserable condition? On the other hand, in this present time of ours they desire to dominate us and be our superiors; they even regard us as people who are in some manner dependent on them.[16]

Indian resourcefulness saved the French garrison at Niagara in 1688 when they were almost annihilated by a severe epidemic; the Miamis kept them well supplied with deer and wild turkey throughout their ordeal.[17]

In addition to resourcefulness, the natives were noted for their flexibility and adaptability in the wilderness environment. This stood in sharp contrast to the French stress on routine and careful advance planning. The natives seem to have been virtually free of the compulsions which dominated French character. This quality made them appear very undependable in European eyes. Perrot drew from this a sound maxim for French policy-makers:

> But you can, as a result of what I have set down, easily understand what are the traits of the savages. The instance of the Tsonontouans will readily convince you that it is impossible to depend on any of the tribes; and that it is much better to let them settle their quarrels among themselves than to meddle therein, unless this is to reconcile them.[18]

Another trait which set the Amerindians apart was their ability to retain an emotional aloofness and a social detachment of which Frenchmen were incapable. The French over-emphasized emotional ties, gave the fullest vent to their emotions and were unrestrained in their spontaneous affective expression. Sagard reported that the Hurons called Frenchmen "women" because they were too hasty, "excited in their movements," and often "speak all together and interrupt one another." Visitors to the Hurons, for example, recorded that they paid honour to their dead and greatly lamented the death of any tribesman. Yet, Sagard was amazed by their very restrained burials:

> But the Hurons bury theirs with tears and in sadness, yet with such restraint, and so governed by the standards of reasonable behaviour that this pitiful tribe appears to have an absolute control of their tears and their feelings, so that they only give way to them as a matter of duty, and only check them under a similar sense of duty.[19]

From their tenderest years, the children of the aborigines were taught to endure hardships, take abuse quietly, and generally conduct themselves with the sobriety and gravity of Veneian doges. Sagard recounted that he could barely eat the ill-prepared and dirty food his Huron hosts prepared for him but he decided to bear his cross as stoically as he could. He tried to remain cheerful in spite of his hunger and weakness and said he "often sang hymns for my spiritual comfort and to please my savages." His hosts did not fail to notice his quiet resolution and patience, which accorded so well with their own values. Sagard concluded from this experience:

> This gave me much to reflect on, and made me wonder at their firmness and the control they have of their feelings, and how well they can bear with one another and support and help one another if need be. And I can truly say that I found more good in them than I had imagined, and that the example of their patience often led me to force myself more resolutely to endure with cheerfulness and courage everything vexatious that happened to me, for the love of God and the edification of my neighbour.[20]

In other words, the Amerindian example enabled him to overcome the normal French reaction to his situation.

Closely related to this dominant cultural trait in Amerindian societies was the deference reported among all the tribal groups. They took care to avoid arousing anger or hostility in others. Emotional aloofness and social detachment could, in tense or suspicious situations, be interpreted at secretiveness, inscrutability and stolid non-committal.

Hennepin aptly described the emotional atmosphere of a French conference with the Seneca in 1679:

> Notwithstanding that seeming Approbation, they believe what they please and no more; and therefore 'tis impossible to know when they are really persuaded of those things you have mention'd unto them, which I take to be one of the greatest Obstructions to their Conversion; For their Civility hindering them from making any Objection, or contradict what is said unto them, they seem to approve of it, though perhaps they laugh at it in private, or else never bestow a Moment to reflect upon it, such being their Indifference for a future Life.[21]

This deference was, at least in part, to maintain personal esteem and assure the individual that he was liked and respected. It was often shown in a conscious antipathy to aggression: "They think every one ought to be left to his own Opinion, without being thwarted."[22] Sagard reported Hurons solemnly accepting reparations from the French for a wrong done them, but laughing greatly at the French action when they returned to their own villages.

These qualities in Amerindian society were in the long-run contributing factors to the disruption of the aboriginal cultures. Freedom in Huron society, for example, was so accentuated by the great emphasis on individual self-expression, the permissiveness of child-rearing, and the independence of the kin-group that it actually threatened cohesive action and established authority.[23] In the face of the internal threat posed by French missionary work, the devastating epidemics and pandemics, the growing reliance on the French fur trade, and the external threat of the Iroquois, the Huron tribes required cohesive action, a highly disciplined community and ideological unity to survive. Their downfall may be explained largely in terms of this fundamental weakness.

The Amerindian admiration for European technology, for manufactured goods — particularly knives, kettles and guns — fundamentally altered native ways of living and brought them into a state of dependence upon European suppliers. The economic contact, in other words, undermined native self-sufficiency and self-reliance. Denys noted that the Micmacs came to rely more and more on trade goods "the use of which has become to them an indispensable necessity." He concluded that this dependence on the French could only increase with the passing of time:

> They have abandoned all their own utensils, whether because of the trouble they had as well to make as to use them, or because of the facility of obtaining from us, in exchange for

skins which cost them almost nothing, the things which seemed to them invaluable, not so much for their novelty as for the convenience they derived therefrom. Above everything the kettle has always seemed to them, and seems still, the most valuable article they can obtain from us. This was rather pleasingly exemplified by an Indian whom the late Monsieur de Razilly sent from Acadia to Paris; for, passing by the Rue Aubry-bouché, where there were then many coppersmiths, he asked of his interpreter if they were not relatives of the King, and if this was not the trade of the grandest Seigniors of the Kingdom.[24]

Denys noted a number of changes in Micmac practices as a result of prolonged contact with the French. The natives were abandoning their custom of placing valuable possessions in the graves of the deceased, not so much because they were being disabused of their former religious beliefs but "as much through a spirit of self-interest as through any other reason." Iron weapons had increased their success in hunting and "the axes, the kettles, the knives, and everything that is supplied them, is much more convenient and portable than those which they had in former times."[25]

The scientific knowledge of the French was sometimes used to advantage in dealing with the Amerindians. The missionaries on more than one occasion used their knowledge of impending eclipses to impress the natives, to inspire them with fear, or to gain their admiration. Sagard reported that the Hurons were not entirely ignorant of celestial order and regional differences although their concepts were very imperfect compared to the new concepts gaining acceptance in Europe:

> The savages, like many simple folk, had never imagined that the earth is round and suspended in space, and that one can sail around the world, and that there are nations beneath our feet, nor even that the sun takes journey round the earth; for they thought that the earth had a hole in it, and that the sun went into this hole when it set and remained hidden there until the next morning, when it came out at the other end. Nevertheless they quite understood that night fell earlier in some countries and day began earlier in others; for a Huron, coming back from a long journey, told us in our hut that it was already night in the parts he came from, and yet it was full summer among the Hurons and at the time only about four or five o'clock in the afternoon.[26]

The Amerindians frequently expressed their admiration for the scientific knowledge displayed by the Jesuit missionaries, who were of the intellectual élite of France. Isaac Jogues' tormentors, for example, questioned him at some length about scientific matters and they were so impressed by his wisdom and explanations that they expressed regrets for the tortures they had inflicted upon him.

The permissiveness of Amerindian child-rearing drew many un-flattering remarks from the French. The Récollets noticed that although little account was taken of the legitimacy or illegitimacy of births, all the children seemed to be loved, provided for and offered the necessary security:

> Nevertheless they love their children dearly, in spite of the doubt that they are really their own, and of the fact that they are for the most part very naughty children, paying little respect, and hardly more obedience; for unhappily in these lands the young have no respect for the old, nor are children obedient to their parents, and moreover there is no punishment for any fault.[27]

Sagard's comments revealed as much about French child-rearing as it did about Huron culture. The French could not conceive of any child-rearing not accompanied by a harsh discipline, demands for instant and complete obedience and submission to parents and elders, and the inculcation of an elaborate ritual of etiquette and subservience to one's superiors. The French thought of children as small adults and even imputed to them the knowledge of guilt and dishonesty that would be culturally acquired only as they grew into adolescence.

The permissiveness of Amerindian child-rearing was the natural concomittant of a society that enjoyed more freedom and tolerance than the authoritarian and disciplined society in which Frenchmen were reared. Sagard believed that this permissiveness led to many disorders in the general society, and that it was "too shocking and smacks of nothing less than the brute beast." Bad example and bad upbringing, without punishment or correction, bred insubordination, wilfulness and a lack of respect for established authority. These were the very traits believed to be at the root of the numerous disorders in France in the early decades of the seventeenth century.

There was not complete agreement among observers that permissive up-bringing produced a disorderly and chaotic society. Many of the traits common to the Amerindians already discussed belied such a conclusion. Nicolas Denys said:

> Their children are not obstinate, since they give them everything they ask for, without ever letting them cry for that which they want. The greatest persons give way to the little ones. The father and the mother draw the morsel from the mouth if the child asks for it. They love their children greatly.[28]

However, the freedom and liberty of the New World troubled the power élite of France.

Among the numerous instructions given the first Intendant sent to Quebec (1665) was the injunction to introduce manual labour early in the educational programme of all the children in the colony because, as Louis XIV had said, laziness in the children was the cause of most adult traits of weakness.[29] The first colonial bishop said that in compliance with the expressed desires of the King himself he was attempting to raise some native children "in the manner of life of Frenchman" in order "to discipline them little by little."[30] How did the Amerindians view these efforts and how did they react to them? Marie de l'Incarnation said that the children the Ursulines received "cannot be restrained and if they are, they become melancholy and their melancholy makes them sick."[31] None of the early schools were able to keep the majority of their wards; the Récollets, the Jesuits, the Sisters of the Congregation, the Ursulines, the Vicar Apostolic of New France all found that after some weeks or months the native children became depressed, homesick and so disoriented that they ran away, sometimes knowing they would not be able to reach their homes but unable to endure any longer the restraints and disciplines of formal schooling. As one group of students acted "like wild asses' colts" and escaped, it was replaced by others who were subjected to the same regimen and association with French children who were supposed to assist them in accommodating themselves to the new education. The results were invariably the same as the Jesuits reported:

> . . . these new guests, giving themselves up . . . to thieving, gourmandizing, gaming, idleness, lying and similar irregularities, could not endure the paternal admonitions given them to change their mode of life, and above all the tacit reproofs, conveyed by the example of their companions, who showed as much restraint as they did lawlessness and immoderation.[32]

The Intendant Jean Talon reported in 1670, on his return to New France after a year's absence, that he found the number of children in these schools "greatly diminished" and that the Jesuit missionaries and Bishop Laval had promised to seek new candidates "to raise in our ways, our customs, our language and our teachings."[33] Talon did not understand that it was precisely the ways of the French, their methods of teaching, their curriculum, and their conceptualization that was so foreign, even abhorrent, to the native mind.

The Amerindians frequently expressed their surprise at the harsh disciplinary methods of the French, the "porcupine-like" affection of French mothers who so readily accepted separation from their small children, and the practice of confining children for months in boarding schools. Education in the aboriginal cultures of North America was part of the everyday life of work and play; unlike French education, it was completely integrated with the rhythm of the adult community. Travellers and missionaries reported how the young girls worked with their mothers in the fields, in preparing meals and clothing; how the young boys learned to hunt, fish, trap and fight; how the youth were initiated into tribal customs and taught the ideals and traditions of the group. French education would not only retard their own cultural indoctrination but would unfit them for life with their own people.

It was commonly reported during the years of early contact that the Amerindians parted readily with their children. Were this so, it was surmised that it would be possible to begin the assimilation of the native population through the education of the children, and to effect their conversion by similar methods. It was true that the tribesmen did send their children to live with other tribes as tokens of friendship and alliance but such exchanges, for the act was usually reciprocated, did not involve the cultural stress that resulted from French schooling. Nor did the Amerindians readily part with their children as sending them to other tribes was a form of adoption and not a renunciation of responsibility. Giving their children to the French, on the other hand, meant they had virtually to abandon them.

In 1535 Jacques Cartier had been offered a girl of ten to twelve years of age by Donnacona and another of eight to nine years of age by the chief of Achelacy (Portneuf) to take to France. The older girl escaped from the French vessel anchored in the St. Lawrence. The chieftain intervened and had her returned with the explanation "that they had not advised her to run off, but that she had done so because the ships' boys had beaten her," whereupon the unfortunate child was returned with her companion to the tender care of the French crew.[34] Champlain, in petitioning Louis XIII for funds to help the Récollets establish a seminary for the education of native children, said "the children are daily offered by their parents to your petitioners to be instructed."[35] However, in January, 1628 he was astonished when he was offered three girls to raise because he had learned that they did not part readily with their children nor did they hold French educational methods in high esteem. He could only conclude that the offer was motivated by a desire to cement an alliance or to compensate for the murder of twe Frenchmen.[36] Most subsequent instances of children being offered to be educated by the French were the result of renewed insistence by the missionaries, or part of military and political alliances or pacts, or in a few cases probably abductions.

Apart from the role rewards and punishments played in French education, the entire concept of punishment and correction differed greatly from Amerindian values and behaviour. This was especially clear in the treatment of adult misdemeanours and crimes. The basic and fundamental difference between the two views was that Amerindian societies stressed compensation for the injured party whereas French justice emphasized punishment of the guilty party. French justice demonstrated all the rigidity, lack of flexibility, impersonality, authoritarianism and excessive concentration of power at the top of the administrative pyramid that characterized European societies at the time. The Huron or Iroquois procedures, as shall be seen, were democratic and reflected the values and the personal considerations of the tribe for each individual case. When Sagard complained to the Huron chiefs that an attempt had been made on the life of one of his companions, a general council was assembled. After lengthy investigation and deliberation the council censured the guilty man, awarded Sagard compensation and then called a village feast "to forget the past completely and to remain good friends as before."[37] The council took the occasion to remind the Récollets it preferred that they leave their isolated lodge, where the incident had occurred, and come to dwell in the village proper, sharing one of the long houses with a good family. But the missionaries preferred their comparative privacy to the assurance of provisions and a measure of protection. In 1622 another Récollet missionary baptized and then buried at sea a tribesman who had been taken to Dieppe and had died on the return voyage to Canada. However, he later regretted not having kept locks of his hair and clippings of his nails to offer his relatives as proof of his decease because he feared they would suspect foul play and demand compensation. The only remaining course open was taken:

> We did not omit nevertheless to make presents to the closest relatives of the deceased, to remove from them all subject of complaint, and to assure our position in the matter.[38]

Compensation was not so much blood money as it was an attempt to repair injury, to satisfy the injured parties and to offset revenge. The custom was observed not only with relatives, but sometimes with entire tribes and even tribal spirits.

Galinée described his party's fear in 1669-70 about passing near a Seneca village because shortly before they had left Montreal three French soldiers had murdered a Seneca hunter and stolen his furs. The culprits were brought to trial and were executed in public in the presence of several Senecas. Nevertheless, as Galinée said, "although the bulk of the nation was appeased by this execution, the relatives of the deceased did not consider themselves satisfied and wished at all hazards to sacrifice some Frenchmen to their vengeance, and loudly boasted of it. . . ."[39]

Another source of concern and friction between Europeans and Amerindians was the spread of diseases of pandemic proportions. France itself was still subject to outbreaks of the bubonic plague in the seventeenth century, besides the rapid infection of entire regions through the movement of troops, beggars, pilgrims, unemployed and pedlars. The French may not have been particularly aware of increasing Amerindian mortality rates in New France because they accepted a high mortality in the general population, particularly among infants, a high casualty rate among soldiers (primarily attributable to non-combatant causes), and a cycle of epidemics as normal conditions of life. The average life expectancy was extremely low and it was not unusual for pandemics to carry off a third of the urban population. In addition, severe famines had plagued France in 1594-97 and again in 1659-62. As for the colonies, the long and dangerous ocean crossings from the motherland were fraught with many risks, not least among them infections. Many vessels arrived in Acadia, at Tadoussac or Quebec, with large numbers of the crew and passengers seriously ill; usually these illnesses were traced to the unsanitary conditions on board ship, the poor food, and the presence of contagious diseases. The first winterings by Frenchmen in Canada in the sixteenth century had been marked by serious illnesses, now generally assumed to have been scurvy. It had been the aborigines who provided the clue to better health and survival for these unfortunates.

Infections brought on vessels from France quickly spread to the population of the ports, especially to the hospital at Quebec, and were then carried to the hinterland by missionaries, traders and soldiers. Disease may rightly be termed one of Canada's first importations.[40] In 1659 a typhus epidemic spread from the infected crew and passengers of the *Saint André* arriving at Quebec from France. Similar outbreaks were introduced by vessels from France in 1663, 1665, and 1670, perhaps even more frequently, but the records are not too explicit.[41] In 1663, for example, no fewer than sixty of the two hundred and twenty-five immigrants died on the high seas. Tracy's troops were seriously weakened by a typhus outbreak in the crossing of 1665. As the royal vessels seem to have been particularly subject to outbreaks of disease, Governor Denonville asked that in future colonists be sent on merchant ships where living conditions were better and disease less rampant than on the royal vessels.

The arrival of infectious diseases from France had far graver consequences for the Amerindians than for the handful of Frenchmen in Canada and Acadia in the first half of the seventeenth century. In the native encampments and villages, measles, whooping cough, smallpox, influenza, typhoid, diphtheria, colds, chicken pox, scarlet fever, tuberculosis, and strep infections — in short, all the microscopic parasites of humans which had found their way from diverse corners of the globe to Europe — quickly took on pandemic proportions, decimating the native population and taking a particularly heavy toll among the elderly, who were the guardians and custodians of the tribal traditions, and among the very young, who were the hope for the future of the tribe. Indeed, the comments of seventeenth-century writers lead one to conclude that the early fishing contacts of the fifteenth and sixteenth centuries resulted in widespread epidemics among the Atlantic coastal tribes prior to 1600. In pre-contact days, according to Denys, "they were not subject to diseases, and knew nothing of fevers." He observed without furnishing statistics that "there was formerly a much larger number of Indians than at present." Dièreville noted that by 1700 the Micmac population had declined very markedly.[42] These comments suggest a protohistoric disaster which continued well into the seventeenth century.

The Gaspesian Micmacs, according to traditional lore recorded by the missionary Christian Le Clercq, had sought ot protect themselves spiritually from the first waves of infections to hit North America. They looked first to the sun for protection but then a "beautiful man" holding a cross revealed himself to them in a dream and instructed them to make crosses for their preservation. This cult of the cross, according to the tale related to Le Clercq, did not afford the tribesmen the salutary effects desired so they abandoned their veneration of the symbol. Le Clercq continued:

> Since this Gaspesian nation of the Cross-bearers has been almost wholly destroyed, as much by the war which they have waged with the Iroquois as by the maladies which have infected this land, and which, in three or four visitations, have caused the deaths of a very great number, these Indians have gradually relapsed from their first devotion of their ancestors. So true is it, that even the holiest and most religious practices, by a certain fatality attending human affairs, suffer always much alteration if they are not animated and conserved by the same spirit which gave them birth. In brief, when I went into their country to commence my mission, I found some persons who had preserved only the shadow of the customs of their ancestors. They lacked respect for the Cross, and they had abolished the habit of meeting in Cross-Assemblies, those in which, with the Cross in the centre of the circle and of the Council as we have related, they decided, as a court of last resort, the affairs of the nation.[43]

Le Clercq's observations relate to the first instance of spiritual collapse and moral disorganization as a result of the introduction of great epidemics and pandemics. The *shamans,* ridiculed by the French as impotent frauds and jugglers inspired by the devil, found themselves unequal to the challenges offered by the new infections and their herbal treatments, rituals and incantations were shown to be disconcertingly ineffective. This undermining and subversion of the belief system of the Algonkian tribes was to have far-reaching consequences.

The French in the colony were soon aware of this pestilential scourge of the native population. Between 1634 and 1640, for example, epidemics of either measles or smallpox carried off an estimated fifty percent of the Hurons, "there remaining only a few old men, very few persons of skill and management." The Hospital Nuns had established their hospital at Quebec in 1639 primarily as a naval and military hospital but within a year outbreaks of smallpox forced them to take in large numbers of natives who came to be treated. Mother Johereau had to have bark cabins erected in the hospital yard and the kitchen converted into an additional ward for the sick and dying.[44] By 1672, the Intendant Talon obtained a more generous subsidy from the King to operate this institution and for some modest expansion. Most of the Amerindians never came near the hospital, of course, and had they all had recourse to the French when struck down by infection all the hospitals of France would not have been sufficient to meet the emergency. As it was, the facilities were never adequate in times of epidemic. In 1687-88, for example, purple fever, as it was called, was alleged to have carried off about five hundred French and three hundred domiciled Amerindians. Epidemics of monstrous proportions were part of the contact experience.

The Amerindians did not understand the precise source of these epidemics, but they did establish a causal relationship between contact and infection. Biard reported as early as 1616 from Acadia that:

> They are astonished and often complain that, since the French mingle with and carry on trade with them, they are dying fast, and the population is thinning out. For they assert that, before this association and intercourse, all their countries were very populous, and they tell how one by one the different coasts, according as they have begun traffic with us, have been more reduced by disease; adding, that the reason the Armouchiquois do not diminish in population is because they are not at all careless. Thereupon they often puzzle their brains, and sometimes think that the French poison them, which is not true. . . .[45]

The charge of poisoning may have been more accurate in Acadia in 1616 than the general context of epidemic infections would suggest because French surgeons had bartered poisons to the natives and French crews had also traded adulterated and spoiled food. The observation that infection spread along the bays of the Atlantic Coast as trading contacts were established with the French was undoubtedly an accurate one; the Jesuit missionaries also recorded the spread of epidemics among the various tribes which had frequent contacts with the French.

In 1635 epidemics were reported among the Montagnais and the Hurons; in 1637 among the Ottawa and Iroquois; in 1638 among the Neutrals, Tobaccos, Nipissings and Algonkians; in 1645 among the Abenakis and in 1694 among the Illinois. Le Jeune related in 1637 that Entaraha, a Huron chieftain, blamed a "porcelain collar they had accepted the year before" at a general council of the tribes on the occasion of the Feast of the Dead as "the cause of their death," or the source of the infection.[46]

The major role played by the missionaries in contact with the Amerindians soon narrowed down the source of infection to the evangelical labourers, their doctrine and their religious objects. There is no doubt that the fur traders, explorers and soldiers who went into the interior of the country also carried infections to the native populations, but the Amerindians rarely singled them out as they did the missionaries and early fishermen as heralds of death. Also, there is no doubt that the Amerindians themselves contributed much to the spread of disease through their journeys to the fur markets and especially to the ports when infection-laden vessels arrived from France. The common rats brought over on French vessels probably helped to spread disease too, besides invading the native lodges to eat their provisions and, in Lescarbot's words, "suck their fish oils."

Bressani admitted in 1653 that with the new religion "the scourge of God came into the country; and, in proportion as the one increased, the other smote them more severely."[47] He wrote that their hosts in various missions, "commonly prosperous when they received us," soon felt the effects of this scourge "usually losing in the same year either wife, or children, or some other of the nearest relatives; or encountering some disastrous accident." Brébeuf's observation that the epidemics were becoming a serious obstacle to evangelization merely indicated the very rational causal relationship the natives had discovered. He wrote:

> The second obstacle arose from the tales spread among the people by followers of the devil, — that our Frenchmen and we in particular, were the cause of this pestilence, and that our sole purpose in coming to their country was to compass their destruction. . . .[48]

Chaumonot confirmed three years later that the epidemics were still "the occasion for many calumnies and persecutions" the Hurons directed against the missionaries because it was commonly believed that they were "the authors of the scourge."[49] The *Relation* of 1640 said that "these barbarians nearly all desired our death as passionately as they craved the preservation of their own lives."[50] Most commentators have emphasized the Huron reaction to the coming of the French and have underestimated the panic that seized the communities when faced with what was in their eyes genocide. The Neutrals were discouraged from trading with the French who "had tainted the air of their country and poisoned many." Huron captives warned the Iroquois against receiving the Jesuits because they would bring the dreaded infection to their villages. The Iroquois charge that Isaac Jogues carried the epidemic to their country in 1646 was not far off the mark.[51] Bressani attempted to dismiss the charges by saying that this association in the Amerindian mind between contact and infection was founded on the word of jealous magicians and ill-willed chieftains. However, the tribesmen seemed all the more convinced of the deliberate attempt to exterminate them by means of infection (an early case of alleged germ warfare) when they noticed that most of the French who fell ill during the epidemics recovered. Also, the warning given to the reservation natives not to return to their encampments in the upper country and the North in order to avoid the epidemics seemed to prove that the French knew the areas of infection because they were its authors.[52]

Opposition to contact because it was a source of infection came to focus more on the new religion, probably because trading with the French had obvious beneficial aspects for the tribesmen. Catholicism was singled out as the magical origin of the new sicknesses and high mortality rate. Marie de l'Incarnation reported in 1640 that:

> The Savages who are not Christian are in this error, that it is Baptism, instruction, and living among the French that were the cause of this mortality; which made us think that we would be given no more girls, and that those we already had would be withdrawn.[53]

In 1647, the Jesuit missionaries, who had given the Ursulines information about reactions in the mission, admitted:

> The Algonquins and Hurons — and next the Hiroquois, at the solicitation of their captives — have had, and some have still, a hatred and an extreme horror of our doctrine. They say that it causes them to die, and that it contains spells and charms which effect the destruction of their corn, and engender the contagious

and general diseases wherewith the Hiroquois now begin to be afflicted.[54]

In the same year, some of the northern tribes coming down to Tadoussac to trade and visit the mission house returned to their hunting territories with religious instruction and disease "which destroyed a great number of them." The pagans concluded that the new religion was the cause of the violent epidemic that raged through the northern districts for the next decade.[55] In some cases, the source of the infection was specified as the missionary himself, who hurried about from lodge to lodge ministering to the dying or who, with a companion, walked from village to village spreading the new doctrine. In other cases, the source of the infection was believed to be the holy water, a relic, the sacrament of the altar, or the motions of making the sign of the cross or of the priest blessing the people. The missionary report of 1653 from the Huron country included the following observation:

> They said the same thing about some images, etc. the prayers that we made, and the masses which we said at an early hour, with closed doors; the litanies; even walking abroad, — a new thing in those countries, — were superstitions which we practiced in order to destroy them.[56]

Some Hurons believed the missionaries kept a corpse brought from France in the mission house to spread diseases among pagans. Transubstantiation invited such interpretations, especially in communities on the verge of panic. Every unaccustomed, unusual or secretive act became the object of suspicion.

If the fear and suspicions of the natives can be understood, the courage and faith of those who converted is greatly to be admired. Conversion was more than a renunciation of certain tribal beliefs and practices; it was a defiance of death itself. As the mortality rate rose it took a very great faith on the part of the neophytes to resist the accusations of the pagans. One woman is reported to have affirmed to one of the Jesuits in 1647 that:

> God gave me children and has taken them from me; I have lost three of them this Winter, almost at the same time. If I had not the Faith deeply in my soul, I would believe, like some, that the new creed which we have embraced causes us to die; but I cannot suffer this thought in my heart.[57]

What may seem incongruous to the modern reader is that the French missionaries, while rejecting the aboriginal idea that disease was caused by the religion of the French and its emissaries, themselves believed these diseases were sometimes the result of God's displeasure.

In other words, they were not always far removed from an Hebraic association of disease with sin. The *Relation* of 1672-73 told of an infidel who settled among the sedentary converts near Quebec where he "sacrificed meats to the demon." When reproved for this pagan act he showed much displeasure and he professed no fear of the wrath of the Almighty with which the missionaries and native converts threatened him. The missionary account of the incident concluded:

> The missionary retorted that perhaps he would soon feel the effects of the just anger of that all-powerful God. These threats were accomplished before long; for, at the end of three months that Savage's three children, who were then in very good health, were all taken from him by death. This example of Divine justice has strongly confirmed our Christians in the Faith, and has inspired the infidels with terror.[58]

Probably the most significant admission made by the evangelist was that the pagans were inspired with terror as they viewed the progress of the new religion and the new diseases in their villages and encampments.

Another factor that helped to inspire fear and insecurity was the apparent good health of the Amerindians upon initial contact with Europeans. Only after contact with the French for several years do we find mention of fevers, catarrhs, and tuberculosis among them. Dysentery seems to have been common at the time of initial contact but the natives had effective remedies for dealing with it. Denys recorded the apparent good health and absence of epidemics among the Atlantic coastal tribes at the beginning of the seventeenth century:

> They were not subject to disease, and knew nothing of fevers. If any accident happened to them, by falling, by burning, or in cutting wood through lack of good axes, theirs being unsteady through failure to cut well, they did not need a physician. They had knowledge of herbs, of which they made use and straightway grew well. They were not subject to the gout, gravel, fevers, or rheumatism. Their general remedy was to make themselves sweat, something which they did every month and even oftener.[59]

In the matter of personal hygiene the Amerindians seem to have been more advanced than the French (judging by the standards adopted by the French in later centuries), who avoided washing because they believed it both unhealthy and immodest. Some of the French practices of the time were severely ridiculed by the Amerindians. The Jesuits reported native reactions to Europeans' use of handkerchiefs:

> Politeness and propriety have taught us to carry handkerchiefs. In this matter the Savages charge us with filthiness — because, they say, we place what is unclean in a fine white piece of linen, and put it away in our pockets as something very precious, while they throw it upon the ground. Hence it happened that, when a Savage one day saw a Frenchman fold up his handkerchief after wiping his nose, he said to him laughingly, "If thou likest the filth, give me thy handkerchief and I will soon fill it". . . .[60]

French medical knowledge in the seventeenth century, particularly with the decline of the Paris faculty, was not especially advanced even by European standards, whereas aboriginal knowledge of basic medicine for survival in the North American environment was remarkable.[61] The natives were skilled in the use of medicinal herbs, ointments, potions and steam baths. Their skill in curing wounds amazed the French. Their ability to heal rapidly indicated general good health, and their practice of minor surgery had a high success rate. Jogues had an abscess lanced by the Iroquois; Crépieul was skilfully bled by an Eskimo; a captive had shot removed from a deep wound; and François Gendron, who served as surgeon at Sainte-Marie from 1643 to 1649, introduced the native cure of *pierres Eriennes* into French medical practice.[62] Sagard saw much that was commendable in Huron medical practice. He approved of their emphasis on exercise, sobriety, the use of emetics, the practice of quarantining, the taking of hot baths, and the liberal use of medicinal herbs. He believed that an important factor in their health was the harmony that prevailed among them. The primitive society he admired did not produce the ulcers, bile and cankers that French physicians attributed to the social turmoil of European life:

> They have no law-suits and take little pains to acquire the goods of this life, for which we Christians torment ourselves so much, and for our excessive and insatiable greed in acquiring them we are justly and with reason reproved by their quiet life and tranquil dispositions.[63]

The Franciscans would hardly have included themselves in the general condemnation of European acquisitiveness and its malevolent physical consequences.

Sagard went on to describe the medicine men, or *Oki,* as being "physicians and surgeons," skilled in employing herbs to cure sickness, in dressing wounds, and as "great soothsayers and devil-raisers." The incantations and "antics and usual foolishness," as Sagard described them, did indicate they were "not so unsophisticated that they cannot make the common people believe in them" and enabled them "to become influential and have the lion's share of the feasts and gifts." Sagard did not discount their ability to restore both physically and mentally ill patients and, in describing the illness of a French youth among the Tobacco tribe, observed that he had turned to the medicine man and "some good natural remedy would not have been refused if there had been any suitable to this illness."[64] In the realm of mental illness, Sagard wrote that both men and women had been reported subject to fits of madness during which they broke objects, shrieked and jumped about. Sagard believed that probably they were not temporarily insane but they believed "they must act like a demoniac in order to cure their imaginations or disturbances of their mind." These outbreaks greatly disturbed village life he found:

> This was partly the reason why the masters of the ceremony and the members of the council often begged us to pray to God in their behalf and teach them some efficient remedy for their diseases, candidly admitting that all their ceremonies, dances, songs, feasts, and other trials were good for nothing whatever.[65]

Among the Micmacs the *shamans* occasionally acted as psychotherapists, tracing the source of the illness to the breaking of some taboo, to failing to perform a ritual act, or to offending a supernatural spirit. The remedy, as among all Algonkian and Iroquoian peoples, was symbolically to remove the immediate cause from the sufferer's body.

French medical practices, bleeding and purges in particular, were held in low esteem by the Amerindians. Lescarbot told of one Micmac warrior who, upon being treated by Poutrincourt's surgeon for a badly cut heel, returned two hours later "as jauntily as you please, having tied round his head the bandage in which his heel had been wrapped."[66] In 1640, the annalist of the hospital at Quebec reported that the natives avoided her institution, holding it in horror, calling it "the house of death," and refusing to come there for treatment.[67] Du Creux repeated the story of the anxious relatives who urged a converted widow to abandon French medical treatments for her ailing son, "and told her that she was more like a cruel beast than a loving mother in deserting her son at such a time." They believed that his recovery depended upon her allowing the use of remedies "which all their tribe had always used before the coming of those cursed Europeans."[68] The fear inspired by French medical practitioners, whose treatments often caused much suffering to their patients, was evident in many accounts. In time, more natives came to the hospitals at Montreal and on the reserve at Sillery, although the early reluctance never left them entirely.[69] The French also adopted aboriginal remedies with considerable success, adding to their pharmaceutical knowledge.[70]

Europeans were not entirely immune to infections resulting from their contacts with Amerindians. Syphilis, the origin of which has been one of the most controversial issues in medical history, was widespread in Central and South America as confirmed by archaeological evidence of pathological damage to the skull and long bones of arms and legs of skeletons in pre-Columbian burial grounds. There was also a vocabulary referring to syphilis in the various languages of the area. Historically, there have been two opposing views on the provenance of syphilis. One view, generally held by Frenchmen in the sixteenth and seventeenth centuries, was that it was of American origin, that the Spaniards had acquired it in Hispaniola and had infected the Italians and French at the siege of Naples. The other view has been that syphilis had been known in Europe since classical times but it was only in about 1500 that it was properly diagnosed. It was the *mentagra* of ancient Rome and the *morbo gallico* of the Renaissance. The existence of four related types of human *treponematoses* — pinta, yaws, endemic syphilis, and venereal syphilis — served to confuse proper diagnosis.

The discovery of the New World had two immediate and observable consequences. Firstly, there was a rapid spread of virulent yaws and venereal syphilis throughout Europe after 1494. Secondly, growing out of the ancient maxim that where a disease existed, there in the same place God had created a remedy, there developed a thriving trade in curative guaiac wood which was soon monopolized by the enterprising Fuggers. The Spaniards were using guaiacum on a large scale by 1508, and by 1517 it had become the usual remedy throughout Europe.[71] Cases of syphilis among Algonkin peoples may have been traceable to European infection.

Venereal diseases raised moral problems as well as medical problems. It is certain that the Amerindians did not always have a high regard for French standards of morality and ethics. Biard observed that the Micmac girls and women were very modest, that the men were well-behaved and "very much insulted when some foolish Frenchman dares meddle with their women." Indeed when a "certain madcap" took liberties with their women, the Amerindians came to complain to the French sea captain and threatened to kill any Frenchman who attempted to do so again. Complaints were made to Poutrincourt by a Micmac chieftain that some Saint-Malo fishermen "had stolen away his wife and were abusing her." Lescarbot observed that "as for the maidens who are willing, if any man has abused them, they will tell it at the first occasion, and therefore it is dangerous to dally with them; for one ought not to mix Christian blood with infidel . . . ."[72]

Lescarbot questioned Cartier's remark that the Micmacs kept "meeting houses and, as it were, colleges, wherein the girls are prostituted, until they marry." He remarked, on the contrary, on the lack of any association between pre-marital incontinence and guilt or immodesty on the part of the native population:

> The maidens of Brasil have the same liberty as those of Canada to prostitute themselves as soon as they are able. Indeed, the fathers act as their pandars, and think it an honour to give them to the men of these parts, in order to have children of their blood . . . and we see, to our great hurt that God has severely punished this vice by the pox, which was brought by the Spaniards from Naples, and by them transmitted to the French, a disease which before the discovery of those lands was unknown in Europe.[73]

That the aboriginal peoples should have been hostile to European contact did not seem strange in this context. The Jesuits believed, for example, that Eskimo hostility to Europeans could be traced directly to Basque outrages. The missionaries concluded that they had "paid well for their cursed incontinence," but the innocent — in this case, the Malouins — had also suffered "and still suffer a great deal every year."

There is no doubt that the fishermen who had long frequented the coasts, and who landed to dry their fish, mend their nets and sometimes winter in America, entered into liaisons with Amerindian women. In fact, native customs favoured offering travellers the company of their womenfolk during their sojourns. From these unions there were numerous half-breed children, which according to some historians explains the origins of the name Malecite.[74] They were said to be the descendants of Saint-Malo fishermen and sailors and native women.

The fur trade encouraged the sexual laxity that the missionaries greatly deplored. The *coureurs-de-bois*, sent to the hinterland to consolidate economic ties for French merchants and traders, led dissolute lives by French moral standards. The Récollet missionaries reported this unfortunate consequence of contact from the first mission station established in the interior country:

> They vie with one another as to which shall have the most lovers, and if the mother finds none for herself she freely offers her daughter and the daughter offers herself . . . they were full of admiration and approval of the propriety of the girls in France of whom we told them. This gave us hopes of great amendment and alteration of their mode of living in a short time, if the Frenchmen who came up with us, most of them, had not told them the contrary, in order always to be able, like beasts, to enjoy their sensual pleasures to the full, in which they

wallowed, even keeping together groups of these bad girls in several places, so that those who should have seconded us in teaching and being a good example to these people were the very ones who went about destroying and obstructing the good that we were building up for the salvation of the tribes and for the advancement of the glory of God.[75]

There has been no estimate of the number of half-caste children born of these casual alliances. The Amerindians never troubled about legitimacy. That French dissoluteness could offend the aborigines, if carried beyond the broad permissiveness allowed the young unmarried men and women, is borne out by a number of references to the comparative lack of French restraint.

The permissiveness of aboriginal life allowed a broad interpretation of what was involved in showing hospitality to strangers. Since there was little privacy, French writers sometimes found the natives lascivious and immodest; some described indiscriminate sexual intercourse in public "with great brutality." Perrot gave a more judicious appraisal of native standards of decorum and morality:

> Although the savages have not, at bottom, much esteem for modesty they nevertheless surpass the Europeans in external propriety; for in all their love-affairs they never utter in conversation a word which can wound chaste feelings. There are among them some who, after being married, have remained six months or even a year without intercourse, and others the same for more or less time. The reason which they give for this is, that they marry not for lust, but purely through affection.[76]

The presence of garrison troops at Montreal and at posts in the upper country further exacerbated the problem. At the end of the seventeenth century Etienne de Carheil deplored the commerce in brandy and in women. He declared the military posts to be virtual bordellos, and the soldiers almost without exception dissolute drunkards. In adapting the aboriginal method of transportation into the interior, the French had also imitated the natives by taking along women to cook, to cut wood and serve as mistresses:

> They are all the prostitutes of Montreal, who are alternately brought here and taken back; and They are all the prostitutes of this place, who are carried in the same way from here to Montreal, and from Montreal here. At present this is the usual manner in which their journeys are carried on; and voyages are no longer performed without a continual flow and Ebb of That tide of prostitutes — whom we see ascending and descending,

going and coming from one mission to another, without cessation, — to the most Heinous and loathsome scandal of the people.[77]

Governor Callières was asked to intervene for "the good of the missions" and for "the good of the trade," without "ever separating one from the other" so that both the economic and spiritual interests of the colony might bring order and justice to all regions where the French had penetrated.

The most vexing and the most persistent cluster of problems growing out of French-Amerindian contact was the liquor traffic, its attendant disorders, and alcoholism. There is no doubt that the natives had been innocent of the effects of alcohol prior to contact, nor is there any doubt that they had a low tolerance to alcoholic beverages. Only in limited areas of South and Central America did Columbus and Ovieda find some Amerindians who were acquainted with the art of brewing. The closest equivalent in New France was *leinhody*, or "stinking corn," which Sagard described as cobs of corn left to ferment in stagnant pools of water and consumed at important feasts. He found it unpalatable; "the taste and smell are very strong," he wrote, "and the stink worse even than sewers."[78]

How the Amerindians came to acquire a taste for brandy and other intoxicants, and how they became addicted to these is a sad and well-known tale. Denys believed that when the French fishermen first contacted the Micmacs "it needed little wine or brandy to make them drunk." By the mid-seventeenth century, "and since they have frequented the fishing vessels they drink in quite another fashion" he reported. The Dutch version of Denys' account reports that the aborigines stood along the shores where fishing vessels were known to come, and made smoke signals to the crews of vessels they sighted inviting them to come and barter for furs:

> These skins are bartered for brandy, for which they ever since they have begun to trade with fishermen are very greedy; and they herewith fill themselves up to such an extent that they frequently fall over backwards, for they do not call it drinking unless they overload themselves with this strong drink in a beastly fashion.[79]

To the dismay of Champlain, liquor was traded to the natives at Tadoussac from the time fur trading started at that post.[80] Thereafter, the illicit trade flourished whether officially prohibited or merely regulated. The Jesuit *Relation* of 1648 told of the ships from France bringing out more strong liquor than previously to sell secretly to the aborigines, and of the deplorable disorders that ensued.[81] Marie de l'Incarnation explained to her son in France that the natives had had no knowledge of brewing before the French arrived, that the French "having let them taste brandy and wine, they find these much to their taste," and that very quickly they became drunk, "almost mad and raging." She attributed this low tolerance to alcohol to the lack of salt in their diet.

Although Governor Montmagny had issued an order of prohibition, the trade flourished: "when the vessels arrive it is not possible to prevent the sailors from trafficking in it with them secretly."[82] Wherever the French traders and *coureurs-de-bois* went into the far interior they carried with them the "fire-water" which the natives wanted and which assured good bartering. And always the disorders and excesses followed. The missionaries wrote apprehensively about those tribes which had not as yet been introduced to liquor, but they praised the converted natives who resisted the traffic and imposed severe penalties, sometimes even expulsion from the reservation, on the backsliders.

The nature of the evils incumbent on unrestricted trafficking in brandy were succinctly described by the Jesuits:

> There have been some whose mania was so extravagant that, after stripping themselves of everything for liquor, they sold even their own children to obtain the means of intoxication. Children, too, when they were overcome with drink, beat their parents without being punished for it; young men used it as a philter, corrupting the girls after making them drunk; those that have any quarrels pretend to be intoxicated, in order to wreak vengeance with impunity. Every night is filled with clamors, brawls, and fatal accidents, which the intoxicated cause in the cabins. Everything is permitted them for they give as an excuse that they were bereft of reason at the time, satisfactory hence. One cannot conceive the disorders which this diabolical vice has caused in this new Church.[83]

The first Bishop, Msgr de Laval, adopted the thesis of the abbé de Quéylus, who had preceded him to the colony in the capacity of Grand Vicar of the Archbishop of Rouen. Quéylus maintained that the use of intoxicants was in itself an indifferent matter, but that drunkenness as an end in itself, the charge levelled against the Amerindians, was a mortal sin and should be repressed severely by the secular arm.

The physical effects of insobriety on the natives were almost as frightening to contemplate as the moral consequences. Lahontan said that brandy was of itself "murdering stuff," which was sometimes adulterated with harmful substances, powerful enough "to extinguish their natural heat," to throw them into "a state of consumption," and even cause death.[84] Du Creux described cirrhosis of the liver, more for the benefit of readers and benefactors of the missions in France than for Canadians. Belmont, in his treatise on the brandy trade, wrote that excessive drinking turned the liver black:

> . . . apart from the natural effects which it produces among all men, it makes such strange ones among the Savages from the beginning, that we were not long in perceiving that the drunkenness of the Savages was of a different type from that of the Europeans; for, the Savages having found a beverage so quick acting and efficacious in warming up their coldness, in enabling them to come out of themselves, and through it to gain the strength and impunity which they were seeking after, we were not long, I say, in seeing drunken men killing each other; husbands burning their wives; wives dishonouring their husbands; fathers putting their children to boil in cauldrons. . . .[85]

Both those who favoured strict limitation of the sale of intoxicants in the colony and those who argued in favour of unrestricted sale because brandy was an important element in the highly competitive international fur trade, were agreed on the harmful effects excessive drinking had on the Amerindians.

Some French cherished the stereotype of the Amerindian female as highly accessible or promiscuous in her sexual relations, particularly when intoxicated. Denys had observed that, from the very beginning of culture contact, drunkenness was intimately related to sexual laxity and, what was for Europeans at least, deviation:

> The women and the older girls also drink much but by stealth, and they go to hide themselves in the woods for that purpose. The sailors know well the rendez-vous. It is those who furnish the brandy, and they bring them into so favourable a condition that they can do with them everything they will. All these frequentations of the ships have entirely ruined them, and they care no longer for Religion. They blaspheme the name of God, are thieves and cheats, and have no longer their former purity, neither women nor girls, at least those who drink.[86]

The disorders caused Bishop Laval to reserve the absolution of confessed brandy traffickers for himself alone. Bishop Saint-Vallier, his successor, pursued the question with even greater vigour but with no more tangible results. Fines, liquor licensing, whippings and brandings did not stem the tide of the nefarious trade. Governor Denonville outlined to Seignelay, Minister of the Marine responsible for the colonies, his plan to punish French traders who debauched native women, to discipline the youth by military training, to remove all natives near the French settlements to reserves, and to regulate further the sale of brandy. Three years later he reported as follows:

> All the savages are fond of it and when they drink it they become mad and enraged, howling and biting like dogs and wanting to kill everybody. Good regulations have been issued here but their execution is found every day to be more and more difficult because of the deceit of the vendors and buyers. The Intendant has some knowledge of the difficulties as a result of the tour he made last year. Besides, Monseigneur, it is pointless to speak of discipline or police or of being able to live with the savages, so long as brandy can be sold or traded to them, especially when they are so numerous.[87]

It was a frank admission that the social controls both church and state wished to impose were ineffective in the over-extended French sphere of influence in North America. Nor did the Amerindian societies have the will, much less the cohesion and authority, to impose controls.

Why did the Amerindians drink so excessively? The French, like their Puritan neighbours in Massachussetts, in attempting to assimilate some of the tribesmen believed they should learn the civilized use of alchoholic beverages for it was "not fit to deprive them of any lawful comfort which God alloweth to all men." The universal observation was that the Amerindians drank in order to become completely inebriated. Denys wrote from Acadia:

> If the brandy they have is not sufficient to make them drunk they will give everything they possess to obtain more. That is only a way of saying they will not cease drinking so long as they possess anything. Thus the fishermen are ruining them entirely.[88]

Biard reported that liquor was the cause of as many disturbances among the French as among the Amerindians of Acadia, but the latter had a greater craving for it than did the Europeans and drank expressly to become drunk.[89] Pierre Boucher, who went to France to describe conditions in the colony in the 1660s to the Court, was of the opinion that all the Amerindians living near Europeans became drunkards and this greatly hindered the progress of the missions. In spite of the attempts of the early Governors and the missionaries to control the sale of brandy to the natives, they had little or no success. He concluded, "The Indians drink only to get drunk, and when they have begun they will give everything they own for a bottle of brandy in order to drink to oblivion."[90] Lacking toleration to alcohol, the cultural conditioning for its social use, and the moral and social inhibitions to drunkenness of Frenchmen, the natives drank to become intoxicated. Bruyas reported in 1668 after a few months in Oneida country, that these Iroquois were "Drunkards only since they have associated with the french and dutch," that although the French had ceased supplying them with brandy the Dutch had not, and that they had "such a mania to get possession of this baneful drink" they would uncomplainingly travel many leagues to obtain a few pots to bring back to their villages where "when they have drunk it, they are demons."[91]

The abbé de Belmont maintained that the Amerindians drank for three principal reasons: to break down their natural inhibitions; to acquire the aggressiveness which their culture suppressed; and to have an excuse to commit illegal and unconventional acts.[92] A more recent rationalization of Amerindian drinking patterns maintains that the Iroquian groups in particular accepted alcohol with eagerness, not for its taste, but to produce intoxication as a means of stimulating vision experiences which were highly regarded in the native cultures.[93] Then, at a later period, alcohol came to serve as a release for tensions, but the dream-making concept never disappeared entirely. This theory related the contact experience to the now widely accepted hypothesis that "the primary function of alcoholic beverages in all societies is the reduction of anxieties."[94]

Insobriety was so excessive and so often accompanied by extreme aggression because subsistence anxieties were high, sorcery operated freely, sexual restraints were low, and there was an absence of super-ordinate social control. Neither French church nor state could effec-tively prevent the sale of intoxicants; nor could native chieftains or *dogiques* among the converted tribesmen enforce abstinence. The lack of control mechanisms effectively to punish drunken excesses ensured the continuation and extension to new tribes of the complex problem. It soon became, and remained thereafter, the chief problem of culture contact.

The Amerindians often sought to excuse their violence or crimes, which were contrary to their normal cultural behaviour and accepted values, by pleading non-responsibility for their actions because they were possessed at the time by another spirit.[95] Brandy, like anything else, according to Amerindian cosmogony, was possessed of a super-natural power or spirit. When a person drank brandy the supernatural evil spirit in the liquor took control of the imbiber's spirit and body and became responsible for his thoughts and actions. However, by an edict of August 1536 it became established judicial practice in France not to accept drunkenness as an excuse for crimes committed when in such a state. The laws of France were extended to Canada, and at the trial of a native named Robert Hache, arrested for the rape of a French woman, the chiefs of all the tribes having contact with the

French colony in 1664 were warned by the Sovereign Councillors that the full severity of French law would be applied to the Amerindians in cases of crimes of violence.[96] There were few other cases of an interracial character as most of the violence resulting from drunkenness was turned upon the Amerindian community itself.

It is necessary to distinguish between the motivation for drinking and the function of getting drunk. The Amerindian problems involved drinking to become drunk, drinking exclusively in groups, demanding that the individual in the group conform to its rapid drinking, and indulging to flaunt the missionaries' and French administrators' disapproval of such behaviour. It is possible that this behaviour represented multiple aspects of a common function of integrating tribal groups through conflict with European society. One is tempted to speculate, in other words, that alcohol, while contributing to a breakdown of Amerindian cultural patterns, was a means whereby some tribesmen could create or symbolize in-group solidarity against the French.[97]

Furthermore, the lack of any general concept of personal sin or blame, such as pervaded the self-regarding ideologies of the Europeans, led the Amerindians to regard success or failure of the individual as the result of external forces playing upon him. The problem of drunkenness, accordingly, was of the Frenchman's making, not his own. The militant but futile actions of the civil administrators and the clergy in their war on the brandy traffic was directed, by and large, against those individuals and groups in the French population who gave or sold intoxicants to the natives. In so doing, the temporal and spiritual leaders focussed and crystallized the emerging inclination of the Amerindians to blame all their difficulties on the coming of the Europeans.

The question of the brandy traffic in New France points up the paradox that arose in the *pays d'en haut*, the upper country, or the hinterland away from the three main St. Lawrence settlement areas. It was here that much of the contact between the two cultures occurred. It was an area of freedom from the supervision and paternalistic intervention of the representatives of church and state in the colony. It was also an area of immense hardships, risks, and moral confusion inhabited by the *coureurs-de-bois* and the converted Amerindians who were caught between the ebb and flow of two different cultures, never quite certain how much of their ancestral way of life they would be called upon to renounce in the pursuit of their new life. The French *coureur-de-bois* was at once a libertine and renegade escaping from the constraints of civilized and Christianized European-style society, but also an heroic and romantic figure indispensable to the economic survival and political expansion of the colony. The upper country where the missionaries found martyrdom and the traders imperilled their souls was the same hinterland where Amerindians were converted to Catholicism and explorers erected the skeletal structure of an empire. The conflicting ideological forces in this *pays d'en haut* were a forceful manifestation of the problems of culture contact when an aboriginal self-sufficient pre-literate society met with a technologically advanced, theocratically inclined materialistic civilization.

1. *Collection de Manuscrits contenant lettres, mémoires, et autres documents historiques relatifs à la Nouvelle-France* (Québec: 1883-85), Vol. I, p. 175.
2. Gabriel Sagard-Théodat, *Histoire du Canada et Voyages que les Frères Mineurs Recollets y ont faicts pour la Conuersion des Infidelles* (Paris: 1636), pp. 241-242.
3. William F. Ganong, ed., *The Description and Natural History of the Coasts of North America (Acadia) by Nicolas Denys* (Toronto: 1908), Vol. I, p. 451.
4. Nicolas Perrot, "Memoir on the Manners, Customs, and Religion of the Savages of North America," in E. H. Blair, ed., *The Indian Tribes of the Upper Mississippi Valley and Region of the Great Lakes* (Cleveland: 1911), Vol. I, pp. 134-135.
5. Pierre D'Avity, *Description Générale de l'Amérique, troisième partie du Monde* (Paris: 1637), p. 31.
6. Sieur de Dièreville, *"Relation du Voyage du Port Royal de l'Acadie, ou de la Nouvelle France* (Rouen: 1708), p. 166.
7. George M. Wrong, ed., *The Long Journey to the Country of the Huron by Father Gabriel Sagard* (Toronto: 1939), pp. 70-71.
8. *Ibid.,* p. 79.
9. *Ibid.,* p. 140.
10. *Ibid.,* p. 88.
11. Louis Hennepin, *A New Discovery of a Vast Country in America* (London: 1698), Vol. I, p. 704.
12. *Ibid.,* Vol. I, p. 37.
13. R. G. Thwaites, ed., *The Jesuit Relations and Allied Documents* (New York: 1959), Vol. XII, p. 61.
14. Hennepin, *op. cit.,* Vol. I, pp. 141-142.
15. Perrot, *op. cit.,* Vol. I, p. 145.
16. *Ibid.,* Vol. I, p. 178.
17. Gédéon de Catalogne, *Recueil de ce qui s'est passé en Canada au sujet de la guerre, tant des Anglais que des Iroquois depuis l'année 1682* (Québec: 1871), p. 19.
18. Perrot, *op. cit.,* Vol. I, p. 260.
19. Wrong, *op. cit.,* p. 206.
20. Wrong, *op. cit.,* pp. 58-59.
21. Hennepin, *op. cit.,* Vol. I, p. 47.
22. *Ibid.,* Vol. II, p. 70.
23. Bruce G. Trigger, "Order and Freedom in Huron Society," *Anthropologica* V, No. 2 (1963), pp. 151-170.
24. Ganong, *op. cit.,* pp. 440-441.
25. *Ibid.,* pp. 442-443.
26. Wrong, *op. cit.,* pp. 183-184.
27. *Ibid.,* pp. 130-131.
28. Ganong, *op. cit.,* p. 404.

29. *P.A.C., Series B.* Vol. I, Instructions to Talon, March 27, 1665, pp. 69-70.
30. H. Têtu, *Biographies de Msgr de Laval et de Msgr Plessis* (Montréal: 1913), Laval to Poitevin, November 3, 1668, p. 35.
31. Joyce Marshall, ed., *Word from New France. The Selected Letters of Marie de l'Incarnation* (Toronto: 1967), p. 341.
32. Thwaites, *op. cit.,* Vol. XIV, p. 233.
33. *P.A.C. MG18, E-7,* "Ecrits autographes de Marguerite Bourgeoys," pp. 8-9; *A.S.Q., Fonds Verreau XIII,* No. 27c; Thwaites, *op. cit.,* Vol. VI, p. 24; VIII, p. 226, IX, p. 284; XII, pp. 44-48; Pierre Margry, ed., *Découvertes et Etablissements des Français dans l'Ouest et dans le Sud de l'Amérique septentrionale* (Paris: 1879), Vol. I, Talon to Colbert, November 10, 1670, p. 92.
34. James B. Conacher, ed., *The History of Canada or New France by Father François du Creux, S.J.* (Toronto: 1951), pp. 35-36; Société littéraire et historique de Québec, *Voyages de Découvertes au Canada, entre les années 1534 et 1542, par Jacques Quartier, le Sieur de Roberval, Jean Alphonse de Xanctoigne &c.* (Québec: 1843), pp. 52-53.
35. J. G. Shea, ed., *Chrestien Le Clercq: First Establishment of the Faith in New France* (New York: 1887), Vol. I, pp. 164-165.
36. W. L. Grant, ed., *The History of New France by Marc Lescarbot* (Toronto: 1911), Vol. II, pp. 146-148.
37. Wrong, *op. cit.,* p. 166.
38. Sagard, *op. cit.,* p. 95.
39. James H. Coyne, "Dollier de Casson & De Brehaut de Galinée: Exploration of the Great Lakes, 1669-1670," *Ontario Historical Society Papers and Records* IV, (1903), p. 19.
40. Emile Salone, "Les Sauvages du Canada et les maladies importées de France au XVIIe et au XVIIIe siècles: La Picote et l'alcoolisme," *Journal de la Société des Américanistes* IV (1904), pp. 1-17.
41. John J. Heagerty, *Four Centuries of Medical History in Canada and a Sketch of the Medical History of Newfoundland* (Toronto: 1928), Vol. I, pp. 106-107.
42. J. C. Webster, ed., *Sieur de Dièreville: Relation of the Voyage to Port Royal in Acadia or New France* (Toronto: 1933), p. 116; Ganong, *op. cit.,* Vol. II, p. 415. Estimates of aboriginal population at the time of contact are constantly being revised upwards and have now reached nearly ten million. Henry F. Dobyns, "Estimating Aboriginal American Population: An Appraisal of Techniques with a New Hemispheric Estimate," *Current Anthropology* VII (1966), pp. 395-416.
43. William F. Ganong, ed., *New Relation of Gaspesia, with the Customs and Religion of the Gaspesian Indians by Father Chrestien LeClercq* (Toronto: 1910), pp. 151-152.
44. Jeanne-Françoise Juchereau de la Ferté de Saint-Ignace et al., *Histoire de l'Hôtel-Dieu de Québec* (Montauban: 1751), p. 19.
45. Thwaites, *op. cit.,* Vol. III, p. 105.
46. *Ibid.,* Vol. XIII, p. 209.
47. *Ibid.,* Vol. XXXIX, p. 141.
48. *Ibid.,* Vol. XI, p. 15.
49. *Ibid.,* Vol. XVIII, p. 13.
50. *Ibid.,* Vol. XX, p. 73.
51. *Ibid.,* Vol. XXX, pp. 227-229. The Huron charge against La Roche Daillon made to discourage the Neutrals is found in J. G. Shea, ed., *Chrestien Le Clercq: The First Establishment of the Faith in New France* (New York: 1881), Vol. I, pp. 267-268.
52. *Ibid.,* Vol. XXXIX, pp. 125-131.
53. Dom Guy Oury, ed., *Marie de l'Incarnation, Ursuline (1599-1672). Correspondence* (Solesmes: 1971), XLIII, September 3, 1640, p. 98.
54. Thwaites, *op. cit.,* Vol. XXXI, p. 121.

55. *Ibid.,* Vol. XXXI, pp. 241-243; XXXIII, p. 19.
56. *Ibid.,* Vol. XXXIX, pp. 129-130.
57. *Ibid.,* Vol. XXXI, p. 239.
58. *Ibid.,* Vol. LVIII, p. 87.
59. Ganong, *op. cit.,* pp. 445-446.
60. Thwaites, *op. cit.,* Vol. XLIV, p. 297.
61. F. Speiser, K. R. Andrae and W. Krickberg, "Les Peaux-Rouges et leur médecine," *Revue Ciba,* No. 10 (avril, 1940), pp. 291-318.
62. Thwaites, *op. cit.,* Vol. V, p. 143; XVII, p. 213; XXXIX, p. 73; XLIX, p. 121; LXI, p. 85; LXVIII, p. 61.
63. Sagard, *op. cit.,* p. 192.
64. *Ibid.,* p. 195.
65. *Ibid.,* p. 202; Jean-Baptiste de Rocoles, ed., *Quelques Particularitez du pays des Hurons en la Nouvelle France. Remarquées par le Sieur Gendron, Docteur en Medecine, qui a demeuré dans ce Pays-là fort longtemps* (Troyes: 1665), p. 8.
66. Grant, *op. cit.,* Vol. II, p. 326.
67. Dom Albert Jamet, ed., *Les Annales de l'Hôtel-Dieu de Québec, 1636-1716* (Québec; 1939), p. 25.
68. Conacher, *op. cit.,* Vol. II, p. 651.
69. Thwaites, *op. cit.,* Vol. XXIII, pp. 283, 315-317; XXIV, pp. 31-33, 55-57, 119, 161-163; XXXII, p. 231; XLVI, p. 35; XLVIII, p. 91.
70. *Ibid.,* LXVIII, p. 73.
71. Paul Hermann, *The World Unveiled. The Story of Exploration from Columbus to Livingstone* (London: 1958), pp. 217-235; Thwaites, *op. cit.,* Vol. XLIX, p. 276; LXXI, p. 377. The botanist L'Ecluse travelled throughout Western Europe in search of new exotic drugs and herbs. He persuaded sea captains to include physicians and druggists in their crews so that they could describe the habitat of plants and test their efficacy. In 1601 he obtained samples of guaiac wood from the London druggist James Gareth to carry out a series of experiments on its curative powers which were being hotly debated at the time. F. B. de l'Ecluse, *La Flore sainte et l'apologie de Flore et des floristes contre les critiques, avec un traité de la culture des principales fleurs* (Saumur: 1675), p. 377; Robert S. Munger, "Guaiacum, the Holy Wood from the New World," *Journal of the History of Medicine and Allied Sciences* IV (1949), pp. 196-229; Alfred W. Crosby, Jr., *Columbian Exchange. Biological and Cultural Consequences of 1492* (Westport, Conn.: 1972), Ch. 4 for a reappraisal of the early history of syphilis.
72. Thwaites, *op. cit.,* Vol. I, p. 67; III, pp. 103-105; Grant, *op. cit.,* Vol. III, p. 167.
73. Thwaites, *op. cit.,* Vol. III, p. 69; Grant, *op. cit.,* Vol. III, p. 163.
74. Lucien Campeau, ed., *La Première Mission d'Acadie* (1602-1616) (Québec: 1967), pp. 117-118; J. A. Maurault, *Histoire des Abénakis, depuis 1605 jusqu'à nos jours* (Sorel: 1866), p. 6.
75. Wrong, *op. cit.,* pp. 133-134.
76. Perrot, *op. cit.,* Vol. I, p. 69.
77. Thwaites, *op. cit.,* Vol. LXV, p. 241. See also pp. 193-199, 213, 217, 227-245. The sexual practices of the Amerindians, and more likely the popular belief in their sexual prowess, were a source of attraction to numerous French colonists, traders and soldiers. Richard Slotkin has concluded that "the Indian in our mythology functions as the image or symbol of the American libido — the primitive source of sexual, conceptual, and creative energy that lies below the level of psychological consciousness and is (according to Jung) the root of creative, religious and erotic inspirations." Richard Slotkin, *Regeneration through Violence: The Mythology of the American Frontier 1600-1860* (Middletown, Conn.: 1973), p. 560.
78. Wrong, *op. cit.,* pp. 107-108; Thwaites, *op. cit.,* Vol. XI, p. 275.

79. Nicolas Denys, *Geographische en Historische, Beschrijving den Kusten van Noord-America, Met de Natuurlijke Historie des Lendts* (Amsterdam: 1688), p. 67.
80. C. H. Laverdière, ed., *Oeuvres de Champlain* (Québec: 1870), Vol. III, p. 153.
81. Thwaites, *op. cit.*, Vol. XXXIII, p. 49.
82. Marshall, *op. cit.*, pp. 131-132.
83. Thwaites, *op. cit.*, Vol. XLVI, pp. 103-104.
84. R. G. Thwaites, ed., *New Voyages to North America by the Baron de Lahontan* (Chicago: 1905), Vol. II, p. 466.
85. Abbé de Belmont, "Histoire de l'eau-de-vie en Canada," *Collection de Mémoires et de Relations sur l'histoire ancienne du Canada* (Québec: 1840), p. 8.
86. Ganong, *op. cit.*, pp. 449-450.
87. *P.A.C., Series CIIA,* Vol. X, Denonville to Seignelay, August 10, 1688, p. 126.
88. Ganong, *op. cit.*, pp. 444-445.
89. Pierre Biard, *Relation de la Nouvelle-France* (Lyon: 1616), pp. 14, 31, 69.
90. Pierre Boucher, *Histoire véritable et naturelle des moeurs et productions du pays de la Nouvelle France* (Montreal: 1882), pp. 118-119.
91. Thwaites, *op. cit.*, Vol. II, pp. 123-125.
92. Belmont, *op. cit.*, pp. 5-9.
93. Edmund S. Carpenter, "Alcohol in the Iroquois Dream Quest," *American Journal of Psychiatry* CXVI, No. 2 (August, 1959), pp. 148-151.
94. Donald Horton, "The Function of Alcohol in Primitive Societies: A Cross Cultural Study," *Quarterly Journal of Studies in Alcohol* IV (September, 1943), p. 223. There is evidence in contemporary society that contact with Europeans brings demoralization and distrust of traditional institutions to Amerindians, often causing them to turn to alcohol. Edwin M. Lemert, "Alcohol and the Northwest Coast Indians," *University of California Publications in Culture and Society* II, No. 6 (1954), pp. 303-406. For prevalent modern theories see Theodore D. Graves, "Acculturation, Access, and Alcohol in a Tri-Ethnic Community," *American Anthropologist* 69, Nos. 3-4 (January-August, 1967), pp. 306-321.
95. Thwaites, *op. cit.*, Vol. LIII, p. 257. See André Vachon, "L'Eau-de-vie dans la société indienne," *Canadian Historical Association Annual Report, 1960*, pp. 22-32.
96. *Jugements et Délibérations du Conseil Souverain de la Nouvelle-France* (Québec: 1885), Vol. I, pp. 174-175; *Le Journal des Jésuites* (Québec: 1871), p. 323.
97. The most recent authoritative works on the subject are Craig MacAndrew and Robert B. Edgerton, *Drunken Comportment: A Social Explanation* (Chicago: 1969); Nancy O. Lurie, "The World's Oldest On-Going Protest Demonstration: North American Indian Drinking Patterns," *Pacific Historical Review* XL (1971), pp. 311-332.

CHAPTER IV

BARBARISM AND CRUELTY

Historiography has long been overburdened with tales of Amerindian barbarism and extreme cruelty such as the scalping of helpless victims, the cruel torture of prisoners, the murderous nature of guerrilla warfare, and the cannibalism of some tribesmen. Histories and theses continue to denounce uncritically, and with little analysis of Amerindian rationalization, the Iroquois threat to New France. North American literature dealing with the Amerindians has in good measure kept alive the image of the cruel, barbaric natives, although a more careful reading of this literature might produce some surprising insights. These negative views, based to a large extent on the fear and hostility felt by Europeans living in North America in the seventeenth century, need not be accepted uncritically and without close examination by twentieth-century scholars as being a fair evaluation of Amerindian nature and behaviour at the time of early contact.

To help restore the balance, it ought to be pointed out the degree of cruelty and barbarism that was tolerated in French society at the time should also be taken into account. Only then can a more impartial judgement be made of the Frenchmen's lurid denunciations of aboriginal viciousness. Literary and historical works that give details of the barbaric tortures, experiences in captivity, ambushes and raids of the Amerindians should be balanced against details of the barbarism of European judicial torture, the horrors of its galley fleets and prisons, the monstrous treatment of slaves, the unbelievable cruelty and irrationality in dealing with witchcraft and sorcery, the brutality of warfare ravaging the European countryside, and the great fear of the populace as soldiers, even supposedly friendly troops, entered a town or village. Even the Iroquois in their greatest fury against New France did not fall into the drunken orgies and wholesale rape of captive women that might be expected of a French conquering army at that time. An Iroquois woman prisoner given to the French in 1636 was asked if she feared sexual assault and is reported to have replied "that she was now of their nation, that she did not fear they would do her any harm, that if she were commanded to marry, she would obey."[1] The incident shows that there was little if any torture by sexually abusing women in Amerindian societies.

That is not to say that platform torture and scalping were anything but cruel and barbaric; but, it should be added that judicial torture and capital punishment were just as vicious and cruel in contemporary European societies. Heretics, for example, like people accused of sorcery, could be gnawed by starving rats or torn by raging swine; they could be made to endure the most refined tortures of rack and wheel and other devilish devices, and later beaten with rods in public, hanged, have their entrails burned before their yet living eyes, and their corpses dragged away to the dung heap. That was the measure of mercy and justice of French society against which evaluations of comments about Amerindian barbarism and cruelty should be measured.[2]

There is no doubt that the contact between Europeans and the Algonkian tribes of the Atlantic Coast were not always friendly. From Viking encounters through to the fishing contacts and the early fur traders of the seventeenth century there were instances of violence on both sides. Pierre Crignan reported in 1539 that the natives of Newfoundland "between Cap Ras and Cap de Brettone" were "a cruel and austerer people with whom it is impossible t odeal or to converse."[3] Whatever the origins or reasons for this hostility, the eventual extermination of the hapless Beothuks who were even hunted like animals by the French and Micmacs indicates from where much of the aggression came. André Thévet in 1557 supported the view that they were "extremely inhuman and intractable, according to the experience of those who have gone there to fish for cod."[4] English, Portuguese and French fishermen visiting the coasts, and trading occasionally in furs as a sideline, aroused hostility and fear by seizing natives and carrying them back to Europe as curiosities or slaves. A Dutch journal of a voyage to Penobscot Bay in 1609 reported the following events which reveal much about contact relationships:

> July 19: The people coming aboard, showed us great friendship, but we could not trust them. . . .
> July 20: Then we espied two French Shallops full of the Country people came into the Harbour, but they offered us no wrong, seeing we stood upon our guard. . . .
> July 25: Then we manned our Boat & Scute with twelve men and Muskets and two Stone Pieces of Murderers, and drove the Salvages from their Houses, and tooke the spoyle of them, as they would have done of us.[5]

We do not have the information necessary to evaluate properly the incident, but it is clear that the Europeans imputed to the Amerindians the prejudices and evil motives which they themselves demonstrated by their behaviour.

There were those who defended the Amerindians in these early contact experiences, just as there were those who continued to decry their barbarism. Jean Mocquet included at the end of his second travel volume eight startling illustrations depicting cannibalism, dances and warfare. Arms and legs of victims were depicted roasting over a fire, while the Amerindians sat in the foreground gnawing on human limbs.[6] As late as 1671 a report to the Ministry of the Marine told of natives attacking cod fishermen on the Grand Banks "killing sixteen men of a single vessel called the St. Lunaire which meant that the others instead of doing their fishing put themselves on guard so did nothing, which will cause much harm to trade."[7] Montaigne, however, could not feel sorry for the early fisherman who had, in his opinion and undoubtedly that of other Frenchmen, set in motion this chain of reprisals:

> . . . I think there is nothing barbarous and savage in that nation, from what I have been told, except that each man calls barbarism, whatever is not his own practice; for indeed it seems we have no other test of truth and reason than the example and pattern of opinions and customs of the country we live in.[8]

The problem of interpretation, involving as it does moral assumptions and value systems, when approached from a time distance of three centuries is no less difficult; the prime requirement is still that "one must rigorously separate the description of an action from the interpretation of that action."[9]

Scalping was a practice that was soon associated in European minds with Amerindian warfare. By the seventeenth century it was a sufficiently widespread practice to be considered a characteristic expression of native cruelty, ambush and perfidious raiding. There are doubts, however, that the practice was universal prior to the seventeenth century; if that is the case, the relationship between contact and the spread of scalping, if any, requires examination. It has been argued that, contrary to general supposition, the practice of scalping in the early exploration period was confined to an area stretching along the interior waterways from the mouth of the St. Lawrence to the Great Lakes and down to the Lower Mississippi Valley where it became absorbed in practices of human sacrifice. According to this interpretation, it was unknown to the Atlantic coastal tribes, to the northern tribes, and to most of the tribes of the Prairies and the Pacific region.[10] There is no report of scalping or torturing of captives among the Micmacs during the early contact period; it appears they either kept their captives in slavery or killed them on the spot. By the beginning of the eighteenth century, and the founding of Louisbourg, however, the more brutal practices reported elsewhere were also reported here, though never corroborated on the extensive scale some Europeans alleged.[11]

It is difficult, in many instances quite impossible, to reconstruct pre-contact behaviour and situations. We can be reasonably certain only of the situation reported at the time of contact and can surmise, at best, from attitudes and reported beliefs what the situation was before the Europeans wrote of their contact experiences. Two reports of sixteenth century practices indicate that scalping was known, if not commonplace, among the tribes. Cartier, on his second voyage, encountered evidence of scalping by the Laurentian Iroquois:

> And there was by the said Donnacona shown to the said Captain skins of five men's heads stretched on pieces of wood, like parchment skins; and said to us that they were Toudamans from the country above, who constantly waged war against them.[12]

A second report, an account of an attack on the Timogona which Laudonnière refused to aid, included details of the savage brutality with which such raids were expedited:

> On their arrival in the territory of their enemies, he and his council resolved that five of the chiefs with half of the troops should proceed by the river . . . that on their arrival at daybreak they should rush into the village, and kill all within save the women and little ones. This plan was carried out as arranged, and the dead were scalped. Of prisoners they took twenty-four, whom they carried away in their canoes, singing praises to the Sun, to whom they gave the honour of their victory. Then they placed the scalps on the end of their javelins, and distributed the prisoners among the chiefs, Satouriana receiving thirteen.[13]

These two incidents describe two somewhat different scalping traditions.

The latter incident illustrates the scalping of the southeastern region of North America which can probably be related directly to sacrificial offerings to the supernatural. Scalps were immediately removed from the defeated enemy, put on lances or sticks and carried home in triumph to be set up around the chief's house, where a victory celebration followed. Laudonnière related that the old women carried the scalps in dances praising the Sun for the victory. Jacques Le

Moyne, the artist who accompanied him to America, added that before going on the warpath the Sun had been asked for victory, the women beseeching the leader to avenge the deaths of their relatives, and scalps set up on stakes along the trails as declarations of war.[14] Both Tonty and Iberville reported in the late seventeenth century that scalps in the lower Mississippi region were used to decorate temples and were associated with religious practices.[15]

At the beginning of the seventeenth century the French were made aware of the Huron, Algonkin, Montagnais and Malecite practice of taking scalps and head trophies in battle. Sometimes legs and arms were brought back as trophies, and occasionally ears were taken along with scalps. Le Jeune was horrified to hear that some natives had hollowed out hands of Iroquois victims to serve as tobacco pouches.[16] Champlain mentioned, without indicating any special abhorrence, being shown about one hundred head trophies near Tadoussac in May 1603, and the following month described an Algonkin chieftain as seated between two poles on which "were hung the heads of their enemies." Two months later the Montagnais returned from a raid in Iroquois territory displaying more trophies, apparently the scalps of the slain warriors.[17] The warriors returning from the Iroquois country in 1609 were met by the women, who came out to the canoes to collect the scalps tied to the ends of long poles in the bows of the boats. Sometimes these scalps were hung about the neck "as if they were precious chains." The Jesuit report was as follows:

> The women ran hurriedly at the sight of these palms and these laures, dropped their clothes and leaped into sw'm after those garlands. There was a struggle among them as to which should catch one to hang it on their cabins as a token of the warrior's generosity. The women who had captured it began to boast of it.[18]

Champlain reported one occasion when the Algonkins brought back their trophies, including a body cut in quarters, from the expedition of 1610 in which he participated.[19] In 1642 the missionaries reported that "the standards — that is, the flying scalps — were fastened on the cabins; and all feasted and made merry in their fashion."[20] By this time they had managed to restrain the Montagnais women to the point that they no longer rushed out to claim the scalps, but had been able to achieve no more in attempting to reform behaviour.

The Récollets, upon their arrival in Canada in 1615, were soon acquainted with the practice of scalping. Denis Jamet wrote:

> At the time we arrived at Tadoussac some Montagnais youth were at surprise warfare according to their custom and of the nine they found they killed seven and brought their head skins

to make presents of them to the women, according to their custom. . . .[21]

The practice seems to have been firmly established, if the Récollet account of Amerindian practices is correct.[22]

Champlain's accounts indicate that head trophies, not just scalps, were taken. This relates scalping to head-hunting, a rather widespread aboriginal practice which seems to hearken back to a cult of the skull.[23] This cult of the skull had important religious or spiritual connotations, not entirely absent in Christianity. Possession of an enemy's skull or scalp gave one some control over his spirit; alternatively, it could also, in primitive belief systems, exact respectful treatment in order to avoid the wrath of the deceased's spirit. Such associations were not entirely foreign to Catholicism. For example, a nun at Quebec gave a Huguenot some broth in which she had put a fragment of the martyred Brébeuf's skull hoping thereby to assure his conversion. The nomadic northern tribesmen were reported to avoid scalping and taking head trophies for the same reasons as they avoided corpses and burial grounds. On the other hand, those who took head trophies and scalps had every reason, given their belief system, to regard these not only as proofs of courage but also as signs of power over their enemies. Champlain's account of the 1610 expedition in which his Amerindian allies "cut off the heads of those who were dead, as they have the customs of doing for victory trophies, and carried them off" is meaningful when head in such a context.[24] Europeans were accustomed to seeing the heads of executed criminals publicly displayed. Indeed, the French soldiers who were executed at Montreal for having murdered some natives, stolen their furs and almost setting off a war of revenge, had their heads crushed on blocks by the blows of a sledge hammer.

The Jesuits reported the Iroquois as sometimes scalping a victim and then another warrior cutting off the head which had been left to take as a trophy; on other occasions, heads were cut off those who fell in battle "in order to remove the scalps from them."[25] Of the Hurons they said "the swiftest warriors pursued the fugitives" in battle and after capturing and killing those they overtook they decapitated them "bringing back their heads and scalps." On one particular raid they recorded, "they brought back only seven prisoners, being content to carry off the head of the eighth."[26] Sagard was more explicit in describing Huron practices: he specified that they "after having clubbed them or shot them dead with arrows, they carry away the head, and if they are too much encumbered with these, they are content to take the scalps with the hair on them."[27] The mutilation of corpses left on the battlefield was not unknown in European warfare, but it would appear that a corpse scalped or decapitated by the Amerindians was never offered any further mutilation.

There has been some suggestion that the practice of scalping spread from the Iroquoian tribes to their northern neighbours. If the taking of scalps was a forest raiding technique derived from the taking of head trophies, then the geographical diffusion might well have been from the tribes with the higher religions to the south — the Iroquois, the Cherokee, the Tuscarora and the Susquehannock. The highest expression of such native religion, of course, would be the human sacrifices of the Aztecs. In forest raiding the act of scalping had to be done rapidly, unlike the ritual executions performed in southern temples. To scalp a victim a warrior usually disabled his enemy, placed his foot or knee on his body, seized his hair with one hand and with his weapon cut to the skull, then pulled and tore off his trophy.[28] It was an operation that took only a moment to execute, but sometimes only part of the scalp was torn away and the victims survived the initial shock and bloodloss to fall victim later to septicaemia or meningitis, or the slower and more painful deterioration of the skull itself, necrosis, and the resulting exposure of the brain. The more usual practice, of course, was to tear off the entire scalp "with all the hair from the head of him whom they slay."[29] Yet there were survivors. The Jesuit *Journal* recorded in March, 1646 a woman who was scalped yet "she kept well" and was able to care for her husband who eventually succumbed to the wounds he had received.[30]

There are indications that scalps were used as symbols to taunt and challenge an enemy, as well as to encourage and honour the victors. The deterrent value of exhibiting the heads, or even entire corpses, of executed criminals was widely accepted by the French. The Jesuits wrote in 1634 that Amerindian warriors wore "through bravado, these scalps covered with hair and moustaches," and again in 1642 that the Iroquois had "erected above their fort, as a flag denoting war" a scalp "which they had taken from some Algonquin."[31] Another anonymous report of 1634 stated that the Oneida placed the scalps on images carved like men on top of the main gate to their enclosed village.[32] Such scalps were carried in preparatory war dances and in victory celebrations. Sometimes a post was "scalped" by each warrior before he set off for war. In these instances, scalping was very much part of a war ritual or symbolism, not unlike the emphasis the French placed on flags and the ceremonial associated with the colours of a regiment.

There were three main reasons for the increase in the number of scalpings and the spreading of the practice over a wider area of North America. The economic and international rivalries of the Europeans brought a new kind of warfare to the continent which intensified the already existing tribal warfare. Secondly, the introduction of steel knives and hatchets made it much easier to take trophies. Thirdly, European rivals encouraged and rewarded scalping of the enemy.

Most sources are agreed that paying bounties for taking scalps was an important factor in spreading the practice. The New Englanders were probably the first to pay the Amerindians for scalps and it became a commonly acknowledged policy in most of the colonies from 1689 onwards. Nevertheless, the British government protested vehemently when Amerindian allies of the French were paid the equivalent of 5 *Livres,* or one-tenth the amount the English colonists were paying for scalps, for every English scalp brought in:

> This is so barbarous and inhuman that it ought by any means to be prevented, and therefore you ought immediately to write to the Governour of Canada and signify to him that unless he forbears to encourage such barbarities, and do not effectively prevent it, you shall be obliged to make reprisals and to treat all the French that shall fall into our hands with the utmost severity.[33]

Indeed, at first the bounty offered for a scalp by the English was greater than the return from the sale of a prisoner of war, so an economic premium was placed on inhumanity. There developed a "scalp racket" which so threatened the policy that the Massachussets House of Assembly had to direct its treasurer "to bury the several Indian scalps now in his custody in some private place, so as not to be discovered or produced again." There is also some evidence that after 1690 the French and English themselves resorted to scalping.[34] When the French had to pay their allies, usually converted "mission Iroquois," for proof of active participation in their military campaigns it may have been an indication that conversion had reduced their taste for warfare and brutality[35] Thus, while contact had the general effect of intensifying inter-tribal warfare, as shall be seen, there were also indications that religious conversion introduced new pacifist tendencies.

In the seventeenth century all the tribes continued to prefer taking prisoners alive to taking trophies from the dead.

> The glory of bringing back prisoners alive dazzles their minds; for the sweetest pleasure that a savage can enjoy is to drag his enemy after him.[36]

The objectives of warfare became not so much for a warrior "to return to his country laden with many scalps" but rather, in order to be honoured, to bring back prisoners alive.[37]

In warfare the French and Amerindians often differed greatly in motivation, intensity, tactics and strategy, objectives, treatment of prisoners and concepts of victory. Contact modified both French and Amerindian warfare in North America, with the net gain being decidedly to the advantage of the Europeans. When the French first made contact with the tribes of the Atlantic littoral they soon became aware of the inter-tribal warfare that was part of the normal pattern of the aborigines' existence. Thévet had some difficulty, therefore, in explaining how tribesmen, whom he also described as having no possessions, living in perfect equality, and demonstrating neither ambition nor desire for power, found motives for warfare. Warfare, whether international or civil, was an almost constant condition of French life in the sixteenth and seventeenth centuries. The motivations or rationalizations were known to all but the lower classes of society in France. But, as Amerindian warfare did not always fit the European patterns, it was open to much speculation and comment.

Since there was an apparent prevalence of warfare in America, motives had to be found to explain it. Thévet did not understand the motives for Amerindian warfare and, not being able to ascribe aggression to the desire for economic gain or territorial aggrandizement, he concluded it was due to their base natures which found expression even in "vengeance against lice and bedbugs, which they catch with their teeth, a thing more brutal than reasonable."[38] Sagard, in the seventeenth century, gave further strength to the impression that Amerindian warfare was a normal and continuous state of aboriginal life. He wrote:

> There is scarcely any nation which is not at war and dissension with some other, not for the purpose of possessing their territory and conquering their country, but solely to exterminate them if possible and take revenge for some slight wrong or unpleasantness, which is seldom a great matter.[39]

The experienced fur trader, Nicolas Perrot, later said that all the tribes were likely to wage war against each other, sooner or later, and that none could be completely trusted as allies.[40] He based his conclusion on his experience with the Ottawas, who had sought to arouse the interior tribes who traded with the French against the latter in the hope of obtaining better trading terms from the English.

What were the motivations for tribal wars? During the late sixteenth century, between the visit of Cartier to the Laurentian Iroquois and Champlain's contact with the Algonkian peoples at the beginning of the seventeenth century, an important inter-tribal war raged in the valley of the lower St. Lawrence. It is surmised that this war erupted over Laurentian Iroquois efforts to free themselves from dependence on Algonkian trade, migration pressures, xenophobia, and the vengeance and blood feud which ensued from isolated hostile incidents.[41]

This seems to have been a true war with planning, definite leadership and series of battles, as distinguished from raids and reprisals of a personal or family feuding nature. Champlain and the first Récollet missionaries witnessed the closing incidents of that war between 1605 and 1615. Prior to contact with the French, wars seem to have been motivated by the blood feud and need for vengeance, the desire to replace a deceased person in a maternal family, the need for warriors to assert their manhood, the fulfillment of spirit direction as revealed in dreams, prophecies, divinations or visions, and the human need to release excess energy in a kind of sporting venture.[42] War was some-times a contest of strength and skill which had its own rewards. Le Jeune stressed this very different approach to warfare:

> They go to war at a distance of two or three hundred leagues from their own country, over inaccessible rocks and through vast forests, provided solely with hope, and leaving in their Villages for whole years at a time, only their women and little children. But a few scalps that they bring back, a few prisoners of war, destined to be butchered by them, are the trophies with which they consider their labours happily rewarded.[43]

Another trait which differed greatly from European warfare was that, among the Iroquois in particular, the women wielded much influence in inciting men to go on the war path, or conversely in giving up a projected expedition. There were even isolated incidents when women fought in battles and prepared the ammunition for the warriors.[44]

Champlain reported that the Algonkins and Hurons gave as their reason for going to war against the Iroquois in 1609 revenge for the torture of captives in previous engagements.[45] This traditional moti-vation did not differ externally from the feuding nature of many European wars in which attempts were made to settle old scores. There were, nevertheless, basic differences. The missionary Hennepin indicated the level at which the revenge motive operated and how it was used to involve an entire tribe in war:

> When they undertake a War, 'tis commonly to recover satisfac-tion for some Injury, that they pretend has been done to them: Sometimes they engage in it, upon account of a Dream, and often as Fancy take 'em: Sometimes they enter into it, because other People jeer them: You're a Coward, say they; You never were in Battle; You have kill'd no Body yet. Then are they rouz'd by Honour, and after they have kill'd some Fallow Deer, make a Feast, and exhort their Neighbours to accompany them in their Enterprize.[46]

An early Jesuit report on warfare made the following observations:

They engage in war rashly and savagely, often with no cause or upon a very slight pretext. . . . In civil war they never engage; they carry arms only against their neighbours, and not for the sake of extending their dominion and sway, but usually, in order that they may avenge an injury inflicted upon themselves or their allies.[47]

It can be concluded that much aboriginal warfare was non-economic and non-political in motivation.[48] However, the social and religious character of inter-tribal warfare persisted after contact with the French.

Frenchmen came to a variety of conclusions about the nature of native warfare. Montaigne, who wrote at a time when the French as yet knew little of the diffusion of tribal warfare and before the great Iroquois thrust against numerous neighbouring tribes over a vast territory, assumed there were limited objectives and diffusion of tribal warfare in America. He wrote optimistically:

Their warfare is wholly noble and generous, and as excusable and beautiful as this human disease can be; its only basis among them is their rivalry in valor. They are not fighting for the conquest of new lands, for they still enjoy that mutual abundance that provides them without toil and trouble with all necessary things in such profusion that they have no wish to enlarge their boundaries. They are still in that happy state of desiring only as much as their natural needs demand; anything beyond that is superfluous to them.[49]

On the other hand, many Frenchmen concluded that since the normal European motivations for warfare did not seem to operate in Amerindian societies, aggression could be attributed only to defects of character, religion and social organization.

For their part, the Amerindians did not understand the motivations for European hostilities and therefore did not participate as allies as fully as the French had expected. When they did co-operate with the French, they did not always have the same motives and war aims so that their performance differed markedly from that of the French at times. Piracy and coastal raids on the Atlantic Coasts were sufficiently similar to inter-tribal engagements to be understandable, but the long-range and protracted imperial wars remained a mystery to the aborigines. This was particularly so when the wars centred on Europe, involving as they did naval engagements, complicated alliances and sudden cessation or resumption of hostilities in New France, depending on the course of events in Europe and in diplomatic negotiations independent of actual engagements in the colony.

Frenchmen who found it difficult to accept the native rationalizations for war were quite puzzled at times by Amerindian tactics and strategy. Culturally they shared a high esteem for the exclusively masculine qualities of skill in hunting and prowess in war. Thereafter, differences in conceptualization were quite marked. The French believed the Amerindians fought only skirmishes, had no master plans for attack, were undisciplined and chaotic in the execution of their designs, were improvident in supplying their expeditions, failed to carry through in campaigns to achieve their objectives, and were bestially inhuman in their treatment of prisoners of war.

Jouvency's report, however, did not bear out most of these criticisms of native warfare. He wrote that since "they have obtained swords and guns from the Dutch and English, and, relying upon these weapons, they plan with greater determination and boldness the destruction of their enemies."[50] Given the French technological superiority, in any conflict with them, the Amerindians were forced to rely on surprise, ambush, deceit and all the cunning they knew to defend themselves, or advance their own plans. Jouvency recounted how on one occasion the Montagnais and Iroquois had avoided all-out war and had agreed to settle their differences by single combat reminiscent of European mediaeval duels or jousts. The missionary was particularly surprised by the democratic nature of their war councils:

> They choose as leaders, by general vote, either the eldest members of illustrious families or those whose warlike valor, or even eloquence, has been approved.[51]

The inclusion of "the eldest members of illustrious families" made the statement comprehensible to French readers, but was an obviously unwarranted assertion from what is known about Algonkian and Iroquoian societies.

There are many testimonials of native ability in organizing, supplying, executing and commanding military campaigns. The Hurons and Algonkians made very elaborate preparations for war. Sagard said that the war parties were recruited by "elder or more daring captains" who went from village to village "to explain their intentions, giving presents to some in these villages in order to persuade them and procure their aid and support in the war." These war organizers bore the full expense of assembling the expedition, but all those who agreed to participate were "supported from their own private means without any payment or expectation of reward other than honour and praise."[52] It is obvious that European mercenary armies were quite beyond the understanding of Amerindians. The Amerindian war leader associated his expedition with death, and therefore painted his face and shoulders black and sang his death-song throughout the campaign. Before leaving, a period of feasting and purification was held, then at the time of departure a grand exit was made from the village. The women who were going along to cook and wash for the warriors followed the war party which marched in single file led by their captain. The Jesuits and Lahontan reported that the preparations were virtually indentical among the Iroquois.[53]

Champlain described the siege procedures used in attacking palisaded villages and described the war chiefs discussing with their men the plan of attack before battle. They illustrated fighting formations by scratches on the ground and positioning sticks. Rearguard actions were well planned and every effort was made to save the dead and wounded from falling into enemy hands. Socially acceptable boasting was part of the attack. Hennepin, who spent some years with the interior tribes, praised the leadership qualities of their commanders in war, the devotion and loyalty of the warriors who "will follow them anywhere," the care taken beforehand to have sufficient provisions, and the careful logistical planning essential in forest engagements.[54] He considered their advance preparations, their intelligence scouting, and their mastery of the tactic of surprise attack quite unmatched by the French.

The French soon learned that warfare in Canada, particularly in winter, could be very costly in men and materials. Captain François de Tapie de Monteil reported that the Courcelles expedition of January 1666 cost the French "four hundred men, who while marching fell dead from the cold."[55] Contact with the French had encouraged the natives to embark on winter campaigns and to wage night attacks. The Europeans learned rapidly to depend upon, and incorporate into their own strategy, the logistical and tactical skills of the natives, which were as necessary for survival as for success. The Montagnais and Algonkins, for example, made excellent use of their scouts, and on war marches divided their manpower into scouting, hunting and fighting units, but surprisingly neglected to post sentries when camping.[56] Champlain tried to impress upon them the seriousness of this omission, although he realized that when they were within a day's journey of the enemy villages they travelled principally by night.

Warfare by its very nature is atrocious, cruel, vindictive and immoral. Frenchmen were aware of the horrors of their sixteenth-century religious wars and, like other Europeans, were troubled by the atrocities and effects of the Thirty Years' War. The period of initial contact with the Amerindians was one when, in Europe, attempts were meeting with limited success to circumscribe warfare, to limit it to uniformed soldiery, to prescribe the humane treatment of prisoners, and to re-affirm the protocol and diplomacy of its general conduct.

Francisco de Vitoria and Hugo Grotius did much to define the legitimate conduct of warfare in the European context. In contrast to the formalities observed by Europeans in declaring, conducting and ceasing hostilities, aboriginal warfare seemed inexplicable in its outbreak, unregulated in its conduct, and unrelenting in its ferocity. Despite the numerous accounts of native courageousness, especially during cruel torture when warriors would not yield to any sign of weakness which would dishonour them or their tribe, some Frenchmen were convinced that, taken as a whole, Amerindians were cowardly and vengeful. Perrot left a weighty personal assessment of native character and motivation and their relationship to the conduct of war:

> The vengeance of the savages is more often inspired by ambition than courage, for there are no people in the world more cowardly than they are. That is made sufficiently evident in their fits of passion by the trembling with which their bodies are seized, and the pallor which would appear on their faces if these were not covered with black, red, or other colors. They expose themselves to danger with great rashness; it is that which renders them so enterprising; for if ambition excites them to vengeance they will go stealthily to kill a man in the midst of his friends, and to confront an ambuscade, even though they are sure they can never return from the undertaking. They are so bold that they will approach a hostile camp so near that they can count their foes. But all these extraordinary displays of courage are maintained onl ythrough vainglory, or from a passion to attract praises to themselves, either during life or after death. Notwithstanding, the reproach has quite often been cast on them that they had been cowardly enough to suffer injuries and let them go unpunished; the reason is, that ambition had no share, for there is no extreme to which their passion for it does not carry them, even to desperation, and to treachery in order to take their revenge.[57]

The values which he espoused and by which he judged native behaviour were very clearly based on a French cultural pattern in which it was considered unnecessary and perhaps politically dangerous for the participants to engage in the pursuit of purely personal objectives in war. Everything was to be subjected to the King's policy, to state objectives, and to general welfare. Collectivist and individualistic values marked the different approach the two cultures had to war.

Contact with the French brought a dependence on the fur trade, a desperate struggle for the middleman status, and usually an intensification of inter-tribal hostilities. Alliances, and concerted action among groups sharing a common enemy but not common objectives, gave the new warfare more significance. Victories or defeats had more consequential results and encouraged new hatreds and cruelties for they had a favourable cultural base from which to develop. Le Jeune remarked in 1637 on the unusual vindictiveness and tribal hatred of the Algonkins against the Iroquois. A native, although deathly ill, upon seeing an Iroquois brought to Quebec, threw himself upon "this poor man" like "a mad dog" and bit off an ear "animated by a passion so brutal, that it caused horror in all who saw it."[58] The newly created appetites for brandy, firearms, hatchets, knives and traps encouraged the dislocation of various tribal groups, which in turn created an atmosphere conducive to war and a variety of anxiety situations which provided strong motives for aggressive action.[59]

The introduction of firearms profoundly altered warfare in America. Had the early traders, settlers and missionaries not supplied any firearms to the Amerindians an intensification of tribal warfare and of native participation in European wars could have been avoided. It was just a matter of time, of course, before some guns came into the possession of aborigines as part of the bartering process. This initiation into the use of firearms was variously attributed to the Dutch and English, although Champlain placed the blame at the doorstep of the La Rochelle merchants.[60] Whoever was responsible, it set in motion counter-active measures, which were rationalized later in terms of trade necessities, the right of self-defence, and inevitable technological advance. The French missionaries attempted to keep guns from the natives, just as the English government in 1622 and again in 1630 forbade the sale of firearms to Amerindians. Indeed, the English colonies individually enacted prohibitions, as did the Dutch and French, but to no avail. In the face of growing complaints from European colonists and traders about the danger of aborigines possessing firearms, a commission of inquiry could only reply that the English themselves were to blame:

> . . . . for they first taught the Indians the use of arms and admitted them to be present at all their musters and trainings, and showed them how to handle, mend and fix their musquets and have been constantly furnished with all sorts of arms by permission of the government.[61]

By 1640 guns were common at Quebec and Tadoussac and the trade in firearms flourished.[62] In 1664, Pierre Boucher warned all Frenchmen interested in Canada that the Amerindians in general "are adept in handling firearms, and fire a gun very well."[63] Further attempts were made to control gun sales, such as restricting firearms to converts, but the final result was that the Iroquois were better equipped than their enemies.[64] This defeated the purpose of the French. The natives seem to have been as frustrated as the French by the fact that firearms were not always reliable, and that they deteriorated rapidly. In addition, the Amerindians found themselves becoming dependent on their suppliers for ammunition, repairs and replacements.

Pre-contact and early contact inter-tribal wars had usually consisted of small raiding parties with limited objectives, and consequently their casualties were generally light.[65] Even large armies, numbering several hundreds, dwindled to a few score by the time they arrived at their destination, as Champlain discovered in 1609 and again in 1610. As for leadership, among the nomadic Algonkian peoples it usually existed at the band level only and was not coercive. It was remarkable that the French were able to bring together hundreds of native warriors from several tribes and from widely dispersed areas under relatively competent leadership to fight sustained battles in which the casualties would run higher than normal in native encounters. Nevertheless, the Iroquois remained a superior force and it was left largely to the French to protect the allied tribes and assure their trade.[66] This was the case after 1680 in the French relationship with the Ottawas, centred on Michilimakinac, just as it had been in their relationship with the Montagnais and Algonkins in an earlier period. The behaviour of the Ottawas scarcely justified the Jesuit missionaries' description of them as warlike and extremely aggressive.[67] On the other hand, following contact with the French and other Europeans, Iroquois raiding took on the characteristics of true war involving larger armies, which were better armed and used a cohesive war strategy.

The growing destructive potential of Amerindian warfare, and the fear which gripped the French and English colonies at the close of the seventeenth century when faced with effective native raids described variously as "barbaric," "ferocious," "bestial" and "inhuman," resulted in an attempt to regulate war conduct between the two European belligerents in North America and to control Amerindian "savagery." New York and Massachussetts made proposals to New France in the summer of 1695 to establish rules of war. The three governments came to an understanding on humanizing their frontier warfare. They agreed to try to prevent scalping and burning of prisoners of war, to appoint a special officer in each country to look after prisoners, to maintain jointly a vessel for a more rapid exchange of prisoners, to permit prisoners to work out their ransom at a reasonable wage, and to prohibit the disfigurement of Christians or their sale into slavery. All prisoners of war, including those in the bands of Amerindian allies, were to be cared for and held to be returned home at the end of the war. This agreement on the limitation of atrocities applied only to French and English prisoners of war and did not extend to Amerindian prisoners.[68] This showed that Europeans viewed their war practices as being very different from the Amerindian code of behaviour. The ultimate solution for the French was to reach a *modus vivendi* with the Iroquois in 1701 whereby the Five Nations were able to maintain a neutral status in the growing English-French struggle for the continent.

A distinction must be made between inter-tribal and inter-racial war, that is, war waged between Europeans and Amerindians. The earliest French involvement was in inter-tribal wars, which won them more friends than enemies, whereas the English involvement tended from the outset to be confrontation in racial war. The English experience therefore was one of explicit racism from the outset, but French hostility towards the Iroquois did not become racist until the 1660s.[69] In 1655 Simon le Moyne gave the Seneca, Oneida, Cayuga and Onondaga chiefs "a hatchet to be used in the New War in which they are engaged with the Cat Nation" so that the French and their allies might not be involved.[70] Once the Iroquois wars were regarded as a crusade against fiendish pagans who threatened French missions and colonization with annihilation, unusual measures and reprisals were deemed justified by the French. A Dutch document confirms that there was utter despondency in New France, as in metropolitan France, that unless very strong military measures were taken by the home government all was lost:

> The French prisoners, brought away by the Maquas savages from under their forts every year, and occasionally ransomed by our people, declare unanimously that if the French receive no assistance by soldiers from France, they will shortly be obliged to leave the country; the gracious God may grant, that the Maquas will not begin with us, after they have destroyed and finished with the French.[71]

The Mohawks were always the chief resistors to French negotiation.

The continuing Iroquois threat to New France, even after the arrival of *troupes de terre* to relieve the beleaguered colony, decided the metropolitan government to order Governor Denonville in 1686 to launch a surprise attach on the Iroquois and send as many warriors as could be captured to France to serve in the Mediterranean galley fleet.[72] The Dutch had already tried enslavement and transportation of Amerindian prisoners in 1661 in their efforts to curb hostile pressure on European settlements.[73] Gédéon de Catalogne later gave a version of the incident as it was commonly reported in the colony; this version indicated quite clearly that the unfortunate Iroquois prisoners expected to be treated as captives reserved for death. He wrote:

> The designated feast day having arrived, all the guests were arrested, and as there was no lodging to serve as a prison, they

were attached, a total of 95 men, to trunks, the foot of each one being made fast; a stake served as a back support, where there was a rope which attached them by the collar; their arms were well secured by a line; their women and girls were at liberty to cook for them. In this situation they sang at the top of their voices their death-songs.[74]

Denonville never fully agreed with the orders he had received from Versailles on the matter. Nevertheless, he did send thirty-six Iroquois prisoners, most of whom had been seized by the Intendant Champigny under pretence of a parley near Fort Frontenac, because, as he said, "I believed I had to blindly obey His Majesty's orders." He would have sooner kept the Iroquois as hostages and for prisoner exchanges. In addition, the Jesuits bitterly accused the military of destroying their missions among the Iroquois and undermining any confidence the Five Nations might have had in the French. In 1688 Denonville requested preferential treatment for the Iroquois galley slaves because they might be required for prisoner exchanges in the New World; the following year, he succeeded in having them released. In the autumn of 1689, thirteen survivors arrived at Quebec. The remaining twenty-three had died in hard slave labour or during the dangerous ocean crossings.[75] The incident did not act as a deterrent to Iroquois pressure on the French colony, nor did it appear to have the effect of impressing them with French treachery and cruelty as the Jesuits feared it would. Obviously, inter-racial war was not bound by the rules of conduct of European warfare then gaining universal acceptance.

The aspect of Amerindian warfare that especially aroused Europeans was the treatment of prisoners of war and their death under torture. Writers who found the natives kind and hospitable also noted their cruelty towards their sworn enemies.[76] The fact that the children as well as being taught stoicism in suffering and adversity were taught refined cruelty towards captured enemies aroused the humanitarian sentiments of the French.[77] The French were outraged in 1627 when a Frenchman, Pierre Magnan, was captured on a peace mission to the Mohawks under orders from Champlain and Emery de Caen and made prisoner and tortured to death.[78] In future, the French were not exempt from the common fate of captives. Torture in inter-tribal wars seems to have been commonplace, although the Algonkins and Hurons gave as their reason for going to war with the Iroquois in 1609 the fact that the latter had tortured prisoners taken in previous engagements. The statement as recorded by Champlain may merely have indicated a continuing series of reprisals. The cruel fate awaiting prisoners of war was widely known and was used by the Iroquois as a terror tactic to break the resistance of their foes. Hennepin observed that as a result of their publicized ferocity they "have subdued a very large Country since within these fifty Years; that they have extended their Territories and multiplied their Nation by the Destruction of other People, the Remainder of whom they have made Slaves to encrease the number of their Troops."[79]

Amerindians seem to have accepted the fact that captivity normally meant death under torture. In preparation for such an eventuality a warrior rehearsed his death-song which he would sing while being led into captivity and when undergoing the prolonged trial by fire and knife. He also prepared suitable taunts and mockeries to challenge and deride tormentors. The gruesome ordeal was a ritualistic death which every warrior accepted as normal were he to be captured. The Jesuits wrote from the Huron country in 1642 that a warrior, having dreamed he had been captured by the Iroquois and tortured, informed the tribal council of his dream so that they could take appropriate measures to avert the ill fortune. He was burned by his friends who compassionately seized firebrands to simulate the tortures endured in his dream. After being burned by a number of torches he seized a dog which was killed, roasted in the fires and eaten at a public feast "in the same manner as they usually eat their captives."[80] In Iroquois country in 1661-62 a man, in order to satisfy the demands of a dream, was dragged through the village and set up on the torture platform where the fires were lit and he sang his death-song. Another warrior called for a more realistic enactment of his torture and took six months to recover from his burns.

Although torture of prisoners was a ritualistic function of warfare, it could be interrupted suddenly and the victim be adopted into the victor tribe and shown all the affection accorded natural children by his foster family. Some classes of people were only rarely tortured to death. Le Jeune commented on the Huron and Algonkian customs in 1636:

> It is true that the Barbarians do not usually harm the women or the children except in their sudden attacks. Indeed, many a young man will not hesitate to even marry a prisoner, if she is very industrious; and thereafter she will pass as a woman of his country.[81]

Frenchmen, when captured, were either tortured with additional satisfaction, or more commonly were adopted or held as hostages for prisoner exchanges. There seems to have been no certainty as to whether the fate of a particular captive would be torture or adoption. Some children, for example, were crucified by the Iroquois and by the Sioux.[82] On the other hand, Monique, a blind Algonkin convert, was spared by the Iroquois in spite of her handicap.[83] Treatment of prisoners varied among the tribes and in some cases prisoners were made slaves, rather than being adopted. These were usually called *Panis,* a name derived from the Pawnee tribe which had been completely enslaved. The Abenakis were never reported to torture their captives. In 1660, the Jesuits reported of one of their campaigns that they returned with captives "not to burn them, for that is not their custom; but to hold them in servitude."[84] Negroes were also held in servitude by certain tribes and there is a record of some Negro captives dying under torture.[85]

Torture of prisoners was not a practice unknown to European armies. It was the ritualistic, pre-meditated and widespread "normal" torture treatment of Amerindians that so aroused French sensitivities and civilized outrage. The Europeans, judging from their own frames of reference and relying on their own moral assumptions, could not understand women and children participating in the torture of captives and could not accept that soldiers and even non-combatants should suffer a death reserved in Europe only for the basest criminals. The only explanation they could offer for behaviour so foreign to their preconceptions was the complete depravity, sadism and degeneracy of the Amerindians. The native motivations, ritualistic satisfaction and value system were ignored. Frenchmen did not understand that in most Amerindian cultures retribution was "an act of inspired virtue," the highest expression of their moral system.[86] Futhermore, in Amerindian cultures retribution merged with the concept of collective accountability, ruling out the possibility of innocent non-combatants, so that any tribesmen could be held responsible for the actions of his kinsmen, and anyone could be made to pay the penalty for them.[87] All European nations, at one time or another, used torture against the Amerindians either to extract information or to punish refractory behaviour.[88] But, in European eyes, the context was completely different from the Amerindian ritualistic use of stake and platform torture.

The Catholic missionaries attempted with limited success to eradicate the practice among the converted tribesmen. Le Jeune and Champlain tried to stop the torture of captives in 1636 but received only rude rebuffs for their efforts.[89] The clergy claimed that their converts had abandoned their former practices. As proof of this, Iroquois prisoners brought back to the Christian reserve in 1645 were greeted by Jean-Baptiste Etinechikawat who received his warriors with praise saying to the war-captain:

> Thou knowest well that we now proceed in a different fashion than we formerly did. We have overturned all our old customs.

That is why we receive thee quietly, without harming the prisoners, without striking or injuring them in any way.[90]

The priest in charge then gave a speech "praising the warriors for their courage, congratulating them upon their gentleness, and showing them that it was for dogs and wolves to devour their quarry, but that men should be humane, especially towards their fellow creatures."[91] The startled prisoners, expecting the traditonal torture stake and platform, were well treated in spite of the urgent pleadings of two women, sole survivors of families killed by the Iroquois, to be permitted to avenge themselves on the pagans. A victory feast with dancing was permitted by the Jesuits, and the scalps of the Iroquois killed in battle were hoisted as standards on the cabins.

The success the missionaries enjoyed on this occasion was rarely repeated. Throughout the seventeenth century there were accounts of continuing torture of captives by converted tribesmen and by Frenchmen. In September, 1647 the Governor had to cede to the demands of the converted tribesmen at Sillery and release an Iroquois to them. Allegedly he was one of the murderers of Isaac Jogues, whom he had held prisoner for more than a week. Le Jeune baptized the Iroquois, thus salving his conscience that one more soul had been won for the church triumphant, before he died after an hour of frenzied torments.[92] In 1650, a renegade Huron named Skandahietsi was arrested, whereupon he made a hasty conversion and received baptism only to be delivered the following day to the executioner and sergeant to be tortured by them before being handed over to the Hurons and Algonkin converts at whose hands he died.[93] In 1652, there is again a record of two Iroquois being baptized then released to the converted tribesmen to be put to death by torture.[94] In 1681, two women captives, originally from Maryland, were brought to the chapel for hasty religious instruction and rites and then "were burned as usual, at a slow fire, with heated irons, and were afterward eaten."[95] The missionaries had succeeded only in administering baptism to these women. In 1696, "an old man, 80 years of age, who was almost blind," was taken captive and while the allied Amerindians debated his fate the French "demanded that he be burned at a slow fire, which they themselves did with much zeal" in the sight of his relatives. The only consolation the priests could offer this Iroquois convert was to hear his confession. "Had he not been burned all over" after an hour of tortures at the hands of the French he would have been released by the allied tribesmen.[96] Although the Iroquois had the reputation for being consigned tormentors, these accounts of women and the aged being consigned to torture do not indicate much more delicacy on the part of the Huron or Algonkian tribes — not to mention the French themselves. Not only did the old ways persist in Amerindian society, but the French on occasion took up some of what Governor Denonville described as "the most vicious" qualities in aboriginal culture.

The procedures and forms of torture of captives need to be examined to show their religious and social significance. Among all the tribes, the crippled, the aged, the mutilated, the incapacitated and the women in advanced pregancy were usually rapidly dispatched by a swift blow on the head so as not to slow the homeward journey of the victors. In exceptional cases, prisoners might be treated well on the journey homeward, but generally preliminary torture was inflicted, especially by the Iroquois when they were caught in a French-English squeeze. Father Jogues and Bressani, for example, were continously ill-treated; Jogues reported that they beat them severely, tore out their fingernails, bit and crushed their forefingers, neglected their wounds, transgressed their personal integrity, left them staked as uncomfortably as possible at night, and fed them only scraps of food "under he belief that their success will be greater as they shall have been more cruel." By enacting the victory scene, according to their religious belief, they believed they would ensure its repetition in the future.[97]

Among the Hurons, Montagnais and Iroquois, when the prisoners arrived at the village of their captors, they were forced to run a gauntlet. One report said:

> At their arrival the whole village goes to meet them at 500 paces from the village, and to welcome them, but in a strange way: every one is armed — one with a club, another with a handful of thorns, another with a knife and firebrand. They form in lines on both sides, and mercilessly strike the prisoners until they have reached the platform prepared for the exhibition of their cruelty — they are naked and each has a collar of porcelain around his head to designate him as a victim.[98]

Having run the gauntlet, for the villagers did not kill the captives at this stage, the prisoners had to await the decision of the council (which among the Iroquois was influenced by the women) as to whether they would be adopted by a family to replace a deceased relative, or be made a slave and hostage, or be condemned to death.

The death torture was most elaborate among the Iroquois, suggesting that they introduced it to the neighbouring tribes who observed a much less elaborate, though basically similar, order in torturing their captives. Sagard sent to France one of the earliest detailed reports of stake torture followed by platform torture as practised among the Huron. The Récollet wrote:

> On arrival of the prisoners at their town or village they make them suffer many different kinds of torture . . . . All the modes

of torture and death are so cruel that nothing could well be more inhuman. In the first place they tear their nails and cut off the three principal fingers which are employed in drawing the bow, and then strip off all the skin of the head with the hair, and afterwards apply fire to it and hot ashes, or they drop upon it melted gum of a certain kind. Or else they are satisfied with making them walk with naked body and feet through a great number of fires kindled for the purpose from one end to the other of a large lodge, in which all people, ranged along the two sides, each holding a burning brand in his hand, apply these to their bodies as they pass. Then afterwards, tying him to a stake, with hot iron they give him garters round the legs, and with red-hot tomahawks they rub his thighs from the top down, and thus little by little they burn the poor wretch. And in order to add to his excruciating sufferings they sometimes dash water over his back, and apply fire to the tip of his fingers and of his private parts. Then they pierce the arms near the wrist and with sticks draw the nerves and wrench them out forcibly, and when they cannot get them out they cut them. This the prisoners endure with incredible firmness, and while it goes on they chant a song, but, as I have said, a very sad and mournful song, a thousand threats against their executioners and against that entire nation. When about to give up the ghost the prisoner is taken out of the lodge to end his life on a scaffold made ready for the purpose, and there his head is cut off, then his belly is opened, and all the little children are there to get some small fragment of bowel. . . .[99]

Hennepin, in describing the torture inflicted by the Iroquois on the southern tribes in 1679, said they fastened prisoners on cross-beams and exposed them to the hordes of insects, cut small pieces of flesh from their fleshy parts and ate them boiled and forced the prisoners to eat them also. They tortured them with fire and knife, and, finally, to encourage the cannibalism of their children "give them their Blood to drink in some little Porrengers made of Barks of trees" thus ending the torments that had been extended over a month in some cases.[100] Jogues, in a letter written from New Netherland to his Provincial, described the special hatred the Iroquois had for converted tribesmen:

My sufferings, great in themselves, were heightened by the sight of what a like cruelty had wreaked on the Christian Hurons, fiercer than all in the case of Eustace; for they had cut off both his thumbs, and, through the stump of his left, with savage cruelty, they drove a sharp stake to his very elbow. This frightful pain he bore most nobly and piously.[101]

The many accounts of torture given by the missionaries, Lahontan, Perrot, and Radisson confirm the usual pattern of preliminary torture and dancing in the lodge or at a stake, followed by platform torture, slowing burning, prolonging sufferings by affected kindness and restoring the victim's strength, applying heated irons, piercing the skin, slicing pieces of flesh for eating, sticking burning splinters into the flesh, drawing out nerves and tendons, scalping and pouring hot ashes or hot sand on the skull, and the final dissection of the body. Prisoners held over several days in such tortures were fastened at night to St. Andrew's crosses or stakes, where the women and children subjected them to further indecencies and delicate tortures.[102] The sacrificial nature of these ghastly proceedings was indicated, nevertheless, by the strict insistence on circumspect behaviour on the part of torturers, tortured and spectators. The victim danced and sang his long-rehearsed death-song. Among the Huron and Montagnais the victim was even afforded much kindness and given a feast before his ordeal and death. It was usually hoped the victim would die on the platform and at the hour of sunrise.[103] The belief that death should come by knife, that the heart needed to be exposed, and that the victim should be eaten were further indications of its sacrificial and religious nature. That Frenchmen who believed in transubstantiation and literally eating their Lord in their communion service failed to understand this aboriginal cannibalism is surprising.

The stake torture which the Montagnais women inflicted on captives was a most refined and ingenious brutality:

> You should have seen these furious women howling, yelling, applying fire to the most sensitive and private parts of the body, pricking with awls, biting them with savage glee, laying open their flesh with knives; in short, doing everything that madness can suggest to a woman. They threw fire upon them, burning coals, hot sand, and when the sufferers cried out, all the others cried still louder, in order that the groans should not be heard and that no one might be touched with pity.[104]

The sexual organs were often the object of torture, but the missionary reporters, in maintaining propriety, seldom said more than that fire was applied "to the end of his privy member." Radisson had fewer scruples and wrote of his own experiences:

> In the next place, they clothe you with a suit made of rind of a tree, and this they make burn out on your body. They cut off your stones, and the women play with them as with balls. When they see the miserable die, they open him and pluck out his heart. They drink some of his blood and wash the children's heads with the rest to make them valiant.

That day they plucked four nails out of my fingers and made me sing, though I had no mind at that time, I became speechless oftentimes; then they gave me water wherein they boiled a certain herb that the gunsmiths use to polish their arms. That liquor brought me to my speech again. The night being come, they made me come down all naked as I was . . . .[105]

In the Jesuit *Relations* there is also an account of the Iroquois capturing a French woman who was "cruelly burned by those barbarians, after they had torn off her breasts, cut off her nose and ears."[106] On the other hand, there is no record whatever, despite rumours among both English and French, of women prisoners being sexually molested in captivity.

The torture ceremony ended with a cannibalistic feast. This was the ultimate proof to many Europeans that the Amerindians were by nature sadistic brutes little above animals in moral development. The image of Amerindian cannibals had first been conjured up in Europe after Columbus' encounter with the fierce Caribs. French experiences with New World cannibalism dated from 1528 when Giovanni da Verrazano landed in the Antilles, probably in Guadeloupe, was captured, killed and eaten before the horrified eyes of his crewmen. The French missionaries depicted the Iroquois as the most ferocious of all the tribes. In describing their torture practices, one eye-witness wrote:

Then, they tear the heart from the breast, roast it upon the coals, and, if the prisoner has bravely borne the bitterness of the torture, give seasoned with blood, to the boys, to be greedily eaten, in order, as they say, that the warlike youth may imbibe the heroic strength of the valiant man.[107]

The procedure among the Hurons was reported to be very similar:

After having at last brained the victim, if he was a brave man, they tear out his heart, roast it on the coals, and distribute it in pieces to the young men: they think that this renders them courageous.[108]

Hennepin erroneously believed cannibalism was practised only among Iroquoian tribes but the literature indicates it was common among the Algonkins, Montagnais and Ottawas as well.[109]

When the Amerindians first roasted and ate a captured Frenchman to fulfill their rituals and to acquire his knowledge or bravery, the French interpreted it as diabolically inspired. The natives subscribed to the common aboriginal belief that "bravery and other desirable parts of an enemy pass through actual ingestion of a part of his body into that of the consumer."[110] Had Frenchmen closely examined their own cultural beliefs they would have discovered a parallel religious belief in transubstantiation whereby they professed to acquire grace through eating the flesh and drinking the blood of their Saviour. The Jesuits had consciously avoided inculcating the concept of eating the body of Christ and drinking his blood, a notion which might too readily be equated in Amerindian minds with the ritual cannibalism the missionaries were trying to discourage. Brébeuf translated the Eucharist into Huron as *Atonesta*, which signified an act of gratitude and thanksgiving in the sense of a memorial or purely symbolical ceremony. In Iroquoian culture, eating a captive's heart was the highest tribute the victors could pay to his bravery and steadfast endurance under torture. If they drank his blood, or poured it over themselves, or sometimes put it directly into their veins through a cut,[111] it was because they wished to appropriate his courage. Although most accounts tell of the body being eaten by the villagers, some accounts specify that the head was given to a chief and the trunk was consumed by the common people. Pierre Boucher distinguished between the heart and blood being consumed for ritual appropriation and the body being eaten "out of vengance."[112] Etienne Brulé, for example, seems to have been murdered and then eaten by the Hurons because of his alleged disloyalty in attempting to negotiate a trading alliance between the Iroquois and the British.

There is no evidence that cannibalism was widely accepted outside of a religious context. Quite to the contrary, the unnaturalness of cannibalism is suggested both by reports of unusual visitation dreams and by reports on "windigo psychosis." Lalemant reported in 1642 that an adolescent youth, who had spent sixteen days fasting in the woods, had a vision of an old man who foretold his future and offered him a piece of raw human flesh to eat. The youth recoiled in horror, but he did eat a piece of bear fat he was offered instead. In his later years he converted and was baptized by the missionaries; in reporting the man's account, Lalemant included his mature opinion that "he would have had equal success in war had he eaten the piece of human flesh that he refused."[113] De Quen, in the *Relation* of 1655-56, told of a Cayuga who dreamed that he gave a feast of human flesh, which greatly upset him and the whole tribe because not to satisfy this unusual dream meant evil days for the nation. Eventually, the chiefs gave him a young girl, adorned with ornaments who was unaware of her fate. The Jesuit reported:

> He took her; they watched his actions, and pitied that innocent girl; but, when they thought him about to deal the death-blow, he cried out: "I am satisfied; my dream requires nothing further."[114]

These accounts indicate that Amerindians had an ambivalent attitude towards cannibalism for they seemed loath to eat human flesh except for religious reasons or in extreme circumstances. The Huron refugees, who spent the winter of 1648-49 on Christain Island with some of the Jesuit missionaries, resorted to eating human corpses because of despair and starvation.

The same attitudes were shown among the northern Algonkian tribes where a type of cannibalistic madness, later identified as the "windigo psychosis," and first described by Paul Le Jeune in 1635, was not uncommon. Gabriel Druillettes and Claude Dablon reported a case of such madness among their guides in 1680:

> These poor men . . . are afflicted with neither lunacy, hypo-chondria, nor frenzy; but have a combination of all these species of disease, which affects their imaginations and causes them a more than canine hunger. This makes them so ravenous for human flesh that they pounce upon women, children, and even upon men, like veritable werewolves, and devour them voraciously . . . .[115]

The missionaries recorded two basic Algonkian beliefs about this form of cannibalism: first, that once human flesh was tasted an insatiable desire for it was aroused; secondly, that this anti-social appetite necessitated the exile or immediate death of the cannibals.

Not all French reactions to alleged Amerindian barbarism and cruelty were negative, critical and filled with horrified disgust. Montaigne alleged that the natives must have learned such refined cruelty from the Portuguese, who had made numerous slaving raids on the North American coasts before the French came to trade and settle there. He also commented on the stoic behaviour of captives condemned to death under torture. He noted the ritualistic nature of the proceedings and attempted to acquaint his French readers with the captive's rationalization of his fate:

> I have a song composed by a prisoner which contains this challenge, that they should all come boldly and gather to dine off him, for they will be eating at the same time their own fathers and grandfathers, who have served to feed and nourish his body. "These muscles," he says, "this flesh and these veins are your own, poor fools that you are. You do not recognize that the substance of your ancestors' limbs are still contained in them. Savor them well; you will find in them taste of your own flesh." Consider that certainly does not smack of barbarity. Those that paint these people dying, and who show the execution, portray the prisoners spitting in the face of his slayers and

scowling at them. Indeed, to the last gasp they never stop braving and defying their enemies by word and look. Truly here are real savages by our standards, for either they must be thoroughly so, or we must be; there is an amazing distance between their character and our.[116]

Montaigne did not regret that Frenchmen deplored "the barbarous horror" of such cruelty, but he felt sorry that "judging their faults rightly, we should be so blind to our own." He called for a reconsideration of French values and practices.

Montaigne gave the following comparative evaluation of cruelty and barbarity in French and Amerindian cultures:

> I think there is more barbarity in eating a man alive than in eating him dead, and in tearing by tortures and the rack a body still full of feeling, in roasting a man bit by bit, in having him bitten and mangled by dogs and swine (as we have not only read but seen within fresh memory, not among ancient enemies, but among neighbours and fellow citizens, and what is worse, on the pretext of piety and religion), than in roasting and eating him after he is dead. So we may well call these people barbarians, in respect to the rules of reason, but not in respect to ourselves, who surpass them in every kind of barbarity.[117]

His essay, *Des Cannibales,* unmistakably indicated Montaigne's belief in the myth of a Golden Age metamorphosed into that of the *bon sauvage,* and his acceptance of the relativity of customs and mores, which were to his mind grounded ultimately in human opinions and prejudices. He used the eyewitness accounts of Amerindian bravery under torture to show their difference from Frenchmen and to underscore the decadence of Western Europe. As a humanist, he used the theme of Amerindian natives — good, happy and brave — to document his thesis of modern Frenchmen as moral and psychological pygmies compared to the Ancients.[118]

Similarily, the Huguenot pastor, Jean de Léry, rationalized the aboriginal treatment of captives by contending that the natives wanted to obliterate the enemy or else incorporate his strength and courage by eating him. He found this "excusable cruelty," but European cruelties he found inexcusable. He cited in particular the terrible massacres during the religious wars in France which degenerated to the level of the selling of human hearts and human fat on the streets of Auxerre.[119]

The image of the brutal savages of America was firmly established through the practices of scalping, torture of captives, and ritual cannibalism. Contact with the French intensified these practices among the tribes that came under military and economic pressure, although in the long-run the more humane treatment practised and upheld by the French made an impression and reduced the incidence of brutality among the northern tribes. On the other hand, it has been shown that the long history of injustice to the Amerindians since the seventeenth century springs in some measure from a profound and deep-seated misunderstanding that passed into literary tradition in which emotional speculation and fiction often replaced fact.[120]

Alleged Amerindian barbarity and cruelty needs to be considered in its complete cultural context in order to be understood. This understanding will not necessarily alter evaluations made in the light of present day values, or in the light of the moral assumptions of Frenchmen of the sixteenth and seventeenth centuries. It should bring an awareness, nevertheless, of the cultural gulf that existed between Europeans and Amerindians and it should illuminate the contradictory reports that were given by contemporaries. Sagard's account of the companions of an exhausted hunter who "seeing him in this state and touched and moved by compassion, asked him if he would like them to put an end to him so as to deliver him from the sufferings and weakness he laboured under" should be taken literally as an expression of brotherly concern and compassion.[121] Le Jeune, in contemplating the examples of gentleness, charity and kindness of the neophytes, concluded:

> Some of our Frenchmen must here correct the notion they have had of our Savages, imagining them as ferocious beasts having nothing human about them save the exterior Formation of the body.[122]

One could always find the qualities one wished to find in an alien culture.

1. R. G. Thwaites, ed., *The Jesuit Relations and Allied Documents* (Cleveland: 1897-1901), Vol. IX, p. 269.
2. Robert Mandrou, *Magistrats et Sorciers en France au XVIIe siècle* (Paris: 1968); Raymond Boyer, *Les Crimes et les châtiments au Canada français du XVIIe au XXe siècle* (Montréal: 1966) are essential reading on this subject.
3. Pierre Crignan, "Discorso d'un Gran Capitano di mare Francese," cited in Bernard G. Hoffman, *Cabot to Cartier. Sources for a Historical Ethnography of Northeastern North America, 1497-1550* (Toronto: 1961), pp. 169-170.
4. Paul Gaffarel, ed., *André Thevet: Les Singularitez de la France Antarctique* (Paris: 1878), p. 438.
5. Robert R. Lienny, ed., *Juet's Journal* (New York: 1959), pp. 14-15.
6. Jean Mocquet, *Voyages en Afrique, Asie, Indes Orientales & Occidentales* (Paris: 1617).

7. *Archives de la Marine, Series B3,* Vol. IX, Sieur de Narp to Minister of the Marine, September 23, 1671, fol. 374.
8. Donald H. Frame, ed., *Montaigne's Essays and Selected Writings* (New York: 1963), p. 89.
9. Wilcomb E. Washburn, "Relations between Europeans and Amerindians during the Seventeenth and Eighteenth Centuries: The Epistomological Problem," Unpublished paper presented at the International Colloquium on Colonial History, University of Ottawa, November, 1969, p. 2.
10. Georg Friederici, *Skalpieren une ähnliche Kriegsgebraiëche in Amerika* (Braunschwiig: 1906), pp. 1-172. Cf. Frederica De Laguna, ed., *Selected Papers from the American Anthropologist, 1888-1920* (Evanston: 1960), pp. 665-667.
11. P. A. S. Maillard, "Lettre sur les Missions de l'Acadie et particulière-ment sur les Missions Micmaques," *Les Soirées Canadiennes* III (1863), pp. 316-320; "Letter from Mons. de la Varenne," *An Account of the Customs and Manners of the Micmakis and Maricheets, Savage Nations, now dependent on the Government of Cape Breton* (London: 1758), p. 98.
12. Société littéraire et historique de Québec, *Voyages de Découvertes au Canada, entre les années 1534 et 1542* (Québec: 1843), p. 49; cf. Bruce T. Trigger, "Trade and Tribal Warfare in the St. Lawrence in the Six-teenth Century," *Ethnohistory* IX (1962), pp. 240-256.
13. W. L. Grant, ed., *The History of New France by Marc Lescarbot* (Toronto: 1907), p. 88, Vol. I.
14. Nathaniel Knowles, "The Torture of Captives by the Indians of Eastern North America," *Proceedings of the American Philosophical Society* 82, No. 2 (March, 1940), pp. 195-205.
15. Henri de Tonty, "Memoir sent in 1693," in B. F. French, ed., *Historical Collections of Louisiana* (New York: 1846), p. 61; Thwaites, *op. cit.,* Vol. LXVIII, p. 125; Pierre Le Moyne d'Iberville, "Historical Journal, or Narrative of the Expeditions made to Colonize Louisiana," in B. F. French, ed., *Historical Collections of Louisiana* (New York: 1875), p. 74.
16. Thwaites, *op. cit.,* Vol. V, p. 130.
17. H. P. Biggar, ed., *The Works of Samuel de Champlain* (Toronto: 1922-36), Vol. I, pp. 63-65, 98-101, 103-108.
18. Thwaites, *op. cit.,* Vol. IX, p. 253.
19. Biggar, *op. cit.,* Vol. II, pp. 106, 134.
20. Thwaites, *op. cit.,* Vol. XXVII, p. 237.
21. *B.N., 500 de Colbert,* No. 483, Denis Jamet to Cardinal de Joyeuse, July 15, 1615, fols. 581-582v.
22. R. L. Scheele, "The Treatment of Captives among the North East Indians of North America," M.A. Thesis, Columbia University, 1947, p. 5 argues it was customary, as does Friederici, *op. cit.,* p. 434.
23. Martin Gusinde, "Culte du crâne, têtes-trophées et scalps," *Revue Ciba* 63 (décembre, 1947), pp. 2258-2283.
24. Biggar, *op. cit.,* Vol. II, p. 134; H. H. Turney-High, *Primitive Warfare: its Practices and Concepts* (Columbia, S.C.: 1949), pp. 196-201.
25. Thwaites, *op. cit.,* Vol. XLI, p. 215; XLII, p. 263; LIII, p. 143.
26. *Ibid.,* Vol. XIII, p. 37; XXXII, p. 183.
27. Gabriel Sagard-Théodat, *The Long Journey to the Country of the Hurons* (New York: 1939), pp. 152-153.
28. Gabriel Nadeau, "Indian Scalping: Techniques in Different Tribes," *Bulletin of the History of Medicine* X (July, 1941), pp. 180-193.
29. Thwaites, *op. cit.,* Vol. IX, p. 252.
30. C. H. Laverdière and H. R. Casgrain, eds., *Le Journal des Jésuites* (Montréal: 1892), pp. 37-38.
31. Thwaites, *op. cit.,* Vol. V, pp. 51-53; XXI, p. 61.

32. "Narrative of a Journey into the Mohawk and Oneida Country, 1634-35," in J. Franklin Jameson, ed., *Narratives of New Netherland* (New York: 1909), p. 148.

33. R. O. MacFarlane, "Indian Relations in New England, 1620-1760; A Study of a Regulated Frontier," Ph.D. Thesis, Harvard University, 1933, p. 89.

34. *Ibid.*, p. 82.

35. E. L. Coleman, *New England Captives carried to Canada between 1677 and 1760 during the French and Indian Wars* (Portland: 1925), Vol. I, p. 152; also, Georg Friederici, "Scalping in America," *Smithsonian Institution Annual Report, 1906* (Washington: 1906), p. 433.

36. Thwaites, *op. cit.*, Vol. XXII, p. 53.

37. *Ibid.*, Vol. LXVII, p. 173.

38. André Thévet, *Les Singularitez de la France antarctique, autrement nommée Amérique et de plusieurs Terres et Isles descouvertes de nostre temps* (Paris: 1558), p. 78.

39. George M. Wrong, ed., *The Long Journey to the Country of the Hurons by Father Gabriel Sagard* (Toronto: 1939), p. 163.

40. J. Tailhan, ed., *Mémoire sur les Moeurs, Coustumes et Relligion des Sauvages de l'Amérique septentrionale par Nicolas Perrot* (Leipzig: 1864), pp. 146-147.

41. Ross Brian Snyder, "Algonkian Warfare in Canada and Southern New England, 1600-1680," M.A. Thesis, University of Ottawa, 1972, pp. 35-40.

42. Turney-High, *op. cit.*, pp. 141-152; G. Snyderman, "Behind the Tree of Peace: A Sociological Analysis of Iroquois Warfare," *Pennsylvania Archaeologist* XVIII, Nos. 3 & 4 (1948), pp. 30-37; E. S. Rogers, "Aboriginal and Post-Contact Traits of the Montagnais-Naskapi Culture," M.A. Thesis, University of New Mexico, 1953, pp. 58-59.

43. Thwaites, *op. cit.*, Vol. XLIII, p. 265.

44. Thwaites, *op. cit.*, Vol. XXIV, pp. 177-179.

45. Biggar, *op. cit.*, Vol. II, p. 69.

46. Louis Hennepin, *A New Discovery of a Vast Country in America* (London: 1698), Vol. II, p. 72.

47. Thwaites, *op. cit.*, Vol. I, p. 269.

48. Anthony F. C. Wallace, "The Institutionalization of cathartic and control strategies in Iroquois religious psychotherapy," in Marvin K. Opler, ed., *Culture and Mental Health: Cross-cultural Studies* (New York: 1959), pp. 86-87.

49. Donald H. Frame, ed., *Montaigne's Essays and Selected Writings* (New York: 1963), pp. 10-105.

50. Thwaites, *op. cit.*, Vol. I, p. 269.

51. *Ibid.*, p. 269.

52. Wrong, *op. cit.*, pp. 151-153.

53. Thwaites, *op. cit.*, Vol. XLII, pp. 171-175; R. G. Thwaites, ed., *The New Voyages to America of Baron de Lahontan* (Chicago: 1905), Vol. II, p. 429.

54. Hennepin, *op. cit.*, Vol. II, pp. 95-96.

55. "Le Livre de Raison de François de Tapie de Monteil, Capitaine au Régiment de Poitou (1661-1670)," *Revue d'histoire de l'Amérique française* XIV, No. 1 (juin, 1960), p. 109.

56. W. L. Grant, ed., *The History of New France by Marc Lescarbot* (Toronto: 1914), Vol. III, p. 305.

57. Nicolas Perrot, "Memoir on the Manners, Customs, and Religion of the Savages of North America," in E. H. Blair, ed., *The Indian Tribes of the Upper Mississippi Valley and Region of the Great Lakes* (Cleveland: 1911), Vol. I, pp. 142-144.

58. Thwaites, *op. cit.*, Vol. XI, p. 85.

59. A. I. Hallowell, "Sociopsychological Aspects of Acculturation," in Ralph Linton, *The Science of Man in the World Crisis* (New York: 1945), pp. 193-194.
60. Biggar, *op. cit.,* Vol. IV, p. 3.
61. Nathaniel Bouton, ed., *Documents and Records relating to the Province of New-Hampshire from the Earliest Period to its Settlement: 1623-1686* (Concord: 1867), Vol. I, p. 343.
62. S. J. Gooding, *The Canadian Gunsmiths, 1608-1900* (West Hill, Ont.: 1962), pp. 20-26.
63. Pierre Boucher, *Histoire véritable et naturelle des moeurs et productions des pays de la Nouvelle-France, vulgairement dite le Canada* (Paris: 1664), p. 117.
64. K. F. Otterbein, "Why the Iroquois Won: An Analysis of Iroquois Military Tactics," *Ethnohistory* XI (1964), pp. 58-60.
65. Wayne Suttles, "Subhuman and Human Fighting," *Anthropologica,* New Series III (1961), pp. 148-163.
66. *P.A.C., Series CI1A,* Vol. III, Memorandum of 1671, pp. 261-262.
67. Thwaites, *op. cit.,* Vol. XLIX, p. 240.
68. *Acts and Resolves of the Province of Massachussetts Bay,* Vol. VII, p. 504; *Massachussetts Archives,* Vol. XXX, p. 377a.
69. Thomas Gossett, *Race: The History of an Idea in America* (New York: 1965), pp. 12, 16; also Alvin Josephy, Jr., *The Patriot Chiefs* (New York: 1958), pp. 35, 52.
70. Thwaites, *op. cit.,* Vol. XLI, pp. 109-111.
71. B. Fernow, ed., *Documents relating to the History and Settlements of the Towns along the Hudson and Mohawk Rivers, 1630-1684* (Albany: 1881), Old Series, Vol. XIII, Document xiii, p. 205.
72. *A.N., Colonies, Series B,* Vol. XII, King to Denonville, May 31, 1686, p. 30.
73. Fernow, *op. cit.,* Vol. XIII, p. 194.
74. Gédéon de Catalogne, "Recueil de ce qui s'est passé en Canada au sujet de la guerre tand des Anglais que des Iroquois, depuis l'année 1682," *Manuscript Relating to the Early History of Canada from the Archives of the Literary and Historical Society* (Quebec: 1871), p. 12.
75. *Collection de Documents relatifs à l'histoire de la Nouvelle-France* (Québec: 1883), Vol. I, p. 454; E. B. O'Callaghan and J. R. Brodhead, eds., *Documents Relating to the Colonial History of New York* (Albany: 1856-83), Vol. III, pp. 557-561; *A.N., Colonies, Series CI1A,* Vol. IX, Memorandum of October 27, 1687, pp. 134-135; Vol. X, Denonville to Minister, November 6, 1608, p. 105.
76. Jean-Baptiste du Tertre, *Histoire générale des Antilles habitées par les Français* (Paris: 1667), Vol. II, p. 357.
77. Thwaites, *op. cit.,* Vol. XXI, p. 45; XL, p. 133.
78. J. G. Shea, ed., *Chrestien Le Clercq: The First Establishment of the Faith in New France* (New York: 1881), Vol. I, p. 284; Gabriel Sagard, *Histoire du Canada depuis l'an 1615* (Paris: 1866), Vol. II, p. 445.
79. Hennepin, *op. cit.,* Vol. II, p. 102.
80. Thwaites, *op. cit.,* Vol. XXIII, p. 173; LIV, p. 199.
81. *Ibid.,* Vol. IX, p. 255.
82. *Ibid.,* Vol. XXX, p. 241; LXI, pp. 137, 269-271.
83. *Ibid.,* Vol. XXXV, p. 247.
84. *Ibid.,* Vol. XLV, p. 69.
85. *Ibid.,* Vol. LXVIII, pp. 169, 189, 195-199, 221-223.
86. Washburn, *op. cit.,* p. 9.
87. Snyder, *op. cit.,* p. 168.
88. Knowles, *op. cit.,* pp. 151-161; MacFarlane, *op. cit.,* pp. 31-32; Thwaites, *op. cit.,* Vol. LXV, pp. 27-29.
89. Thwaites, *op. cit.,* Vol. IX, p. 259.

90. *Ibid.,* Vol. XXVII, p. 235.
91. *Ibid.*
92. *Journal des Jésuites,* p. 95; Dom Guy Oury, ed., *Marie de l'Incarnation, Ursuline (1599-1672). Correspondance* (Solesmes: 1971), cxi, p. 338.
93. *Journal des Jésuites,* pp. 140-141.
94. *Ibid.,* p. 173.
95. Thwaites, *op. cit.,* Vol. LXII, p. 59.
96. *Ibid.,* Vol. LXV, pp. 27-29.
97. *Ibid.,* Vol. XXXI, p. 31.
98. *Ibid.,* Vol. XV, p. 187.
99. Wrong, *op. cit.,* pp. 161-162.
100. Hennepin, *op. cit.,* Vol. I, pp. 47-48.
101. John Gilmary Shea, *Perils of the Ocean and Wilderness; or, Narratives of Shipwreck and Indian Captivity* (Boston: 1856), Jogues to Father Provincial, August 5, 1643, p. 25.
102. Thwaites, *op. cit.,* Vol. XXX, p. 243; XXXI, p. 45.
103. Knowles, *op. cit.,* p. 213.
104. Thwaites, *op. cit.,* Vol. V, pp. 51-53.
105. Arthur T. Adams, ed., *The Explorations of Pierre Esprit Radisson* (Minneapolis, 1961), pp. 20-21.
106. Thwaites, *op. cit.,* Vol. XXXVI, p. 165.
107. Thwaites, *op. cit.,* Vol. I, pp. 271-273; the account of da Verrazano's death at the hands of Carib cannibals is found in G. B. Ramusio, *Terzo volume delle navigatione et viaggi nel quale si contego Le Navigationi al Mondo Nuovo* (Venetia: 1556), Vol. III, pp. 420-422.
108. Thwaites, *op. cit.,* Vol. X, p. 227.
109 Hennepin, *op. cit.,* Vol. II, p. 101; Snyder, *op. cit.,* pp. 190-191.
110. E. E. Muntz, *Race Contact: A Study of the Social and Economic Consequences of the Contacts between Civilized and Uncivilized Peoples* (New York: 1927), p. 72.
111. Thwaites, *op. cit.,* Vol. X, pp. 227-229; for Brébeuf's presentation of Catholic doctrine in the Huron language. I am indebted to John Steckley, Memorial University of Newfoundland.
112. Pierre Boucher, *Histoire Véritable et Naturelle des moeurs et productions du pays de la Nouvelle-France, vulgairement dite le Canada* (Boucherville: 1964), p. 132.
113. Thwaites, *op. cit.,* Vol. XXIII, p. 159.
114. *Ibid.,* Vol. XLII, p. 155.
115. Thwaites, *op. cit.,* Vol. XLVI, pp. 263-265. Cf. Raymond D. Fogelson, "Psychological Theories of 'Windigo Psychosis' and a Preliminary Application of a Models Approach," in M. E. Spiro, ed., *Context and Meaning in Cultural Anthropology* (New York: 1965), pp. 74-99.
116. Donald H. Frame, ed., *The Complete Essays of Montaigne* (Stanford: 1948), p. 158.
117. Donald H. Frame, ed., *Montaigne's Essays and Selected Writings* (New York: 1963), pp. 101-103.
118. R. A. Sayce, *The Essays of Montaigne: A Critical Exploration* (London: 1972), pp. 91-94, 192-194, 259, 272-275.
119. Jean de Léry, *Histoire d'un voyage fait en la terre du Brésil, autrement dite Amérique* (La Rochelle: 1578), Vol. II, p. 52.
120. Roy Harvey Pearce, "The Significance of the Captivity Narratives," *American Literature* XIX, No. 1 (March, 1947), pp. 1-20; Howard Mumford Jones, *O Strange New World* (New York: 1964), pp. 54-61; Donald Boyd Smith, "French Canadian Historians' Images of the Indian in the 'Heroic Period' of New France, 1534-1663," M.A. Thesis, Laval, University, 1969, *passim.*
121. Wrong, *op. cit.,* pp. 199-200.
122. Thwaites, *op. cit.,* Vol. XV, p. 77.

CHAPTER V

INTEGRATION AND SEGREGATION

French policy towards the Amerindians from the time of the initial contact was based on assimilationist concepts. The policy of assimilation, which when translated into action became in reality an effort to effect an integration of French and Amerindian societies while maintaining French dominance, was based on the optimistic view that the native people could be civilized by accepting French culture and the Catholic religion. A cultural, not a colour or racial designation, was used to identify them as *sauvages,* which meant uncivilized, ignorant, untutored, unsophisticated natural beings. The Amerindians' inferiority was not considered innate. This dominant attitude among the French can be defined as "minimal racism" because it portrays the natives as "backward or less evolved, different in degree but not in kind . . . therefore capable with training and education to rise . . . to a status of equality with the ruling group."[1] The policies of assimilation devised by the French administration and the missionary superiors aimed to raise a people conceived as culturally inferior to equal status with the Europeans. Montaigne wrote in the sixteenth century of the duty incumbent on colonizing peoples to "gently polish and reclaim" the aborigines "by co-operating with them inasmuch as they are fellow human beings possessing the same dignity as other men."[2]

These attitudes were expressed in various official and ecclesiastical directives pertaining to New France in the seventeenth century. The Sieur de Monts was instructed in the letters-patent granted him in 1603 by Henry IV to arouse the Amerindians "to the knowledge of God and to the light of the Christian faith and religion." This was a general mandate which was made more precise in the instructions of the Viceroy, the Duc de Montmorency, who wrote:

> . . . . to seek to lead the nations thereof to the profession of the Christian faith, to civilization of manners, an ordered life, practice and intercourse with the French for the gain of their commerce; and finally their recognition of and submission to the authority and domination of the crown of France.[3]

Amerindians would be required, according to such policy, to convert, to adopt French manners and customs, and to subordinate themselves to French laws and political jurisdiction. The French thought that the problem of having discovered an inhabited continent could be solved simply by the peaceful process of assimilation.

Assimilation required the co-operation and consent of the natives, as well as certain dispositions on the part of the French. Champlain, as commandant of New France from 1612 to 1627, envisaged a fruitful co-operation between the French church and state through "the help of princes, and ecclesiastics, who alone have the power to do this" to assist the natives to attain the higher cultural plain of the French. He foresaw no resistance on the part of the Amerindians, but assumed that "in course of time and through association with others" they would become civilized and "with the French language they may also acquire a French heart and spirit."[4] The Récollect missionaries, whom he had brought to the colony to work among the natives, deplored native nomadism, which Lescarbot attributed to the fact that "game is not always to be found in a place where people are obliged to live upon it." The Récollects welcomed the initial effect of the fur trade as it gave more stability to Huron sedentary settlements. Denis Jamet held out little hope of a rapid or massive conversion of the Algonkins and Montagnais, on the other hand; he counselled energetic French settlement and some resettlement of the Amerindians nearer to the European settlements.[5]

Assimilation also required that the French be the dominant group not only in the political, military and technological senses but also in terms of population. If the majority of the population had the superior culture and social institutions in the new environment they would be able to absorb the minority or passive group. The Récollets, using common-sense reasoning, were disturbed by "the negligence and lack of interest of the merchants who hitherto have been satisfied to get furs and profit" out of New France without at the same time being willing "to make an outlay for cultivation, settlement, or progress of the country." The French base in Canada was a commercial counter, nothing more, and unless more effort and expenditure were directed to colonization, assimilation would fail. Sagard observed:

> But if they will do nothing more than in the past Antarctic France will always be a name of fancy, and ourselves an imaginary possession in others' hands. Also the conversion of the savages will be always incomplete, for it can only be accomplished through the aid of some settlements of good and virtuous Christians, together with the teaching and example of good monks . . . . I will say with truth that unless colonies of

good virtuous Catholics are established in all these savage countries, Christianity will never be quite strongly rooted in them, though men of the religious life should give themselves all the trouble in the world. It is one thing to have to do with civilized peoples, and another thing to deal with savage tribes who need an example of a virtuous life in order to see themselves therein, more than to be instructed in high theology, although both are necessary . . . .[6]

The desire to convert the Amerindians was not clearly distinguished from the more general aim of assimilating them into French culture. This was a natural confusion because Catholicism was at the core of French culture at the time.

The Récollets had always reported that the way to convert the Amerindians "is to endeavour to make them men before we go about to make them Christians." This approach was described by a Récollet who laboured in the interior of the continent in the second half of the seventeenth century in these terms:

Now in order to civilize them, 'tis necessary that the Europeans should mix with them, and that they should dwell together, which can never be done for certain till the Colonies are augmented: but it must be acknowledged, that the Company of Canada Merchants, have made great Obstacles to the increasing of the Colonies; for out of greediness to keep all the trade in their own hands, these Gentlemen would never permit any particular Society to settle themselves in the country, nor suffer the Missionaries to persuade the Barbarians to dwell constantly in a place. Yet before this be done, there's no way to convert these Unbelievers.[7]

So long as colonization was left largely to the trade monopolists and a few enterprising French nobles there was little hope of laying the broad foundations upon which to erect a new nation or a continental empire.

Cardinal Richelieu's new trading association in 1627 did include a clause in its charter providing that "the Savages who will be brought to the knowledge of the Faith and will make profession of it, will be deemed and reputed to be natural-born Frenchmen, and as such may come to dwell in France when it shall seem good to them." They would also enjoy all the rights of acquiring and disposing of property and goods on the same footing as the metropolitan French themselves without needing special letters of declaration or of naturalization.[8] Although these citizenship rights granted to assimilated Amerindians were more symbolic than anything else, the spirit of this remarkable document remains admirable. The monopoly-holders did not, however, follow up the pious purpose with any significant French settlement to encourage native assimilation into French life.

The Jesuits came to assist the Récollets in their evangelical work and fostered the same policy of assimilation. They dreamed not only of an ideal church of new Amerindian converts, recapturing the pristine purity of the Apostolic church, but also of a utopian French colony:

> If those who will hold the reins of government in their hands are zealous towards the glory of our God, there will be raised here a Jerusalem blessed of God composed of citizens destined for Heaven. It is very easy in a new country, where the families will arrive all disposed to accept the laws which will be established there, to banish the evil customs of several places in old France, and to introduce better ones.[9]

The arrival of a group of pious settlers to found Montreal in 1642, an enterprise organized by the secret, militant, pietistic Company of the Holy Sacrament, seemed to promote the ideals enunciated by the civil officials and the missionaries. This new settlement was strategically located on the water route into the interior, the hub of the fur trade, and the centre of a fertile belt in a generally poor agricultural terrain. The settlers had high expectations about Amerindian acceptance of "right reason" and "right religion" brought by the French:

> . . . . and if once reason obtains the advantage over their old customs, with the example of the French which they esteem and respect, inciting them to work, it seems that they will set themselves straight, withdrawing from a life so full of poverty and afflication, and that they will take their places beside the Frenchmen or Christian Savages . . . .[10]

These well-intentioned planters viewed native cultures as unreasonable and disorganized and their own civilization as orderly and divinely sanctioned.

Although there was agreement about the need to accelerate French settlement in order to promote French institutional life, there was also a growing awareness of the need for select immigration if the absorption of the natives into a new inter-racial society were to be attempted. The natives would have to be converted and civilized to become assimilated, and only select French families could form a suitable host society for such absorption. Increasing the number of French indiscriminately could prove disastrous to achieving the desired objectives. A Jesuit writer warned:

> It is to be feared that in the multiplication of our French, in these countries, peace, happiness, and good feeling may not increase in the same ratio as do the Inhabitants of New France. It is much easier to control a few men than whole multitudes.[11]

The Récollets had been the first to sound the alarm about the contradictions they experienced at the hands of irreligious and unscrupulous French traders. To that opposition, the Jesuits soon added further evidence of organized tribal resistance, a counter-innovative movement, to French efforts to refashion Huron society. Conversion implied not only identification with Catholicism but also with the French lifestyle. Le Jeune wrote in 1641 about "the new Christians who publicly profess themselves Frenchmen." On the occasion of the baptism of Ahatsistcari, the Huron converts resolved to inform their pagan relatives "that we do not wish our bones to be mingled together after our death, since our Souls will be eternally separated, and our affection will not continue beyond this life."[12]

There was considerable discussion among the Jesuit missionaries in New France, especially concerning the Huron mission, about the appropriateness of continuing to tie conversion to Frenchification. The desirability of disassociating evangelization from assimilation gained ground, especially after Jérôme Lalemant (1639) successfully instituted a central missionary headquarters at Sainte-Marie and after Paul Ragueneau (1645) promoted a relativist approach to native culture. Ragueneau firmly believed that the earlier rigourist approaches to pagan practices had not only been a hindrance to evangelical progress but had also been philosophically and morally wrong. The experienced missionaries in the field tended to abandon their preconceived ideas of the need to Europeanize and civilize their hearers as a prerequisite to conversion. Flirtation with the dissociation of religion and culture, however, left them open to serious theological charges in France. Thus while many of the evangelical workers, as opposed to the canonical theorists and theologians, espoused the concept of an Amerindian Catholicism, the general conceptual framework in which colonial missions operated remained officially unchanged.

So it was that towards the end of the seventeenth century Hennepin could report on the objectives, sources of resistance and policies in traditional terms. He wrote:

> So that Christianity is not like to gain much ground among the Savages, till the Colonies are strengthened by a great Number of Inhabitants, Artisans and Workmen, and then the treaty betwixt the Barbarians and us should be freer, and extended to all Europeans: But chiefly it should be endeavour'd to fix

the Barbarians to a certain dwelling Place, and introduce our Customs and Laws amongst them, further'd by the Assistance of zealous People in Europe, Colleges might be founded to breed up young Savages in the Christian Faith, which might in turn contribute very much to the Conversion of their Country-men. This is a proper Method without doubt, to strengthen the Temporal and Spiritual Interests of the Colonies; but the Generality of Mankind are bent upon Gain and Traffick, and are little concern'd to procure God's blessing upon them and endeavour the advancement of his Glory.[13]

As religious conversion remained inseparably bound to the concept of assimilation, so the materialistic outlook of the colony militated against the pursuit of purely spiritual objectives. It could not have been otherwise since French culture was so religiously oriented and since the colony was primarily commercial and materialistic. On the other hand, Amerindian cultures, while differing from region to region, were all basically religious and therefore European innovations caused a certain paralysis of culture-bearing indigenous classes which in turn called forth a counter-innovation or resistance to assimilation.

Did the French in their plan to assimilate the Amerindians dis-criminate against them as inferior peoples? If we accept as a definition of racism a situation where one group, believing its somatic character-istics are superior to those of another group, "applies that belief as justification (or rationalization) for dominating over, discriminating against, and/or in other ways exploiting or denying equal treatment or opportunities to the other, inferior-regarded group," we must acknowledge that the French practised some discrimination against the Amerindians in the seventeenth century.[14]

The predilection of some missionaries to distinguish between evangelization and Frenchification, after the initial disappointments with assimilation attempts, led to avowedly segregationist practices. Of course, the partisans of the earlier view of cultural assimilation as necessary to conversion also defended segregation as a means of achieving their dual objectives. The Amerindians were segregated from the French in processions, in church pews, and eventually in separate churches, just as the children were segregated in the class-rooms and dormitories. One Jesuit let slip the phrase "these savages were indeed given to understand that the french did not resemble them, and were not so base as they . . . ." When the missionaries in Huronia refused to permit the bodies of two Frenchmen to be included in the communal grave at the Feast of the Dead, the Huron converts became very upset and protested vociferously that their opponents would ridicule them because "the friendship was only in appearance, since we had not allowed the bones of our Frenchmen to mingle with theirs."[15] The Algonkins themselves divided a raiding party in 1642 against the Iroquois into Christian and pagan units, probably to maintain some order and peace within their own ranks. The Jesuit superior remarked that the tolling of the church bells at the death of an Amerindian girl was "unusual" and the Hospital Nuns commented on the tolling of the bell of the parish church of Quebec for Cecile Gannondaris, "which is never practiced for the Savages who die at the Hospital."[16] Bishop Laval's reversal of the "usual precedence" by confirming Amerindian candidates before the French children was considered remarkable and audacious. Marie de l'Incarnation felt that segregation was sometimes imposed on the natives "by fear that they imitate the evil ways of some Frenchmen." Nevertheless, she concluded that the Amerindians were "not capable of the honest liberties" of French life, and she remarked in 1663 that they were unsuited to holy orders.[17]

The absence of natives among both the regular and secular clergy and the teaching and hospital nuns of the colony could be accounted for in part by a hesitation to admit Amerindians to the first estate. Native chiefs were convinced that in the application of French laws, in the imposition of trading and liquor restrictions, and in the assignment of penance, preferential treatment was given the French over the Amerindians. Whether these allegations were always well-founded or not may be less important than the fact that they existed and they fostered some resentments. One external indication of prejudicial discrimination much in evidence in the Dutch and English colonies was the prohibition to supply the natives with horses or to permit them to ride these animals. The French first imported horses at Saint-Sauveur in 1613 and Quebec in 1647. Although the later increase in the number of horses in the colony brought official restrictions on their breeding, mainly because they were used more for racing than for agricultural work, there is no evidence that they were either prohibited trade items with Amerindians or that the Amerindians had any desire to possess these "moose of France."[18] So, while the public policy was one of assimilation and integration there existed an undercurrent of discrimination that could be detected from time to time in isolated incidents. This undercurrent never became a dominant attitude in the French colony and it never passed into official legislation.

In contrast to neighbouring colonies, the question of Amerindian proprietary rights never gave the French or their native allies much concern. The Spaniards in the fifteenth century had considered it beyond doubt that Spain possessed a legitimate right to conquest and to occupation of the Americas; what was subject to some controversy was the precise basis of that right. Some contended on the basis of the papal donation and others on the right of conquest; the one required effective evangelization of natives and the other argued that "the lack of faith and the vice of the natives demanded their extirpation as a Christian duty." Later disputes raged in the Spanish colonies between the partisans of the *encomienda* system and the regalists who advocated the freedom of the Amerindians as a means of retaining all political jurisdiction in the King's hands.

The French never employed the argument of Henry of Susa, elaborated in the thirteenth century, that heathen peoples lost their political jurisdiction and their right to wordly possessions to Christ when he became King of the earth.[19] They did not require such a convenient political and canonical theory to assert their monarch's title to all the lands they ceremoniously and systematically claimed in his name. Like the English, the French did not admit legally that the Amerindians had "sovereign rights" in the land or that they possessed "absolute ownership." Although the French wrote about Amerindian kingdoms and made kings of chiefs and priests of *sachems*, they never recognized the native tribes as sovereign powers and they never accorded them any diplomatic recognition because they did not belong to the accepted "family of nations." The English, on the other hand, did recognize aboriginal "possessary rights" and either bought tracts of land or negotiated its formal cession for settlement and agricultural development. Because the French Laurentian settlement area was largely a no-man's-land at the beginning of the seventeenth century, there was no problem of dispossession or of native surrenders as in the English experience. Indeed, the French were soon aware of the English land hunger pressing upon the sedentary agricultural tribes to the south of New France and the tensions that resulted. During the last decade of the French régime the Governor told some Iroquois chiefs who were visiting Montreal:

> Go, and examine the forts which our king has erected; you will see that the land beyond their walls is still a hunting ground. Our forts have been set up, not as a curb upon the tribes, but to be useful for your trade with us. While, no sooner do the British enter upon possession of your lands, than the game deserts them. The forest falls below their blows, the soil is bared, and hardly will you find a bush left upon your own domains to shelter you by night.[20]

When the French established seigneurialism in Canada and Acadia they did not make land concessions to the Amerindians. In the St. Lawrence Valley, Amerindians were never displaced to make way for French agricultural settlement. On the contrary, the reservation system represented a resettlement of Amerindians within the French seigneurial tract and area of white habitation on lands which the Amerindians had not occupied at the time of contact. The Algonkin chief, Charles Packiriny, received a plot *en roture* of a little over two thirds of an arpent in the bourg of Trois-Rivières, but the land was administered for him by the Jesuits. At the Sillery reservation the fief was held for the converted tribesmen "under the management and direction" of the Jesuits. In fact, through an alleged lack of Amerindian claimants the land was divided into "70 grants, given in the name of the said Savages to as many French habitants, who reside there." The reservation at Sault St. Louis was granted to the Jesuits although nominally it had been set aside for resident converts. Natives settled on the Sulpician reservation were no more title-holders than others. Governor La Barre and Intendant de Meulles, in setting aside a tract of land on the Chaudière river for the Abenakis, registered it in the name of the missionary clergy. The situation at the Lorette reservation was much the same, as indicated in the following report prepared by Claude Dablon in 1674:

> In the afternoon, he made a feast for the Savages, to whom — among other presents that he made them in the way of blankets, cloths, and hatchets, — he gave the contract of concession for the lands which have been granted them. The principal clause of this contract is that the Savages are obliged, by way of dues, not to take liquor to excess; and that those who shall henceforth become intoxicated shall be driven from Lorette and shall lose their fields, whatever work they may have accomplished.[21]

There is little indication that the converts living on the reservations ever took up agricultural work with much enthusiasm, although Marie de l'Incarnation repeated the belief that clearing the land was the first step in making the natives sedentary and amenable to assimilation.[22] The French official view persisted that hunting and fishing constituted a life of idleness and that agricultural labour was the only true work that should be imposed on the Amerindians.

Another means of promoting integration was miscegenation. Since the first contacts between fishermen and sailors and the native women of the Atlantic Coast there had been a certain amount of racial admixture. But these illicit and usually temporary liaisons produced a half-breed population the numbers of which were never recorded although the physical traits are still discernible in descendants who claim to be "pure blood" Europeans or Amerindians. It is believed by some authorities that the Malecites were not a genuine Algonkian tribe but were the half-caste descendants of unions between Micmac women and the fishermen of Saint-Malo.[23] There were, beyond doubt, numerous half-breed children wherever the French *coureurs-de-bois* carried French trade and in the vicinity of forts garrisoned by French soldiers. But the results of such liaisons did not help assimilation as planned by church and state because the children were raised as Amerindians in the native villages and encampments. The casual liaisons with the natives occurred in the towns as well, according to Dièreville:

> Savages though they be they do not fail to attract the Youth of both sexes in Quebec who are inclined by their evil impulses toward wrong doing; the Boys become worse than the Iroquois themselves, & that is the reason they are so well-received; otherwise they would not be worth having. Their kindred appeal to them in vain, these Renegades will not return to them; they prefer the Iroquois. The wanton Maidens, they appear Shapely and tall, and fit for their delight, So unafright-ened by their horrid mien, They go with them to gratify their lust. Women are always pleased by size and strength . . . .[24]

The number of these liaisons convinced both church and state officials that the preponderance of men in the French population needed readjusting and that stable Catholic peasant family life needed to be encouraged through renewed immigration. The sending of "king's daughters" and, after 1666, the encouragement for soldiers to settle were designed to alleviate the problem.

Since mercantilist officials feared a depopulation of metropolitan France and were also aware of the unattractiveness of the majority of the colonies for metropolitan Frenchmen, the absorption of the large native population through inter-marriage was proposed as an alternative to large-scale immigration from France. The idea of a racially mixed empire in North America had been in Champlain's mind when he told the Hurons that, if they accepted the Catholic religion brought by the Récollets, the French would go to live among them, marry their daughters, and teach them their arts and trades. One Huron chieftain observed that this proposal contained nothing new because the French had taken wives in the past "in whatsoever way they had desired" with no special permission or sanctions being required. To this a Jesuit replied "that the Frenchmen who had hitherto married in the country had not made such a stir about it, but also that their intentions were far removed from ours." He insisted that "their purpose had been to become barbarians," whereas the new proposal was designed to make the Hurons "like us" and to induce marriages which would be both "stable and perpetual."[25]

Theoretically, miscegenation could solve the problems posed by a marked preponderance of men in New France and a preponderance of women in Amerindian society. The pious founders of Montreal were in favour of inter-marriage with the Amerindians to effect large-scale conversions, increase the French population, and develop agriculture.[26] These optimistic projects ignored the fact that the fruit of such legitimate alliances would be little different from the fruit of the illicit encounters. The native way of life would be reinforced rather than French colonization being promoted.

There is evidence that the Amerindians did not always approve of the kind of inter-marriage the French wished to encourage. In 1635, the commissioner general of the Company of New France reproached the natives around Trois-Rivières for marrying only within their own tribe and for avoiding alliances with Frenchmen. The following year, a chief from Tadoussac replied to French charges that his people "were not yet allied with the French by any marriage" and that their dislike of the French was evident because "they did not care to be one People with us, giving their children here and there to their allied Nations, and not to the French." He told an assembly at Quebec that when young Frenchmen joined with Montagnais warriors in war and returned "after the massacre of our enemies" they would find native girls to marry. As for placing children among the French, he retorted boldly, "one does not see anything but little Savages in the houses of the French; there are little boys there and little girls." He concluded with a strong argument:

> . . . . what more do you want? I believe that some of these days you will be asking for our wives. You are continually asking us for our children, and you do not give yours; I do not know any family among us which keeps a Frenchman with it.[27]

While the French viewed educating native children as part of their assimilation policy, the Amerindians continued to think in terms of exchange of children as a token of unity and alliance which ought to be reciprocated. The early practice of sending French youths, such as Etienne Brûlé and Nicolas Marsolet, to live among the natives to learn their languages and ways, accommodated the Amerindian cultural pattern. That exchanges should become a one-way process was unacceptable and incomprehensible except in terms of attempts to assert dominance over them or to acquire hostages.

Thereafter, mixed mariages were scrutinized very carefully. A trader named Chastillon wanted to marry a native girl who had been educated for four years by the Ursulines. He gave the Ursulines a rescript of 300 *livres,* of which 100 *livres* was to serve as his pledge to the sisters, "but it was found that the girl did not want him at all, and preferred a savage and to follow the wishes of her parents."[28] The natives did see some advantages in alliances with Frenchmen when the

French state began to provide dowries to Amerindian girls who were raised in French customs and who consented to marry Frenchmen. Dowries were used to strengthen the marriage bond and to hold the natives to their new religion and new way of life. One report of the response to the policy ran as follows:

> They would be very glad to know what a husband would give his wife; that among the Hurons the custom was to give a great deal besides, — that is to say — a beaver robe, and perhaps a porcelain collar. Second, whether a wife would have everything at her disposal. Third, if the husband should decide to return to France, whether he would take his wife with him; and in case she remained, what would he leave her on his departure. Fourth, if the wife failed in her duty and the husband drove her away, what she could take with her . . . .[29]

The missionaries favoured giving dowries to circumvent the thorny problem of illicit unions because "a husband will not readily leave a wife who brings him a respectable dowry" and "a woman having her possessions near the French settlements, will not readily leave them, anymore than her husband."[30]

The Jesuits had always had reservations about the policy of inter-marriage, probably because they realized it originated in the attempt to overcome the lack of French women in the colony. Such marriages were usually between a French man and a native woman, not between French women and Amerindian men. Therefore, although the children of such unions were, in European terms, French by paternity, they were raised in the native way of life by their native mothers. If Amerindian brides were isolated from their ancestral environment, educated in the colony, and continued to live with their French husbands in the French settlements there was less reason to oppose inter-marriage. Pierre de Sesmaisons prepared a lengthy justification in 1648 to obtain a papal dispensation allowing Frenchmen to marry native girls who were receiving religious instruction but were not as yet baptized.[31] In 1662, Laurent DuBoc took a native bride and was given 500 *livres* to set up his household; a week later, Jean Durand was given 260 *livres* when he married a Huron girl.[32]

In general, the Jesuits continued to oppose such marriages. In April, 1660, for example, Father Albanel was moved from his mission station at Tadoussac because he had solemnized a marriage between a certain François Pelletier and a Montagnais woman "without the publication of banns, or advice given beforehand to the relatives, to Mons. the Bishop, nor Mons. the Governor."[33] Eleven years later, François de Crepeuil repeated the same advice to another incumbent at Tadoussac:

> Let him not marry with the rites of the Church any Frenchman to a Savage woman without the consent of the parents, and without Monseigneur's approval.[34]

The need for approval from the highest officials of the French church and state in the colony suggests the practice was controversial and irregular, and the need for approval of the native parents indicates that Amerindian culture patterns had to be respected to avoid unpleasant incidents. There were some notable exceptions. Pierre Boucher married a Huron girl, educated by the Ursulines, in 1649. The Baron de Saint-Castin was an even more notable exception for he seems to have had two children by the daughter of the chief of the Penobscot tribe, then two other children by her sister and, finally, after marrying her in 1684, to have had eight more children.[35] In general, the practice of inter-marriage was not common and was not a fruitful means of promoting assimilation of the aboriginal population. Governor La Barre discovered in 1683 that the policy had in practice been abandoned in the colony before Versailles became aware of it:

> You placed 3000 *livres* at my disposal in the list of gratuities for 1682 for the dowries of Indian maidens. This has been a mistake, for none of them married; and as this fund has always been employed for the dowries of French girls, it is necessary, if you believe it to be appropriate, to correct the designation in the estimates we have prepared, and apply it instead to the support of two Hospitalières.[36]

Thus official policy eventually came into line with colonial practice.

Education of the children was seized upon very early as a means of converting and assimilating the natives. Traditionally, Europeans have placed much faith in formal education to spread their culture. It was believed that by educating Amerindian children in French schools they would adopt certain French norms and would be exposed to European beliefs and values. Conversion would help them identify with French society and, in theory, education and resettlement on reservations would complement the evangelization efforts of the missionaries and would introduce them to the social and material goals of a new community.

Almost immediately upon their arrival in Canada in 1615 the Récollets began educating native children. Following the example of the Capuchins who sent six Brazilian natives to Paris in 1613 for instruction and baptism, the Récollets decided to send their most promising young scholars to France. It was reported in 1618 that they had two boys who were "brought to France, baptized and put in boarding at the college of Calleville," one of whom "was very well educated."[37] In 1620 they sent Pierre-Antoine Patetchoanen, a Montagnais, to Angers, and in 1626 they had arranged to send a Huron youth, Louis Amantacha, but the Jesuits intervened and succeeded in having him sent instead to Rouen, where they arranged a splendid public baptismal service in the cathedral in order to attract attention to their role in the Canadian missions.

Champlain petitioned Louis XIII for financial support for the Récollets who had decided to establish a "seminary" to educate a number of Huron boys to form the nucleus of a new church and new nation:

> That it may please Your Majesty to found, and endow for six years only, a seminary for fifty Indian children, after which time they can be supported from the increased returns of the lands which will by that time be under cultivation. The children are daily offered by their parents to your petitioners to be instructed by them and brought up in the Christian religion.[38]

Not only was capital required for buildings, equipment and the overhead expenses of such an enterprise, as Champlain suggested, but funds were also necessary to induce the Amerindians to part with their children. In 1620 the "seminary" was opened at Notre-Dame des Anges, near Quebec, on land which, after ten years hard work, ten settlers had not been able to make productive. The Grand Vicar of Pontoise sent much needed supplies and food in 1622 to keep the institution functioning.[39] Two years later the Récollets expressed hope for the future of the assimilation programme without indicating too much success in their efforts to date:

> It must be hoped that as the Colony is peopled we shall civilize the Indians. This is necessary first of all . . . . They will be regulated by French laws and modes of living . . . for all that concerns human and civil life is a mystery for our Indians in their present state, and it will require more expense and toil to render them men than it has required to make whole nations Christian.[40]

Three French boys had been joined by six native boys, all of whom received elementary instruction in catechism, reading and writing.

Sagard reported on the beginnings of the Récollet educational programme:

> We had made a beginning of teaching them their letters, but as they are all for freedom and only want to play and give themselves a good time, as I said, they forget in three days what we have taken four to teach, for lack of perseverance and

for neglect of coming back to us at the hours appointed them; and if they told us that they had been prevented because of a game, they were clear. Besides, it was not yet advisable to be severe with them or reprove them otherwise than gently, and we could only in a complaisant manner urge them to be thorough in gaining knowledge which would be such an advantage to them and bring them satisfaction in time to come.[41]

Eventually all the native boys left and when no more pupils were forthcoming the Récollets reluctantly closed their "seminary." They were very disappointed by the failure of their plan to assimilate the Hurons and Montagnais through schooling. Even the youth they had educated at the college of Calleville reverted to his ancestral way of life.[42]

The Récollets themselves were forced to leave the colony in 1629 when Quebec temporarily fell into enemy hands, and were not permitted by the state officials to resume their missionary work in Canada until 1670. Upon their return, they placed less stress on education of the youth although they did establish a school for the Cayugas living near Fort Frontenac. Hennepin reported in 1679:

> We made frequent Visits to the Savages, whom we had persuaded to settle themselves near the Fort, who, together with their Children, whom we had taught to read and write, lamented much our Departure; and assur'd us, That if we did return in a short time, they would persuade the rest of the inhabitants of the Village of Ganeousse to come and settle themselves in the Neighbourhood of the Fort.[43]

The previous year, Hennepin had visited the Senecas and concluded that at that time there was little hope of converting them, short of a miraculous intervention by the Divinity, "till they are subdu'd by the Europeans, and that their Children have another sort of Education."[44] The Récollets did not propose at that time to give the Iroquois the necessary type of education.

The Jesuits returned to Canada in 1632 with a monopoly in missionary work. They followed the Récollet example of sending a few select pupils to France as their Provincial considered it desirable to send at least one child to the metropolis each year. They had little success with these efforts, however, as a lad named Fortuné fell so ill in France that he had to return before his education was completed. In 1635 a youth named Bonaventure returned from France; a girl being educated by the Hospital Nuns at Dieppe was reported to have died suddenly; and a Nipissing girl was being sent to France. There was some Jesuit opposition to this policy because of the apparent failure of these visits to France to keep the Récollet protégés to the Catholic faith and French life-style after their return to New France. Nevertheless, in 1636 five natives were sent to France: a young Iroquois woman to be trained as a teacher; a young boy; and three Montagnais girls, one of whom went to the Hospital Nuns at Dieppe, and the two others to the Carmelite convent in Paris where they were baptized the following year. In 1638, a chieftain's son was sent to join those already at school in France.[45]

The Jesuits were now coming to the conclusion that it was preferable to attract native children to schools where they could be brought into close contact with the children of the colonists. Le Jeune drew up an educational programme on the premise that native children had the same intellectual potential as French children, and that "if animals are capable of discipline, the young savage children are much more so."[46] No concession was made to the native educational pattern which was completely integrated into everyday life or to their permissive approach to child-rearing. Native children would be subjected to the same classroom techniques, discipline, curriculum and formal approach as French children and as prescribed in the *Ratio Studiorium*. There were, therefore, many exhibitions of student achievements; public awards and public exhibits were used to create incentives and foster competition; academic awards were much emphasized; and, in the classroom, memory recitation, repetitions, concertations, and examinations were the usual fare. Brébeuf wrote about "weekly reviews," "awarding prizes of merit," "the stimulation of learning through awards," and "holding public exercises for children before both French and adult Indians."[47] The unaccustomed discipline, the rigidity and inflexibility of routine learning, and the competitive spirit added to the loneliness and disorientation of the native students and made life for them in these French boarding schools intolerable.

In 1635 the Jesuits began teaching elementary subjects at Notre-Dame des Anges, the former Récollet monastery near Quebec. French and Amerindian children were segregated and taught by different teachers, but soon the two classes were integrated because only six frightened, homesick, under-nourished and practically naked boys had come. Before long they reacted to the strict discipline and tedious curriculum like "wild asses' colts" and all ran away.[48] The Jesuits realized how wide the cultural gap was that separated their young Amerindian students from the French way of life:

> . . . these new guests, giving themselves up . . . to thieving, gourmandizing, gaming, idleness, lying and similar irregularities, could not endure the paternal admonitions given them to change their mode of life, and above all the tacit reproofs, con-

veyed by the example of their companions, who showed as much restraint as they did lawlessness and immoderation.[49]

The permissiveness of their upbringing and their close kinship ties made the strict regimen of Jesuit pedagogy quite unbearable.

The Jesuits then decided to attempt educating the young in the controlled atmosphere of reservations. In 1637, a small number of Huron and Algonkian children came to Sillery where converts were being settled on agricultural land near the mission house and church, but by the following spring they had all left.[50] More children came the following year but disease soon thinned their ranks.[51] The Jesuits did, however, manage to keep a few boys at the reservation schools and were often encouraged by their apparent progress. In 1679 the missionaries at Prairie de la Madeleine were surprised that the native students had learned the chants, the psalms, and not less than thirty different hymns:

> The boys, who have learned to serve at mass, and who are very eager to serve, are vested at all these ceremonies as little acolytes, and know their office so well that no one loses his place. People are every day astonished, and with reason, that savages have so soon learned all that — they whom one hears yelling in the woods when they sing in their own fashion, and who have an education so contrary to the civilized manners of other nations.[52]

But the final result was almost always the same; the children tired of school and reverted to their old tribal ways.

All the clergy were expected to participate in the educational programme. The Capuchins in Acadia, for example, operated separate schools for the French children and the Micmac children at La Hève as early as 1632.[53] On January 13, 1640, Cardinal Richelieu gave them revenues of one-fifth part of "the rights and concessions" in the Company of New France belonging to Razilly for "the seminaries that will be established, the food, education and maintenance of the children of the savages of the said country under the conduct of the said Capuchin fathers."[54] The secular Sulpicians graciously followed the Intendant Talon's advice "to open a school to teach the Indians, and render them capable by marriages to form a blood community with the French." They first, however, made sure that they would not be the instruments of the state policy of exploiting community rivalries to serve secular purposes and of being "disquieted in these exercises of charity by those who claim to be the sole directors of the said Indians."[55]

Two years later, state officials praised the Sulpicians for their efforts to raise native children "in the maxims of our religion and in the civil life of the French" and instructed the civil officers of New France to render special assistance to these missionaries "in order to render them capable of uniting the Indians and French" and to bring the natives into closer contact with "those who possess the legitimate authority of His Majesty."[56] The Sulpicians found no more favourable response than did the other missionaries; they placed the blame on the Jesuits, whom they accused of having spread rumours among the tribes that the Sulpicians were Jansenists and priests of the Anti-Christ. These accusations, of course, were meaningful only to Frenchmen and not to Amerindians.[57] In 1677 the Sulpicians were quite embarrassed by Colbert's personal gift of 1,000 *livres* for the education of native children at Quinté because they no longer had any children in their care. The Sulpician Superior in Paris advised dissimulation:

> Perhaps among the savages to whom we give assistance there are some children who could take the place of those it is expected we educate and to the maintenance of whom it is believed we contributed.[58]

When instructions came from Paris that the Minister of the Marine "had it very much in his heart that we should apply ourselves to it, therefore see what can be done to make him happy," Dollier de Casson asked for state permission, which was granted, to remove all Sulpician schooling to the reservation at La Montagne.

Bishop Laval, who upon his arrival in the colony as Vicar Apostolic was very hopeful of mass conversions and a thorough-going assimilation of the native tribes,[59] himself resolved to undertake the education of some native boys. He was all the more determined when he learned of the displeasure of the state officials with the lack of success of clerical efforts to date. Laval described the situation to a friend interested in the new church:

> As the King told me that he hoped we would attempt to raise in the manner of life of Frenchmen the little children of the Savages, in order to discipline them little by little, I have formed a seminary, into which I have taken a number of children for this express purpose; and in order to succeed better, I have been obliged to join with them some little French children, from whom, by living with them, the Savages could learn more easily both the customs and the language.[60]

The seminary was opened on October 9, 1668, and received modest royal subsidies in 1669 and 1670 to assure its initial success. But Laval soon discovered that the Amerindians wanted their children at home to teach them the ancestral beliefs and way of life, and in particular their responsibilities to their kinsmen and band. He admitted that it could be foreseen that these children would not remain long in a French environment and under a new discipline.[61]

Two years later the Bishop disclosed to a sympathetic friend the difficulties he was encountering in his enterprise:

> There is no means which I did not employ nor any care I did not take for the education of Savage Children, especially the last two years and although in my Seminary I spent twice as much for each of them, and even more, than for the French children, I had nevertheless very little success. The difficulties, concerning which I have written you these past two years, and which I apprehended, are found to be real in the carrying out of the design and render the matter very difficult. I have some children nevertheless at present in our seminary and accept as many as I can obtain from the parents, from whose hands it is almost impossible to acquire them, or to retain the children against their will no matter what means we have been able to employ, neither gentleness nor the authority of the Governor can prevail. The inordinate passion which they all have, even the Children, for intoxicating liquors gives ample inclination to their Liberty.[62]

Actually, Laval had not founded a new school, as the French authorities believed, but he provided the students with board and room and sent them to the Jesuits for their lessons.[63] Only one of the boys remained more than one year with the Bishop, and by 1673 not a single child of the original class remained. Thereafter, the Bishop accepted no new students, with the exception of one Iroquois boy who came for a few months only in 1679. A half-breed boy was also enrolled in 1679 but he was soon sent home on the vague grounds that he was totally unfit for the school environment. By 1680 the Bishop had no more Amerindian boys in his seminary and he never permitted any to enroll in his model agricultural and trades school at St. Joachim.[64]

The education of girls was an important part of the French assimilation programme, as has been seen. The Jesuits sent several native girls to the house of Guillaume Houbou in Quebec where the widow of Louis Hébert gave them some elementary instruction. In 1636 several Amerindian families had given their daughters to be raised with French families at Quebec but the arrangement proved mutually unsatisfactory.[65] When the Ursulines arrived at Quebec in 1639 they were immediately given some native girls to educate. The same practice was followed with the Hospital Nuns although they were supposed to be exclusively a nursing order. Four months later, Mother Marie de l'Incarnation of the Ursulines reported to the Jesuit Superior on the progress of their Amerindian pupils: three girls were commended by name for their progress, the three last pupils received were said to have left "their Savage humour at the door," and another two were simply described as "not yet baptized."[66] One of the pupils commended for "suffering no indecency on the part of her companions" had run away from school four days after arriving, but her father, a notable convert, had forced her to return. By March, 1640, three of these girls were prepared for their first communion and by September of the same year the Ursulines had charge of eighteen girls in the "seminary" and were promised two more Hurons and two more Algonkins, as well as a number of French girls in the separate day schools.[67] The Mother Superior gave the following account of these girls' reception:

> When they give them to us they are as naked as a worm, and it is necessary to wash them from head to foot, because of the grease with which their parents anoint their entire body; and whatever care we take, and although we change their linen and clothes often, it is a long time before we can rid them of their vermin because of the abundance of this grease. One sister spends part of each day at this task. It is a task which every one desires ardently.[68]

Seven sisters taught the French girls and one taught the Amerindian girls.

In 1655 some Iroquois came to visit the Ursuline monastery and the sisters permitted one of their model students, a Huron girl named Marie Arinadsit, to go beyond the grille and gates of the cloister to eat with the visitors and offer them some presents. She was reported to have encouraged the Iroquois to send their children to the French to be educated:

> Live, she said to them, with us henceforth as with your brothers, let us be only one people, and as a mark of your affection send some of your daughters to the Seminary; I will be their elder daughter, I will teach them to pray to God, and all the other things our Mothers taught me. And thereupon she started to read before them in Latin, in French and in Huron; then she sang spiritual Hymns in those three languages. Thereat those good people were quite taken aback, asked how long it took to learn so many things and to francize well a Savage girl, promising they would not miss sending their children to such a good school.[69]

By 1668, the Ursulines had to limit their boarding school to sixteen French girls and three native girls, "of whom two are Iroquois and one a captive to whom it is desired that we should teach the French language," Although they had been offered seven Algonkin girls they had to refuse them because they did not have the funds necessary to clothe, feed and educate so many students who did not pay fees nor anything towards their board.

The girls were accepted at all ages, and some were virtually kidnapped and sent to the Ursulines by the missionaries to be raised in French customs. Marie de l'Incarnation continued her description:

> Others are here only as birds of passage and stay with us only until they are sad, something which savage humour cannot suffer; the moment they become sad, the parents take them away for fear they will die. We leave them free on this point, for we are more likely to win them over in this way than by keeping them by force or entreaties. There are others who go off by whim or caprice; they climb our palisade like squirrels, which is as high as a stone wall, and go to run in the woods. There are some who persevere and we bring them up as French girls; we then arrange their marriages and they do very well.[70]

As time passed the Ursulines became more experienced and less optimistic of the success of their educational endeavours.

Finally, in 1668, the state officials began to press for more results from the assimilation programme. The Mother Superior was, however, not over-optimistic and when a Huron chieftain said that the King and the Governor "desired that their children and those of the French should marry one another so as to make but one people," she wrote to her son:

> He based this proposition on that he learned that His Majesty desires, so it is said, that the Reverend Fathers raise a number of small Savage boys, and we a number of girls in the French manner. If His Majesty desires it we are ready to do it by the obedience we owe him, and above all, because we are all prepared to do whatever will be to the greater glory of God. It is however a very difficult thing, not to say impossible, to francizize or civilize them. We have had more experience in this than any others, and we have remarked that out of a hundred that have passed through our hands scarcely have we civilized one. We find docility and intelligence in them, but when we are least expecting it they climb over our enclosure and go to run the woods with their relatives, where they find more pleasure than in all the amenities of our French houses. Savage nature is made that way: they cannot be constrained and, if they are they become melancholy and their melancholy makes them sick. Besides, the Savages love their children extraordinarily, and

173

when they know that they are sad they will do everything to get them back, and we have to give them back to them.[71]

The Ursulines had dealt mostly with Huron and Algonkin girls, and although the Iroquois girls were "the prettiest and most docile of all" there was not much more hope of success with them than with the others. Marie de l'Incarnation felt that "they are Savages and that suffices not to hope." The expense of such education was very heavy, especially as by 1668 only two benefactresses remained in France assuring the Ursulines of 100 *livres* revenue each year for native schooling. The Superior, however, had calculated it cost on the average 200 *livres* in fees, while the natives paid nothing "and even so, their parents who care passionately for their children believe they are doing us a great service."[72]

But state pressure required the religious communities, regular and secular, male and female, to fulfill their roles as public service institutions. There was no escaping the fact that the Canadian church, even in its missionary aspects, was part of the Gallican church. Each community contributed what it could to the programmes, and hoped for the approval of the Ministry of the Marine which was responsible for colonial developments. According to the Ursulines:

> Monseigneur our Prelate keeps in his house a certain number of young Savage boys, and as many French, so that being raised and fed together, the former take on the manners of the latter, and become francized: The Reverend Fathers do the same: Messieurs of the Seminary of Mont-Réal are going to imitate them. And as for the girls, we have some Savages too with our French Boarders for the same purpose. I do not know where all that will end, for to speak frankly with you, it seems very difficult to me. Since the great number of years we have been established in this country, we have been able to civilize but seven or eight, who were francized; the others who are numerous all went back to their kinsmen, although very good Christians. The savage life is so charming to them because of its liberty, that it is a miracle to be able to captivate them to the French way of doing things which they esteem unworthy of them, for they glory in not working except at hunting or navigation, or making war.[73]

Although the Ursulines were convinced it was impossible to achieve the Colbertian objective of assimilating the natives, their work was much appreciated by the missionary clergy and was not without its good effects. Father Millet reported from the Iroquois country in 1674, for example, that two former students of the Ursulines were having a good influence in their villages. One of them in particular "was able to assume and ever to maintain a certain ascendancy over all the other Christians," and so effective was her catechizing that "the men themselves willingly listen to her as their teacher."[74]

The non-cloistered Sisters of the Congregation, founded by Marguerite Bourgeoys, made some attempt to raise native girls in the French fashion too, although they became more occupied with the *petites écoles* for French children. The Sulpician priest, abbé Souart, paid an Iroquois a wampum collar worth 30 *livres* to release a nine-month-old baby to Marguerite Bourgeoys to be raised as a French child. The child's father later came to Montreal to claim back his daughter "but he could not discover where she was and was constrained to return without getting her back."[75] The child died in 1663 at the age of six, and may have been the first Iroquois to be baptized in New France. An Algonkin girl was taken in to replace her but also died at the age of seven or eight; a third girl, from the Illinois tribe, replaced her, but she also died in a matter of months. These three children, all successively baptized and named Marie des Neiges, were of little help to the Frenchification policy since they died so young. In 1660, an eighteen-year-old girl had also been accepted but she died the same year.[76] Some of these children were acquired virtually by abduction.

Both Colbert in France and Jean Talon in Canada were convinced that the missionaries had been more interested in religious conversions and particularly in baptismal statistics than in assimilating the natives. They cited what seemed to them an obvious deficiency in the missionary technique: had French only been used to communicate with and preach to the natives they would soon have adopted the European tongue and would have been brought more readily "to constitute one people and one race" with the French.[77] By 1668 the King had been advised of the lack of success in assimilating the Amerindians. Although the former programme of giving the native children a French and Catholic education even if the adults resisted integration had previously failed, the King recommended a return to that policy.[78] The mercantilist idea that the natives were idlers and vagabonds, since they practised no trades, professions, or agricultural labour, had already been voiced in royal instruction in 1665. It was thought that manual labour should be introduced early in the curriculum of native boys because the King believed that laziness in children was the cause of most later traits of weakness and insubordination.[79] Colbert informed the Intendant Bouteroue in 1668 to guard against Jesuit arguments in favour of racial segregation. He insisted that the missionaries had ignored or obstructed the royal policy in three respects: they had failed to encourage inter-marriage; they had failed to grant lands to natives near French *censitaires* who could serve as models to them; and they had not educated the children in the same schools as French children.[80]

So the tenor of royal instructions remained unchanged in 1671. The royal vessels brought the following orders:

> Always strive by all manner of methods to excite all the clergy and nuns who are in the aforesaid country to raise among them the greatest possible number of the said children in order that through instruction in the matters of our religion and in our ways they might compose with the inhabitants of Canada a single people and by that means also fortify the colony.[81]

Frontenac accused the Jesuits in 1672 of insincerity in their assimilation efforts, and the following summer he boldly asserted that the state would set an example for the church. He asked the Iroquois for some children which he would personally raise in a French manner of life. The Iroquois replied insolently that they did not part with their children as would French mothers, who seemed to have little more maternal instinct than a porcupine. Nevertheless, they did send six girls (not boys) whom Frontenac placed with the Ursulines rather than raise them in his own household as he had boasted.[82] He continued to boast about the success of the state, as opposed to the failure of the church, and accused the Jesuits of wishing to keep the natives in perpetual tutelage for fear they should become independent and demand a share in the Jesuit lands which had been granted in many cases for the benefit of the aborigines. To the surprise of everyone, the Iroquois brought four boys to Frontenac in 1674: he placed two in boarding school and the other two he kept in his household but sent them daily to the Jesuits for instruction.

By 1675 Versailles began to caution colonial officials about forcing the missionaries to submit to the assimilationist policy, and redefined the need to diminish the number of itinerant savages and raise them to a proper civilized state. Although this might not be equal to the level of the French, the natives should be raised "to the condition in which God has placed him at birth."[83] The Intendant Duchesneau adopted three native boys in 1680 but he had no sooner outfitted them with French clothes than they all ran away. He tried again with two other boys but was less optimistic of success in this venture:

> If I allowed them freedom I would be able to hold them, but my intention is to accustom them gradually to our ways in my home, and the slighest constraint rebuffs them.[84]

The Intendant De Meulles, who succeeded him, prepared a comprehensive report in 1682 on the progress of education. He observed that the Sulpicians taught the natives both French and Latin, some handi-crafts and agriculture; the Sisters of the Congregation provided prac-tical training in domestic subjects; the Jesuits stressed the mother tongues to the neglect of French and Latin; and the Ursulines taught them only "to say prayers and to speak French."[85] The immediate response from Versailles was to order that Amerindian girls no longer be given the élitist education given to girls from French families:

> His majesty does not wish that they be placed with the Ur-sulines, and His Majesty has given orders to have three women sent to teach them knitting, and three others to teach them to spin, and to make lace, in order to introduce these manufac-tures which will be advantageous to the colony.[86]

Amerindians as well as overseas Frenchmen were to be brought within the bounds of the mercantilist state.

The Jesuits, like all those involved in assimilation through edu-cation of the young, concluded that "one saw no notable fruit among the savages, beginning the instruction of the people by the children," and confessed that "God has confounded our thoughts and upset the foundations."[87] Education was not the cornerstone of assimilation of the Amerindians, although the conviction that this was the solution would continue to surface. Faith was therefore placed in the reserva-tion system as it forced the natives to become sedentary agricultural-ists, after a fashion living close to the French. One missionary expounded the theory in this manner:

> Now, I must state, in passing, that there are four great works bound together by a single tie — the settlement of the savages, the Hospital, the seminary for little savage boys, and the seminary for little savage girls. These last three depend on the first. Let these barbarians remain always nomads — then their sick will die in the woods and their children will never enter the Seminary. Render them sedentary and you will fill these three institutions, which all need to be vigorously aided.[88]

Emphasis was now shifted to the resettlement of the Amerindians rather than on the possibility of influencing them in any appreciable way while they lived in their traditional fashion in their hunting territories.

The Jesuits said the reservations, or *réserves*, first introduced in 1637, were consciously modelled on the *reducciones* of Mexico and Paraguay.[89] This was no doubt correct, although in point of fact it was the Franciscans who had originated the concept of racial segrega-tion in the New World in order to promote the conversion of the natives. Geronimo de Mendieta (1525-1604) had stated that the segregation of the Amerindians from direct contact with the Europeans was the *sine qua non* for the creation of the millenial kingdom in the New World.[90] Gabriel Sagard and Denis Jamet had both advocated some form of segregation before the Jesuits became the principal missionaries in the colony. The Jesuits probably owed as much to the Récollets, a branch of the Franciscans, as to their own experiences in South America.

Assimilation was a policy; segregation was a device which could achieve diverse objectives. It was a device that some believed would enable the French to assimilate the aborigines; it was also a device whereby others hoped the natives would be isolated from the forces of rapid change and protected from the ruthless and excessive assimilationist pressures. In other words, segregation could either hasten or retard the assimilation of the Amerindians into a European way of life. Some viewed it as a means of accelerating the process of acculturation while others viewed it as a transitional stage which would enable them eventually to integrate elements of each cultural group to form a new Amerindian Christian civilization. Between these two opposing views there existed a number of compromises or transitional possibilities. In fact, the result was most often simply social disorganization.

As first conceived at Sillery, the reservation was to be a socially controlled environment affording Amerindians a favourable milieu in which to adapt at their own rate to a French way of life. Paul Le Jeune had become convinced during his missionary journey of 1633-34 that the northern nomadic tribes should be resettled near Quebec and Trois-Rivières, the two main plantations at the time, in order to become isolated Christian cells and the nucleus for a New Israel. The basic aim of the plan he outlined in 1635 was to make the natives sedentary, to draw them away from their nomadic hunting economy, and to raise entire family units under missionary supervision. Thus the settlement started by Father Jacques Buteux on the left bank of the St. Maurice River near Troix-Rivières stressed agricultural labour, but as the natives showed little interest or aptitude, French settlers took up the concessions after five years. Similarly at Sillery, the old nomadic ways were never entirely abandoned and farming remained a very seasonal occupation rotating with hunting and fishing activities. All in all, Sillery was the most promising reservation. By 1645 there were no less than one hundred and sixty-seven domiciled and converted Amerindians living there. They were such models of piety and good behaviour that it became customary to refer to them as "the true believers."[91] However, there were indications of problems ahead. The persistence of quasi-nomadic ways was but one source of concern to the missionaries and to the administrative officials to whom they reported on their success in implementing the royal policy of assimilation of the aborigines. Proximity to French settlers meant not only that the natives could observe European Christians practising their Catholic religion and European agriculturalists bringing the virgin soils under cultivation, but that they could also see the weaknesses in the French character and in French society and could obtain brandy and trade goods more easily. The Jesuit missionaries noticed, in addition, that numerous Hurons remained at the hospital opened on the reservation at Sillery, taking up the space required for the sick and dying, as long as the free rations of wheat and eels were forthcoming. It was apparent that the natives' motives for resettlement were not always those the French had had in mind when organizing the reservations.[92]

The reservations had also been conceived as "republics" under the paternal authority of the missionaries and the native cathechists. A puritanical order was enforced by the *dogiques* not only on the professed converts but also on the young and the pagan relatives. Normally residents had formally to renounce their belief in dreams, give up their spouse-sharing practices and renounce alcoholic beverages. At Sault St. Louis, near Montreal, the curious visitors were sometimes drawn into the closed community of the reservation:

> Some came to it as agents of the demon, to corrupt others; and yet they all found themselves caught by the nets of the gospel — little by little, cabin by cabin, and man by man. Thus it is that the beginning of the mission have been like the grain of mustard seed. These visitors, seeing the corn very fine, resolved to remain there and build their cabins. The first cabin did not stay long alone; in less than a year there were four. Among others, we saw there that of an Onnatague who was baptized in France, — to whom the King gave his name, with a handsome silver medal, which he constantly wears suspended to his neck.[93]

Much of the agricultural work was done by the Jesuits themselves and the French settlers rather than by the Amerindians. The chief success seemed to be a spiritual victory rather than an overall cultural conquest. Father Allouez praised the residents of the Prairie de la Magdeleine reservation and remarked that "these Savages will rise up against us on the day of judgment." He said:

> They glory in being Christians, and make so public a profession of it that no one ventures to come and dwell among them unless he is fully resolved to embrace the Faith; for he is convinced that he would soon be driven away if he were not fully inclined to live as a good Christian. This causes the unchaste and the

drunkard to say: "I go not to la Prairie, for there are neither women nor liquor there." . . . I believe that there is a guardian angel of this village, who wards off all such occasions for sin: and that, if he were to leave it, and liquor were to come in, there would be no more Christianity in it.[94]

Before long, there were complaints from the reservations near Montreal, just as from those near Quebec, Trois-Rivières and Tadoussac, that the fanatical religious leaders were persecuting the pagans and lukewarm believers.

The Jesuit reservation at Prairie de la Magdeleine, and later at Sault St. Louis (Caughnawaga), aroused special interest in France because they were designed to attract Iroquois converts. The comments sent in the King's name to Governor Frontenac in 1680 merit attention:

I have accorded to the Jesuit Fathers the grant of land which they requested at the place known as the Sault . . . for the settlement of the Iroquois, and I added to this grant the conditions which they asked of me because I esteem this establishment advantageous not only for their conversion and maintenance in the Christian religion, but even more for familiarizing them with the habits and ways of the French. Although you may have known that the conversion of the savages in their habitations was not satisfactory because they readily returned to their idolatry, nevertheless when entire villages come to live within the settlements which are inhabited by my subjects their establishment can only be advantageous, and you must always encourage them in this, and favour their settlement by the protection you must and can provide them.[95]

Before long there were disputes over Frenchmen using the reservation lands to raise cattle, the opening of a cabaret at a convenient distance from the native settlement, and the recurring charges (which the missionaries tended to discount) that the converted and domiciled natives engaged in illicit trade with Albany and New York.

Reservations rapidly became refugee camps for native converts who were persecuted in their pagan villages, and for survivors from tribal wars. Iroquois refugees and Abenakis survivors came to swell the population of the reservations. As early as 1672 this role was acknowledged by one of the missionaries:

La Prairie has, then, always been the asylum of those who wished sincerely to pray to God and be Christians. These holy fugitives began to make, in the woods round about here, well-beaten hunting paths; for the chase was the pretext which they then adopted, in order to come to live at la prairie. The christians who left la prairie, in going to hunt beasts, went also to hunt men; the hunters always brought back some of their kinsmen or acquaintances in the spring, in the guise of a visit — wherein, God touching their hearts, they had themselves instructed and became christians. All those who had come from the iroquois had thus eluded, as it were, the fury of the drunkards and the enemies of prayer. This made the elders distrustful; in their councils, their declamations all concerned the destruction of their land by the french and by the missionaries. The more they complained, the more people were desirous of coming to see what was going on; and among these curious ones some always remained.[96]

The largest and most famous reservation which became a refuge for the persecuted was the Lorette mission near Quebec.

The reservation was becoming a substitute for native organization, just as the missionaries had hoped, but their success in converting the natives to Catholicism was not always as sincere a case of acculturation as the missionaries hoped it would be. Rather, it was often a mere addition of Catholicism as a cultural overlay. Hennepin pointed out the advantages of the reservations over mission stations in the interior, but he believed more in cultural overlay than in genuine assimilation of the native population:

> There are two villages in the Neighbourhood of Quebec, and two other higher up upon the River of St. Lawrence, near Mont-royal, which are separated from the Commerce of the Europeans. It's therefore in those Parts that the Church of the Savages is to be found. Tho their Language as well as Manners are altogether savage, yet for all that those Neophytes are kept in their Devoir. Great pains is taken to educate them in Piety, yet not much is gain'd upon their Spirit. There are some that are Christians in good earnest; but there are many entire Families who escape from the Missioners after having abode with them ten or twelve Years, and return to the Woods to their first mode of living.[97]

Assimilation of the adults seemed no more successful than education of the children had been.

Frontenac's accusation that the Jesuits were not interested in Frenchification of the natives because they kept them isolated from the French and taught them in their own languages rather than in French, was a reminder to the Court that in Huronia the Jesuits had attempted to establish a new nation and a new indigenous church on the Paraguayan model. The Jesuits had never openly committed themselves on how they proposed to organize the indigenous church with reference to the church of the European settlement, or how they proposed to associate Huronia with New France politically. Frontenac's thesis could only be tested by observing the methods and success of the other religious communities in the colony.

In 1673, three years after their return to New France, the Récollets assumed responsibility for a mission to the Cayugas at Quinté. They moved it to the vicinity of Fort Frontenac where they also served the French settlers and acted as chaplains for the troops. The beginnings were as promising as those of the other reservations:

> After having discours'd them some time, we return'd, bringing with us a considerable number of the Natives, in order to form a little Village of about Forty Cottages to be inhabited by them, lying betwixt the Fort and our House of Mission. These Barbarians turn'd up the Ground for sowing of Indian Corn and Pulse, of which we gave them some for their Gardens. We likewise taught them, contrary to their usual custom of eating, to feed upon Soupe, made of Pulse and Herbs, as we did.[98]

The Récollets insisted on mixing the French and Cayugas and brought up the children of both communities to be bilingual. It was as close as any missionaries came to succeeding in getting the Amerindians to learn French. Actually, the Sulpicians had already had considerable contact with these natives. Donations from wealthy patrons of the Sulpicians and royal subsidies, obtained by the Intendant Talon, had furnished agricultural equipment, grind-stones, furniture and household utensils for the Bay of Quinté mission but the assimilation programme had collapsed when Fort Frontenac had been built, for it held a much greater attraction for the natives. The Superior in Paris tried vainly to save the experiment:

> I see by the particulars you have sent me that the mission at Kenté is tottering. The discouragement of M. Trouvé, the ruined buildings, the lack of proper order seen there, the frequent journeys, the dissipation of individuals, and the instability of the Indians are strong reasons for convincing us that this establishment will not endure. But I cannot believe them sufficient reasons for abandoning it if means can be found to keep it going.[99]

A year before writing in such discouraging terms about Quinté, the Superior had authorized the secular clergy of St. Sulpice to open a mission station at La Montagne, near Montreal, where in 1671 eight warriors and their families had come to settle. The mission soon became a refuge for Hurons, Algonkins, Pawnees, Fox, Sioux and Iroquois living together in concord and united by their new religion. In 1680 the Sulpicians decided to move all their domiciled Amerindian converts to this reservation.[100] Within a few years all the problems that had arisen on the other reservations occurred at Lac des Deux Montagnes with additional disturbances over supposed cases of witchcraft. In the end, it was seen that the Récollets and Sulpicians were no more successful than the Jesuits.

By 1685 the missionaries had abandoned all hope of assimilating the Amerindians and making Frenchmen of them and the civil officials were slowly accepting this failure as an inevitable fact of life in the New World. Governor Denonville stated the failure of assimilationist policy in unmistakable terms:

> It was believed for a very long time that domiciling the savages near our habitations was a very great means of teaching these peoples to live like us and to become instructed in our religion. I notice, Monseigneur, that the very opposite has taken place because instead of familiarizing them with our laws, I assure you that they communicate very much to us all they have that is the very worst, and take on likewise all that is bad and vicious in us . . . .[101]

Although there had been a massive assault on traditional Amerindian society the natives had not been assimilated. On the contrary, French moral fibre had been weakened as each race had tended to absorb the worst features of the other's culture. The Governor did not conclude, on the other hand, that the device of segregating the converted Amerindians was necessarily valueless, and the missionaries continued to defend segregation of domiciled converts on reservations. The seventeenth-century experience with the reservation system, however, has been defended:

> Some there are who think, and therefore write, that the soil of Canada is thoroughly sterile and unfruitful; that the heralds of the Gospel reap there from hardly any fruit in return for long and painful labour. This single village of Lorette can teach them otherwise. In fact, I make bold to say that all the other missions of Canada are by no means as fruitful as this one. Drunkenness, — a vice inborn in barbarians, and spread far and wide by the greed of European traders, — and the corrupt morals and criminal example of Europeans, deplorably oppose the Gospel. These obstacles are, however, surmounted, although not everywhere with the same promptness and facility. They have been thoroughly abolished and destroyed in the village of

Lorette, where the savages enjoy the most ample liberty, and have made it a custom ot practice piety openly and in security.[102]

Thus when hopes of assimilation dwindled the segregationist practices were continued in order to isolate and insulate the aboriginal nucleus that was the hope of a New Israel.

On the other hand, there is some evidence that the French became more barbaric and Americanized. The trend was established by Cartier, who in 1541 sent two French youths to learn the Laurentian Iroquois language and to study their ways, and by Champlain, who sent young men to live among the natives as *coureurs-de-bois* and interpreters. It soon became evident that the freedom of Amerindian life held more attractions for the independent and self-reliant Canadian youths than did the contraints of Catholic and European civilization for native youths. Denonville observed in 1685:

> I could not, Monseigneur, adequately express to you the attraction which the young men feel to this savage way of life which consists of doing nothing, in being restrained by nothing, in pursuing all one's urges, and placing oneself beyond the possibility of correction.[103]

The system of *congés*, or special licences to carry on trade in the hinterland, encouraged a flow of men into the interior which neither church nor state could curb. Perrot wrote of the effects living in the wilderness had on men who tended to become less civilized and forget their French culture and Catholic religion.[104] The natives, on the other hand, regarded the process as a natural one in which Frenchmen were adapting to the environment and the cultural ways that had evolved over centuries in the New World. They openly urged the French to adopt their ways and come to live among them and teach them some of their technology. Bressani wrote in 1653:

> Our Christians had informed us of all their customs, and exhorted us to observe them exactly, unless we could arouse prejudice not only against ourselves, but also against the cause of God and of the faith.[105]

The tendency was never effectively reversed throughout the French régime. Peter Kalm observed that although "many nations imitate the French customs," his travels in the New World convinced him "on the contrary, that the French in Canada in many respects follow the customs of the Indians." He believed there was some miscegenation but, as for assimilation, the French had been quite unable to absorb the native population or Frenchify them:

Hence the Indian blood in Canada is very much mixed with European blood, and a large number of the Indians now living owe their origin to Europe. It is also remarkable that a great number of the people they had taken during the war and incorporated with their nations, especially the young people, did not choose to return to their native country . . . .

There are likewise examples of some Frenchmen going amongst the Indians and following their mode of life. There is on the contrary scarcely one instance of an Indian adopting the European customs.[106]

It was an unequivocal assertion of the failure of French policies.

Life in the New World could, however, never revert to pre-contact conditions. The coming of the French altered much in Amerindian society at the individual, the kin-group, the tribal and the inter-tribal levels. French life in the New World was never an exact replica of the Old World nor of basically unchanged fragments of that metropolitan society. Environmental forces left their mark. In addition, the demographic weakness of the French detracted from the technological and cultural superiority which, they believed, they enjoyed over the Amerindian inhabitants. The French never ceased to marvel at how successfully Amerindian tribes could integrate non-members, including some European captives, into their societies. This was especially remarkable in view of the lack of success of their own programme of Frenchification of the natives.

The French were hardly conquerors and masters in America: they continued to depend on the natives for supplies of furs, for allies in wartime, and for their own safety and convenience. The Amerindians had been quick to realize the material superiority of Europeans, had adopted certain aspects of that culture for their own purposes and in so doing had helped create an inter-dependency from which neither party could withdraw or escape. The church was fearful of cultural decline in the New World, especially as emigration from France never increased beyond a mere trickle. Instead of forging ahead to establish the millenial church of the Third Age of the Holy Ghost, it began fighting what often appeared to be a rearguard action to preserve French Catholic culture in what might develop in time into an urban and agrarian rural life not too dissimilar from provincial France.

1. R. A. Schermerhom, *Comparative Ethnic Relations* (New York: 1970), pp. 73-74.
2. André Labrouquère, *La Notion d'Assimilation en législation et économie coloniales,* (Hanoi: 1934), p. 9.
3. W. L. Grant and H. P. Biggar, eds., *The History of New France by Marc Lescarbot* (Toronto: 1907), Vol. II, p. 217.

4. W. L. Grant, ed., *Voyages of Samuel de Champlain, 1604-1618* (New York: 1917), Vol. I, pp. 264, 323.
5. *P.A.C., 500 de Colbert,* Vol. CDLXXXIII, Denis Jamet to Cardinal de Joyeuse, July 15, 1615, fols. 581-582v.; Bruce G. Trigger, "Settlement as an Aspect of Iroquoian Adaptation at the Time of Contact," *American Anthropologist* 65 (1963), pp. 92-93.
6. George M. Wrong, ed., *The Long Journey to the Country of the Hurons by Father Gabriel Sagard* (Toronto: 1939), pp. 52-53, 176.
7. Louis Hennepin, *A New Discovery of a Vast Country in America* (London: 1698), Vol. II, p. 60.
8. *Etablissements de la Compagnie de Canada sous le titre de Nouvelle France par les Articles des vingt-neuf Avril et sept May, mil six cens vingt-sept* (Paris: 1725), Article xvii, p. 10.
9. Paul Le Jeune, *Relation de ce qui s'est passé en la Nouvelle France en l'année 1635* (Paris: 1636), pp. 19-20.
10. *Les Véritables Motifs de Messieurs et Dames de la Société de Notre-Dame de Montreal* (Paris: 1643), p. 106.
11. R. G. Thwaites, ed., *The Jesuit Relations and Allied Documents* (Cleveland: 1896-1901), Vol. VIII, p. 9.
12. *Ibid.,* Vol. XXI, p. 57; XXIII, p. 31.
13. Hennepin, *op. cit.,* Vol. II, p. 61.
14. The definition is that given by Donald G. Baker, "Color, Culture and Power: Indian-White Relations in Canada and America," *Canadian Review of American Studies* III, No. 1 (Spring, 1972), p. 5.
15. Thwaites, *op. cit.,* Vol. X, p. 311; LXIII, p. 221.
16. *Histoire de l'Hôtel-Dieu de Québec* (Montauban: 1751), p. 201; Thwaites, *op. cit.,* Vol. LII, p. 244.
17. Dom Guy Oury, ed., *Marie de l'Incarnation, Ursuline (1599-1672). Correspondance* (Solesmes: 1951), pp. 221-222, 718.
18. B. Fernow, ed., *Documents relating to the History and Settlement of the Towns along the Hudson and Mohawk Rivers, 1630-1684* (Albany: 1881), Vol. XIII, pp. 72-73, 113; F. G. Roe, *The Indian and the Horse* (Norman: 1951), p. 67-68. By the eighteenth century the Iroquois were raising horses and the Pawnee used them to hunt: Thwaites, *op. cit.,* Vol. III, p. 261; LXVIII, p. 275; LXIX, p. 227.
19. Henry Folmer, *Franco-Spanish Rivalry in North America, 1524-1763* (Glendale: 1953), p. 21.
20. Cited in R. C. Alberts, *The Most Extraordinary Adventures of Major Robert Stobo* (Boston: 1965), p. 125.
21. Thwaites, *op. cit.,* Vol. LX, p. 89. Land grants are mentioned in Vol. XXXVI, p. 250; XLVII, p. 263; LIX, p. 285; LXII, pp. 266-267, 276.
22. Oury, *op. cit.,* p. 94; Thwaites, *op. cit.,* Vol. XVI, p. 74; XVIII, p. 108.
23. J. A. Maurault, *Histoire des Abénakis, depuis 1605 jusqu'à nos jours* (Sorel: 1866), p. 6; Lucien Campeau, *La Première Mission d'Acadie (1602-1616)* (Québec: 1967), Introduction, p. 118. The first *coureurs-de-bois* were probably the two youths sent by Jacques Cartier in 1541 to live with the chief of Achelacy (Portneuf).
24. John C. Webster, ed., *Relation of the Voyage to Port Royal in Acadia or New France by the Sieur de Dièreville* (Toronto: 1933), p. 186.
25. Thwaites, *op. cit.,* Vol. X, p. 26; XIV, pp. 17-19.
26. *Les Véritables Motifs,* p. 107.
26a. Thwaites, *op. cit.,* Vol. IX, pp. 216-218.
27. *Ibid.,* Vol. IX, p. 233.
28. C. H. Laverdière and H.-R. Casgrain, eds., *Le Journal des Jésuites* (Québec: 1871), p. 77-78.
29. Thwaites, *op. cit.,* Vol. XIV, pp. 19-21.
30. *Ibid.,* Vol. XIV, p. 263.
31. *A.R.S.I.,* Gallia 110, Vol. III, fols, 356-357. On the seigneury of Bou-

cherville, during the first decade of the eighteenth century, three Amerindians married French women: Pierre Voisin, a Panis domestic, married Marie Martin in 1703; Laurent Léveillé, a *sauvage,* married Marie Demers in 1705; and Nicolas Dyon, a Panis blacksmith, married Marie Gareau in 1710.

32. *Journal des Jésuites,* p. 312.
33. Thwaites, *op. cit.,* Vol. XLV, p. 148; *Journal des Jésuites,* p. 281.
34. Thwaites, *op. cit.,* Vol. LXIII, p. 267.
35. Clarence J. d'Entremont, "The Children of the Baron de St.-Castin," *French Canadian and Acadian Genealogical Review* III, No. 1 (Spring, 1971), pp. 9-28.
36. E. B. O'Callaghan, ed., *Documents Relative to the Colonial History of the State of New York* (Albany: 1883-87), Vol. IX, La Barre to Seignelay, November 4, 1683, p. 207.
37. P. Margry, ed., *Découvertes et Etablissements des Français dans l'Ouest et dans le Sud de l'Amérique septentrionale* (Paris: 1879), Vol. I, pp. 5-6; Thwaites, *op. cit.,* Vol. V, pp. 107-109; VI, pp. 85-87, 97.
38. J. G. Shea, ed., *Chrestien Le Clercq: First Establishment of the Faith in New France* (New York: 1887), Vol. I, pp. 164-165.
39. *A.N., Series E.,* Vol. 72B, Arrêt of Council of State, August 11, 1622, fol. 191.
40. Shea, *op. cit.,* Vol. I, p. 214.
41. Wrong, *op. cit.,* p. 133.
42. H. Harrisse, *Notes pour Servir à l'histoire, à la bibliographie et à la cartographie de la Nouvelle-France et des Pays adjacents, 1545-1700* (Paris: 1872), p. 71.
43. Hennepin, *op. cit.,* Vol. I, p. 57.
44. *Ibid.,* Vol. I, p. 47.
45. Thwaites, *op. cit.,* Vol. VII, pp. 287, 297; IX, pp. 105, 201, 223-225; XI, pp. 93-99; XII, p. 125; XV, pp. 223-235, 233-237.
46. *Ibid.,* Vol. XVI, pp. 179-181.
47. *Ibid.,* Vol. XI, p. 225. Cf. Cornelius J. Jaenen, "Problems of Assimilation in New France, 1603-1645," *French Historical Studies* IV, No. 3 (Spring, 1966), pp. 265-289; J. V. Jacobsen, *Educational Foundations of the Jesuits in Sixteenth Century New Spain* (Berkeley: 1938); A. P. Farrall, *The Jesuit Code of Liberal Education, Development and Scope of the Ratio Studiorium* (Milwaukee: 1938).
48. *A.S.Q., Fonds Verreau XIII,* No. 27c; also Thwaites, *op. cit.,* Vol. VI, p. 196; VI, pp. 150-152, 242; VII, p. 265; VIII, p. 226; IX, p. 284; XII, pp. 44-48.
49. Thwaites, *op. cit.,* Vol. XIV, p. 233.
50. *Ibid.,* Vol. XII, pp. 42, 221.
51. *Ibid.,* Vol. XIV, p. 242; XVI, p. 187.
52. *Ibid.,* Vol. LXIII, p. 211.
53. Candide le Nant, *Pages glorieuses de l'Epopée canadienne* (Paris: 1927), pp. 141-142.
54. *Ibid.,* p. 313.
55. *A.C., Series F3,* Vol. III, Bouart to Tracy, October 7, 1667, fol. 353.
56. *P.A.C., Series B,* Vol. I, Colbert to Quéylus, May 15, 1669, pp. 216-219; Colbert to Courcelles, May 15, 1669, p. 208.
57. Margry, *op. cit.,* Vol. I, p. 372.
58. *B.S.S.P., Tronson Correspondence,* Vol. I, No. 32, Tronson to LeFebvre, June 6, 1677, p. 106.
59. *A.S.Q., Lettres N,* No. 5, Alexander VII to Laval, April 3, 1660; Sacra Rituum Congregatio, Sectio Historica, *Quebecen. Beatificationis et Canonizationis Ven. Servi Dei Francisci de Montmorency Laval* (Rome: 1961), Doc. XXIII, No. 1, Laval to Alexander VII, July 31, 1659, pp. 74, 76.

60. H. Têtu, *Biographies de Msgr Laval et de Msgr Plessis* (Montréal: 1913), Laval to Poitevin, November 3, 1668, p. 35.
61. *A.A.Q., Lettres I,* Laval to Poitevin, November 8, 1668, p. 128.
62. *P.A.C., MG 18/E9,* Laval to abbé de l'Isle-Dieu, September 30, 1670.
63. *P.A.C., A.S.M.E.,* Vol. CCCXLV, Pt. I, Histoire du Séminaire de Québec, fol. 3, p. 27.
64. *Ibid.,* p. 28.
65. Thwaites, *op. cit.,* Vol. IX, pp. 102-104.
66. Oury, *op. cit.,* p. 91.
67. *Ibid.,* p. 95.
68. *Ibid.,* p. 97.
69. Oury, *op. cit.,* p. 995.
70. *Ibid.,* pp. 801-802.
71. Oury, *op. cit.,* p. 809.
72. *Ibid.,* pp. 821, 852.
73. Oury, *op. cit.,* p. 828.
74. Thwaites, *op. cit.,* Vol. LVIII, p. 199.
75. *B.S.S.P., Carton B,* Mélanges, No. 28(h), p. 199.
76. *P.A.C., MG 18/E-7,* "Ecrits autographes de Marguerite Bourgeoys," pp. 8-9.
77. *P.A.C., Series C11A,* Vol. II, Talon to Colbert, November 13, 1666, p. 332; Colbert to Talon, April 5, 1667, pp. 476-477; Talon to Colbert, October 27, 1667, p. 518.
78. *P.A.C., Affaires Etrangères: Amérique,* Vol. V, Louis XIV to Laval, March 2, 1668, fol. 243; *A.S.Q., Lettres N,* No. 27, Colbert to Laval, March 7, 1668.
79. *P.A.C., Series B,* Vol. I, Instructions to Talon, March 27, 1665, pp. 69-70.
80. *Ibid.,* Vol. I, Instructions to Bouteroue, April 5, 1668, p. 82.
81. *Ibid.,* Vol. III, Instructions to Talon, February, 1671, p. 67.
82. *P.A.C., Series K,* Carton 1232, No. 1, p. 12; *P.A.C. Series C11A,* Vol. IV, Frontenac to Colbert, November 14, 1674, pp. 163-164, 197-198.
83. *Collection de Manuscrits, contenant lettres, mémoires, et autres documents historiques relatifs à la Nouvelle-France* (Québec: 1883-1885), Vol. I, King to Frontenac, April 22, 1675, pp. 235-236.
84. *P.A.C., Series C11A,* Vol. I, Duchesneau to Colbert, November 13, 1680, pp. 178-179.
85. O'Callaghan, *op. cit.,* Vol. IX, De Meulles to Seignelay, November 12, 1682, p. 199.
86. *P.A.C., Series B,* Vol. XI, King to De Meulles, April 10, 1684, p. 28. For an elaboration of the meaning of mercantilism for the development of the colony see our article "Le Colbertisme," *Revue d'histoire de l'Amérique française,* XVIII, No. 1 (juin, 1964), pp. 64-84; No. 2 (septembre, 1964), pp. 252-266.
87. Thwaites, *op. cit.,* Vol. XXIV, p. 102; XXIX, p. 192.
88. *Ibid.,* Vol. XVI, p. 33.
89. *Ibid.,* Vol. XII, p. 221; Jacques de Machault, *Relation des insignes Progrez de la religion Chréstienne, faits au Paraquai, province de l'Amérique Méridionale* (Paris: 1638), p. 162.
90. John Leddy Phelan, *The Millenium Kingdom of the Franciscans in the New World* (Berkeley: 1956), pp. 1-159.
91. *Journal des Jésuites,* p. 24.
92. *Ibid.,* pp. 10, 14, 36, 42-44.
93. Thwaites, *op. cit.,* Vol. LXIII, p. 159.
94. *Ibid.,* Vol. LVIII, pp. 81-83.
95. *P.A.C., Series C11A,* Vol. V, King to Frontenac, April 29, 1680, p. 193.
96. Thwaites, *op. cit.,* Vol. LXIII, p. 169.
97. Hennepin, *op. cit.,* Vol. II, p. 158.
98. *Ibid.,* Vol. I, p. 19.

99. *B.S.S.P., Tronson Correspondence,* Vol. I, Tronson to LeFebvre, April 5, 1677, p. 54.

100. *Ibid.,* Vol. I, Nos. 23, 24, 32, 48, 60, 71, 73, 98, 105, 106, 107, 118.

101. *P.A.C., Series C11A,* Vol. VII, Denonville to Seignelay, November 13, 1685, pp. 46-47.

102. Thwaites, *op. cit.,* Vol. LXVI, pp. 147-149.

103. *P.A.C., Series C11A,* Vol. VII, Denonville to Seignelay, November 13, 1685, pp. 45-46.

104. J. Tailhan, ed., *Mémoire sur les moeurs, coustumes et relligion des sauvages de l'Amérique septentrionale de Nicolas Perrot* (Leipzig and Paris: 1864), pp. 130-131.

105. Thwaites, *op. cit.,* Vol. XXXVIII, p. 281; also IX, p. 231.

106. Adolph B. Benson, ed., *Peter Kalm's Travels in North America* (New York: 1966), Vol. II, pp. 456-457. James Axtell has studied the effectiveness of the Amerindian educational and nurturing system in the adoption of Europeans in contrast to the dismal failure of European efforts to civilize the natives. Cf. James Axtell, "The White Indians of Colonial America," *William and Mary Quarterly,* Third Series, XXXII, No. 1 (January, 1975), pp. 55-88. Of interest, if not directly related to New France, is J. Norman Heard, *White into Red: A Study of the Assimilation of White Persons captured by Indians* (Metuchen, N.J.: 1973).

CONCLUSION

The French established contact with the Amerindians on a casual basis through the Newfoundland fisheries as early as the fifteenth century, and probably earlier. In the sixteenth century, voyages of so-called discovery and abortive colonization schemes further acquainted the French with the aborigines whom the Spaniards and Portuguese were in the process of subjugating and exploiting. Swarthy American natives were taken as curios of the New World to be displayed in various public spectacles in Western Europe, raising disquieting theological and scientific questions.

In general, the French were less involved than their neighbours in great controversies about the origins of the American aborigines, their nature, and the possible sources of their civilizations. Indeed, Frenchmen did not contact the same highly developed Amerindian civilizations as did the Spaniards in Central and South America. The French judged the Amerindians in terms of their religious beliefs and their degree of civility. Just as there was no doubt that the tribes were heathen, so there was no doubt that, in terms of the classical distinction between Greeks and barbarians, they were also barbarians. These heathen barbarians were rough and unpolished, to be sure, but views differed as to whether they were men in savage and degenerate form, the prototype of the wild man, or whether they were primitive men without benefit of religion and social institutions. Montaigne observed that "everyone calls barbarian what is his own usage." In whatever way Amerindians were viewed, the consensus was definitely that they were unpolished *sauvages*, and therefore presented a challenge to Frenchmen to civilize them and impart to them the religion, arts and culture of Europe's leading civilization.

One of the early reactions was to equate the Amerindian societies with the lost Paradise of their literary and philosophical tradition. The liberty, equality and fraternity which travellers and missionaries, at least those who tended to be critical of their own society, reported in America provided a very powerful criticism of contemporary France.

The Amerindians were apparently proof that Christian Europe did not have a monopoly on goodness and rationality. Those who looked for noble savages or native utopias as a means to criticize and castigate contemporary French manners, morals and government were well served. These precursors of the eighteenth-century deists and rationalists were, however, a minority whose influence must not be exaggerated.

The French discovery of America brought together many threads to form a twisted skein of perceptions of the New World and its peoples. Theories of lost continents and prehistoric migrations, mingled with myths of concurrent creations and cataclysmic displacements of populations, these in turn being overlaid by tales of fabled isles and monstrous lands given over to the devil, fed the imaginative and beckoned the venturesome. Religious revivalism, pious mysticism and eschatological undercurrents in France raised hopes of ushering in the millenial age, of building the spiritual church and New Jerusalem in the New World. From the excitement of early contact in the sixteenth and seventeenth centuries — for the fishermen never revealed their earlier experiences or their fishing grounds — and the contradictory reports of explorers and exploiters, there emerged a dominant French view of the world and of themselves which stood in sharp contrast to the views of the Amerindians.

Although there was a strain of romantic primitivism, the dominant French view of man was that he was a changer and overseer of nature: a husbandman, a builder, an inventor, a domesticator, a civilizer. As a steward of God in his relationship to other forms of life his normal and divinely ordained role was to change and control by his arts and his technology. Frenchmen regarded their intervention in nature as purposive. The Amerindians, on the other hand, saw themselves as having a contractual or symbiotic relationship with the forces of nature. The contractual relationships of the French were to various authorities — to God, to the king, to the seigneur, to the religious superior, to the monopolist. Amerindians saw themselves and their tribal society as a product of nature and they acknowledged this in the names they assigned their tribes and bands. The Amerindians saw themselves as intimately dependent on nature, while the French saw themselves as superior to nature, as destined to dominate it and to bend its forces to their own objectives and aspirations. Progress in French eyes consisted of manipulating, controlling and subordinating nature and society more and more to man's initiative and enterprise. Insofar as religion and nature were intimately related, Amerindian society was more theocentric than was French society in the seventeenth century.

All in all, the French experience differed markedly from the Spanish or English encounters in day-to-day relations with the aborigines. The conceptual frameworks of all Europeans closely resembled each other, whether they classified themselves as Latins or Anglo-Saxons, as Catholics or Protestants. When the contact with Amerindians did not involve displacing the native peoples or extensive European immigration, which was the French experience as contrasted to the English and Spanish experiences, relations remained friendly. Cooperation and intercourse resulted in a certain degree of interdependence and created an impression of successful accommodation and acculturation. Such impressions were superficial observations neglecting the deeper evidences of social disorganization. The fact that the British, who had such a poor reputation in cultural contact in the Anglo-American colonies, assumed and appropriated the apparently friendly French relationship with the tribesmen after the conquest of Canada and the American Revolution suggests the need for an environmental approach to the question of culture clash. The French contact experience with the sedentary agricultural Iroquoian tribes had been less amicable than had their contact with nomadic Algonkian tribes. In the seventeenth century, the Amerindians seem to have stereotyped the Englishman as a farmer or town-dweller whose activities gradually drove the original agriculturalists deeper into the hinterland, whereas the stereotype of the Frenchman was a trader or soldier laden with baubles and brandy who asked only for furs and hospitality.

These comparatively more amicable relations between Frenchmen and Amerindians resulted in more credence being given in France to the good qualities of native life. The view that they were filthy, depraved barbarians never became a dominant and obsessive view with the French, although it was always present as an undercurrent and occasionally surfaced as in the reaction to the so-called Iroquois scourge. When goodness and virtue were accepted as possible in aboriginal societies a number of purposes might be served: those who sought the lost Paradise found in America a hope of restoring it; those who deplored the evils of sophisticated civilization found in America the noble savages; those who chafed at political oppression and bureaucratic corruption saw in America a land of freedom and opportunity; those who wearied of religious turpitude and theological strife caught a vision of the New Israel in the New World and the imminent end of the world. But those who lived and worked in New France came to believe more in the New World of their own experience than in the America invented by the metropolitan French.

Frenchmen, as a result of contact with primitive peoples, were more convinced that they stood at the pinnacle of civilization. Their society, despite some defects such as religious wars, famines, rural unrest and unemployment, and bureaucratic corruption, was an orderly, rational and Christian one, which all peoples everywhere ought to adopt and emulate if they wished to progress and elevate themselves. Although the French did not discriminate against the Amerindians on strictly racial grounds, they did by their somatic norm image consider them inferior and infantile. Native barbarism and cruelty, which must be seen in the Amerindian religious and social context to be understood, was an important factor in the literature on captivity and the creation of a stereotype of cruel savages. This literary tradition and popular stereotype were largely responsible for later discrimination against the aboriginal peoples in both Canada and the United States.

The Amerindians, for their part, had their own somatic norm image in which Frenchmen were regarded as ugly, effeminate, weak, disorganized, improvident, excitable, domineering, and quite inconsistent in applying their ideals to their everyday living. The French regarded Amerindian societies as devoid of spirituality and basic religious concepts, but it turned out that native society was as religiously oriented as European society. Indeed, many of the aspects of Amerindian life which the French were slow to comprehend — torture of captives, significance of dreams, resistance to conversion — were spiritually based. In the final analysis, it was sometimes French Catholic society that emerged as this-worldly, materialistic and superstitious. True conversion for the Amerindians meant a renunciation of their culture and a loss of their identity, a fact which the French missionaries and civil officials, without realizing the full implications of social disorganization, found quite normal because the French and Catholic qualities of their own civilization were rarely dissociated or conceived as separable.

The fact that the continent was not an empty wilderness but a populated expanse required some accommodation with its inhabitants, and some state policy of occupation. The French response to this challenge came at two levels — the spiritual and the temporal. First, the Amerindians would have to be evangelized and take their place with the Christians of France. Secondly and concurrently, they would have to be assimilated into French society by a process of Frenchification and civilization. As conversion soon proved to be a very disruptive experience in the native communities, religious conversion and cultural assimilation became more closely entwined. Unless the whole community converted and the whole apparatus of French institutions and life-style were adopted, divisions became acrimonious, reversion was likely, and social disorganization always ensued.

In their contacts the French came to sense, although they never fully comprehended or openly acknowledged, that Amerindian societies were well-integrated units. Education, for example, was fully integrated into everyday living. Therefore, French attempts to introduce formal schooling as a means of civilizing and converting the natives cut across traditional belief systems, values, institutional forms and band aspirations. No two societies could have differed more in their conceptual frameworks than did the European and Amerindian. Religion also permeated all aspects of native life, probably to a greater extent than religion permeated French life because the French, unlike the Amerindians, did not always allow their religious convictions to interfere with their economic mores, their warfare, or their personal behaviour. Because the Amerindians sought to live in tune with nature and their religious perceptions, Catholicism as a new religion could only be a disruptive innovation undermining their spiritual concepts as well as their entire way of life, their value systems, and their moral assumptions.

The French considered the Algonkian nomadic peoples as idlers and vagabonds because they were not sedentary agriculturalists or village craftsmen; conversely, the natives occasionally were only too well-informed about poverty and lower-class conditions in France. Amerindian concepts of communal property, hunting territories and kinship responsibilities found no precise equivalents in French views of property rights, legal jurisdictions, contractual agreements, monopolies and sovereignty. There was no common theoretical ground for accommodation. They did not clash, however, because they remained largely isolated and separated from each other. The French towns and seigneuries formed a riparian colony, whereas the majority of the Amerindians, except a small number of domiciled converts resettled on reservations, inhabited the hinterlands. Because of this physical separation, there were few if any confrontations or contests about property rights or civil jurisdiction.

The French in their contacts with the natives admired their ability to grapple with problems in a resourceful manner and often abandoned their abstract speculation to adopt native ways. This utilitarianism, born of a long experience in North America, did not conform to French concepts of artisanal organization, seigneurial subservience, or military logistics, but it gradually became one of the acquired qualities that distinguished a Canadian *habitant* from a metropolitan Frenchman. The superiority of European technology had profound consequences for the Amerindians. As their hunting and warfare became more effective and their artifacts became more sophisticated, their demands grew and correspondingly their dependence on the Europeans increased both for supplies and repairs. Inter-dependence developed between native hunter and French trader, between native canoeman and French soldier, between native catechist and French missionary.

The French contact experience does suggest that the behavioural patterns routinized and institutionalized among the aborigines were rational, at least in the sense that they applied the best available techniques to the resources at hand in order to obtain the greatest benefit and use from them. There is also another conclusion that clearly emerges. Traditional societies cannot respond so readily to external challenges to their institutional system. Since the French were more adaptable than the Amerindians, the transfer of French institutions to North America also involved a transformation as well as a transplantation. It was the French who gained most from the cultural contacts of the seventeenth century The French learned new techniques for building, travelling, dressing, fighting, food-gathering and survival in the wilderness. They acquired new foods and medicines. They brought new areas under their domination and new peoples in contact with their trade and religion. French society was sufficiently cohesive and stable to absorb new elements while remaining basically itself. Amerindian societies, on the other hand, often became disorganized as a result of cultural contact and too frequently exhibited the worst elements adopted from French culture.

French culture in New France, however, lacked sufficient men, materials and money to act effectively as a host society for the assimilation of the socially disorganized Amerindians. The great failure of the French in seventeenth-century America was their inability to integrate the native peoples in appreciable numbers into a new social order, thereby overcoming the continuing stresses of cultural clash and the nefarious consequences of social disorganization. As officials of church and state came to realize by 1685, their relatively insignificant and insecure colony could not acculturate the Amerindians. The French were unable to exert the kind of social control necessary to stamp out the brandy traffic or to prevent the exodus of *coureurs-de-bois* each year to the *pays d'en haut*. They could not, therefore, hope to exert much control over the vast territories in which their traders, soldiers and missionaries lived more as guests and dependents of the natives than as representatives of a ruling power.

What was the effect of cultural differences among Amerindian tribes when contact with the French influenced their traditional way of life? All the tribes contacted by the French showed a certain traditional inertia, an adherence to their ancestral beliefs and conceptualization. To live on good terms with the different tribes the French had to accept a degree of coexistence, which meant renouncing any plan of immediate assimilation of the natives. It was essential to accommodate a certain resistance, both conscious and subconscious and rooted in native religion, on the part of the Amerindians. The aborigines developed counter-innovative techniques when they sensed that their traditional society was threatened by the French intrusion. It was in this aspect of contact that the cultural differences emerged between nomadic and sedentary tribes, and between animists and polytheists. The more advanced Amerindian cultures assimilated more rapidly than the less advanced tribes, but they were also better able to preserve their traditional belief system and social organization. It was the less advanced, northern and eastern, nomadic Algonkian-speaking tribes who were most disorganized in the face of contact and who showed the most signs of social disintegration and cultural confusion.

Numerous Amerindians became zealous Catholics, some to the point of demonstrating excessive zeal in their self-mortifications and adorations, and some of them made genuine efforts to take up French agricultural life on the reservations administered for the state by the missionary clergy. But this should not obscure the evidence that the economic and social problems arising out of French competitive pressures, the new religious divisions, the inroads of drunkenness and diseases of epidemic proportions, and the introduction of a new technology were not resolved. The converted and resettled natives were no more immune than those who continued to hold to their traditional beliefs and life-style. Neither conversion nor resettlement seemed to reduce appreciably the cultural conflicts that engulfed their whole society.

Assimilation meant the adoption of a new belief and value system and the setting of new limits for behaviour. It meant that actions and thoughts considered good and moral in their traditional society might be censured in French society, and that sometimes what was formerly censured might now be permissible or approved. The problems attendant on assimilation arose out of the process of change and the admixture of beliefs and values, and often resulted in the confusion of individuals and whole societies. Assimilation efforts seemed essentially to produce dislocation; they were a breaking-down process in order to reconstruct a new order. But by attacking the value system of Amerindian societies in order to replace it with a new value system, the entire integrated way of life was upset, including folklore, religion and occupational patterns. As ambiguities and inconsistencies marked the changes, it was not unusual to find rather bizarre patterns of behaviour. Personal and social demoralization seemed to be reflected in alcohol addiction which became the curse, and often the identifying characteristic, of Amerindian communities.

Acculturation is a two-way process. The French were affected by contact too. When any culture is transplanted it changes and varies, but such adaptations are more marked when the society comes into contact and into conflict with other cultures. There follows an exchange and interaction of cultures which can, theoretically, enrich or impoverish both. Cultural *métissage* results, out of which a new culture can emerge. In a limited way, this is what began to occur in New France in the seventeenth century. The Amerindian societies were undermined and disoriented in several respects, as has been shown, without at the same time being afforded an opportunity to reorganize and consolidate themselves into Euro-Amerindian cultures. The French, on the other hand, did begin to develop a distinctive Canadian culture from a French Renaissance base, which was somewhat changed in both form and spirit by the North American environment and experience, and which was greatly enriched by and made the beneficiary of the centuries-old Amerindian exprience in North America.

In the French experience, as in the Amerindian, paradoxes were to be found. The highest aboriginal civilizations were those which assimilated most readily to European society, but were also those best equipped to retain their ancestral beliefs and social structures and so resist losing their identity. In French society, the paradox was that in the seminal development of a distinctive Canadian-French culture, owing much to transplantation and to contact with the Amerindians, the efforts to mould the colony in the image of metropolitan France increased with the passing of time. The optimum condition to assert an independent identity passed in the early phase of resource exploitation, missionary dominance, and social disorganization, but as the colony grew older and stronger efforts were made to fashion it more and more in the traditional cadres of the absolute monarchy, the Gallican church, mercantilism, and seigneurialism. A result of the important contacts with the indigenous tribes of New France — contacts which absorbed much evangelical zeal, which sustained the economy, and which threatened or assured military and political survival — was a growing Canadian ethnocentrism. The colonists turned to their culture, particularly their religion, as a source of identity. There they found a sense of stability and security. As New France became more like Old France it follows that the cultural gap between French and Amerindian widened rather than closed.

BIBLIOGRAPHICAL NOTE

What follows is only an indication of the chief sources available for the study of French-Amerindian relations. It is not meant to be an exhaustive bibliography, but rather a guide to the principal works.

The MANUSCRIPT SOURCES are of course abundant. They can be summarized under three principal headings: national or state archives; provincial, departmental, regional or municipal archives, libraries and repositories; the archives and libraries of religious foundations. The chief national or state archives of interest to us are the Public Archives of Canada in Ottawa, the Bibliothèque Nationale de France in Paris, and the various sections of the Archives Nationales de France — Affaires Etrangères, Colonies, Marine, Outre-Mer. There are also the provincial or departmental archives such as the Archives Nationales du Québec, the Archives Judiciaires in Montreal, Trois-Rivières and Québec, the Public Archives of Nova Scotia, the Massachussetts Archives, and the numerous departmental archives in France (Bordeaux, La Rochelle, Nantes, Rouen, Tours, etc.) , and the municipal libraries such as those at Montreal, Honfleur, La Rochelle, Nantes, Orleans, St. Malo, etc. Finally, a very important category is the religious archives: the archdiocesan archives at Quebec, Rouen, Paris; archives of religious communities such as the Récollets at Chantilly, the Jesuits at St. Jérome and St. Louis, the Sulpicians in Montreal and Paris, the Ursulines at Quebec, the Sisters Hospitallers at Quebec, the Sisters of the Congregation in Montreal, the Séminaire de Québec at Quebec and the Séminaire des Missions Etrangères in Paris.

The Principal PRINTED COLLECTIONS OF SOURCE MATERIALS are the Publications of the Champlain Society for the works of Lescarbot, Denys, LeClercq, Dièreville, Sagard, Du Creux and Champlain; the Publications of the Archives of Canada for the *Relations* of Cartier, the early precursors, Bertrand, Cobes and Ronual; the publications of the Literary and Historical Society of Quebec for the works of Dollier de Casson, Belmont, Catalogne; the Ontario Historical Society Papers and Records for the voyages of Dollier de Casson and Galinée. The works of d'Abbeville, d'Avity, Biet, Boyer, Clodoré, du Tertre, de Léry, Le Febvre, Le Roy, Thévet and Verrazzanno are not readily available in reprint editions or in major collections. There are major documentary collections such as the invaluable R. G. Thwaites, ed., *The Jesuit Relations and Allied Documents*, 73 vols. (Cleveland: 1896-1901); the recent addition to the Jesuit monumentary history, L. Campeau, ed., *La Première Mission d'Acadie, 1602-1616* (Québec: 1967) which is a masterpiece of editing and historical criticism; and the very instructive Dom Guy Oury, ed., *Marie de l'Incarnation, Ursuline (1599-1672), Correspondance* (Solesmes: 1971).

There are also the journals and memoirs of Frenchmen who had extensive experience with the Amerindians: A. A. Adams, ed., *The Explorations of Pierre-Esprit Radisson* (Minneapolis: 1961); Pierre Boucher, *Histoire véritable et naturelle des moeurs et productions du Pays de la Nouvelle-France* (Boucherville: 1964); Jean Delanglez, ed., *The Journal of Jean Cavelier* (Chicago: 1938); François Gendron, *Quelques particularitez du Pays des Hurons* (Troyes: 1660); Louis Hennepin, *A New Discovery of a Vast Country in America*, 2 vols., (London: 1698); R. G. Thwaites, ed., *New Voyages to North America of the Baron de Lahontan*, 2 vols., (Chicago: 1905); Nicolas Perrot, *Mémoires sur les moeurs, coutumes et religions des sauvages de l'Amérique septentrionale* (Paris: 1864); M. B. Anderson, *Relations of the Discoveries and Voyages of Cavelier de la Salle* (Chicago: 1901).

The SECONDARY SOURCES are abundant as many new studies of Amerindian history, archaeology, anthropology and related social sciences are published each year in increasing numbers. The periodical literature is particularly important; also a number of significant theses and dissertations relating to French-Amerindian history have appeared in recent years. Among the important publications related to our topic are:

BAILEY, A. G. *The Conflict of European and Eastern Algonkian Cultures, 1506-1700.* St. John: 1937.

BARBEAU, C. M. *Comment on découvrit les Indiens d'Amérique.* Montréal: 1966.

BAUDET, Henri. *Paradise on Earth.* New Haven: 1965.

CHINARD, Gilbert. *L'Exotisme américain dans la littérature française de XVIe siècle.* Paris: 1913.

CHINARD, Gilbert. *L'Amérique et le reve exotique dans la littérature française au XVIIe et XVIIIe siècles.* Paris: 1913.

COLEMAN, E. L. *New England Captives carried to Canada between 1677 and 1760,* 2 vols. Portland: 1925.

DESROSIERS. L.-P. *Iroquoisie, 1534-1646.* Montréal: 1947.

DOUVILLE, R. and CASANOVA, J. D. *La Vie quotidienne des Indiens du Canada à l'époque de la colonisation française.* Montréal: 1967.

FAIRCHILD, H. N. *The Noble Savage: A Study in Romantic Naturalism.* New York: 1928.

FENTON, W. et al. *American Indian and White Relations to 1830: Needs and Opportunities for Study.* Chapel Hill: 1957.

FLANNERY, Regina. *An Analysis of Coastal Algonkian Culture.* Washington: 1939.

GONNARD, René. *La Légende du bon sauvage.* Paris: 1946.

GUERRAND, Roger H. *Indiens et coureurs de bois.* Paris: 1960.

HAGAN, William T. *The Indian in American History.* New York: 1963.

HANKE, Lewis. *Aristotle and the American Indians: A Study in Race Prejudice in the Modern World.* London: 1959.

HUDDLESTON, Lee E. *Origins of the American Indians: European Concepts, 1492-1729.* Austin: 1967.

HUNT, G. T. *The Wars of the Iroquois.* Madison: 1940.

JENNESS, Diamond. *The Indians of Canada.* Ottawa: 1967.

JOSEPHY, Alvin M. *The Indian Heritage of America.* New York: 1960.

KEISER, Albert. *The Indian in American Literature.* New York: 1933.

KINIETZ, W. V. *The Indians of the Western Great Lakes, 1615-1760.* Ann Arbor: 1940.

KROEBER, A. L. *Cultural and Natural Areas of Native North America.* Berkeley: 1963.

MAURAULT, J. P. A. *Histoire des Abénakis depuis 1605 jusqu'a nos jours.* Sorel: 1866.

PATTERSON, E. Palmer. *The Canadian Indian: A History since 1500.* Toronto: 1972.

PEARCE, R. H. *The Savages of America: A Study of the Indian and the Idea of Civilization.* Baltimore: 1965.

PECKHAM, Howard et al. *Attitudes of Colonial Powers towards the American Indian.* Salt Lake City: 1969.

QUIMBY, George I. *Indian Culture and European Trade.* Chicago: 1966.

QUIMBY, George I. *Indian Life in the Upper Great Lakes, 11000 B.C. to A.D. 1800.* Chicago: 1960.

ROUSSEAU, Jacques. *L'Indien et son milieu.* Québec: 1965.

SPECK, Frank G. *The Iroquois: A Study in Cultural Evolution.* Bloomfield Hills: 1965.

SURTEES, Robert J. *The Original People.* Toronto: 1971.

TOOKER, Elizabeth. *An Ethnography of the Huron Indians, 1615-1649.* Washington: 1964.

TRIGGER, Bruce G. *The Huron: Farmers of the North*. New York: 1969.

VACHON, André. *Eloquence indienne: textes choisis*. Montreal: 1968.

WALLIS, W. D. and R. S. *The Micmac Indians of Eastern Canada*. Minneapolis: 1955.

WASHBURN, Wilcomb, ed. *The Indian and the White Man*. Garden City: 1964.

WRIGHT, James V. *The Ontario Iroquois Tradition*. Ottawa: 1966.

Martyrdom of Brébuf from "Novae Franciae
accurata delineato 1657" (F.G. Bressani, S.J.,
Giovanni Frederico Pesca, sc.) Courtesy Public
Archives of Canada, National Map Collection.

Le Moyne, Jacques, painting depicting René de
Laudonniere and Chief Achore from Jacques Le
Moyne de Morgures narrative, *Brevis Narratio
Eorum Guae in Florida Americae,* Frankfurt, 1591
(Courtesy New York Public Library).

A

Abbeville, Claude d' 29, 30, 33, 42, 78
Abenakis 86, 101, 161, 180
Acadia 44, 51, 84, 98, 113
Achelacy 96
Acosta, Joseph de 19, 20
Adamic descent 17-18, 20-21, 78
Agriculture 55, 169, 176, 177-183
Ahatsistcari, Eustache 157
Albanel, Charles 164
Alcohol 65, 67, 71, 110-115, 171, 179,
    183-184, 196
Alexander VII, Pope 13
Algonkians 25, 54, 72, 84, 88, 89, 101,
    106, 107, 121, 128, 131, 135, 138,
    140, 145-146, 161, 194, 196
Algonkins (tribe) 88, 124, 129, 132,
    134, 135, 137, 140, 141, 154, 159,
    171, 173, 174, 175, 183
Allouez, Claude 18, 44, 69, 179
Amantacha, Louis 166
André, Louis 60
Angers 166
Apocalypticalism 8, 48, 49-50, 156,
    178, 184, 185, 191, 192
Arinadisit, Marie 172
Aristotle 15, 19
Arnauld, Antoine 68
Atontinon, Marie-Barbe 75
Auxerre 147
Avaugour, Louis d' 73
Avity, Pierre d' 18, 23-24, 25, 27, 86
Aztecs 126

B

Baptism 56, 66, 67, 68, 71, 72, 140,
    145, 157
Barcia, André Gonzales de 13
Barbarism 16, 27, 120-147, 193
Basques 53, 108
Bear tribe 65
Bellenger, Etienne 14

Belmont, François Vachon de 26,
    112, 114
Benzoni, Giralmo 19
Beothuks 121
Bernières, Henri de 71
Bertrand, sieur 70
Bestiality. See brutishness
Betanzos, Domingo de 16
Biard, Pierre 30-31, 47, 51, 53, 100,
    107, 113
Biencourt, Charles de 51
Biet, Antoine 33, 42
Black Legend 17, 70
Black Robes. See Jesuits
Bodin, Jean 18, 22, 32, 77
Bolton thesis 9
Bordeaux 14
Boucher, Pierre 113, 134, 145, 165
Bourgeois, Marguerite 175
Bouteroue, Claude de 175
Boyer, Paul 30
Brandy traffic. See alcohol
Brazil 14, 67, 108, 165
Brébeuf, Jean de 70, 101, 125, 168
Bressani, Francesco 23, 101, 102,
    141, 184
Bretons 10
Brulé Etienne 145, 163
Bruyas, Jacques 59, 114
Brutishness 18, 27, 42, 131, 144, 190.
    See barbarism, wild men
Beuteux, Jacques 178

C

Cadillac, Antoine de la Mothe 20,
    21, 44
Caen, Emery de 137
Calleville, college of 165, 167
Callières, Louis Hector de 110
Canaanite origin 19-20
Cannibalism 120, 122, 140, 142-148
Cape Breton 67
Capuchins 165, 169

Carheil, Etienne de 109
Carmelites 168
Cartier, Jacques 13, 14, 16, 42, 46, 96, 123, 128, 184
Cat Nation 136
Catalogne, Gédéon de 136
Catherine de Medici 14
Cataracoui. See Fort Frontenac
Cayuga 67, 136, 145, 167, 182
Celibacy. See sexual morality
Chabanel, Noel 54
Chain of being 17-19, 24
Champlain, Samuel de 27, 34, 42, 47, 78, 96, 110, 124, 125, 128, 129, 132, 135, 137, 139, 154, 162, 166, 184
Champigny, Jean Bochart de 137
Charles IX 14
Chastelain, Pierre 63
Chastillon 163
Chauchetière, Claude 23, 69
Chaumonot, Pierre 64, 102
Cherokee 126
Chihouatenhoua, Joseph 70
Child-rearing 94-96
"Chinese rites" controversy 51
Choul, Guillaume de 76
Christian Island 146
Clodoré, Robert de 29
Cobes, sieur de 24, 25, 46
Colbert, Jean-Baptiste 85, 170, 174, 175
Columbus, Christopher 110, 144
Company of the Holy Sacrament 48-49, 84, 156
Company of New France (Hundred Associates) 163, 169
Comte, Robert 20
Conversion 54-56, 65-74, 103-104, 116, 127, 139-140, 155, 158, 165, 180-181, 193
Cord tribe 65
Counter-innovative techniques 44, 53, 56-58, 59, 62, 99, 115, 157, 195
Courcelles expedition 132
Coureurs-de-bois 53, 86, 108, 111, 115, 157, 162, 184, 195
Crépieul, François de 105, 164
Crignan, Pierre 121
Cross 44-45, 61, 99
Crucé, Eméric de 18
Crusade, against Iroquois 70-71, 136
Cultural relativism 50-51, 77, 157

D

Dablon, Claude 146, 161
Deer tribe 65
De Laet, Jan 20
De Monts, Pierre de Gua, sieur 14, 73, 153

Denonville, Jacques-René de Brisay, marquis de 71, 98, 112, 136, 137, 141, 183, 184
Denys, Nicolas 30, 85, 92, 93, 94, 99, 104, 110, 112, 113
De Quen, Jean 59, 145
Dieppe 13, 97, 167, 168
Dièreville, sieur de 86, 99, 162
Dollier de Casson, François 170
Disease 58, 59, 90, 92, 98-107, 170
Display in Europe of Amerindians 12-15
Dogiques 56, 70, 71, 74-75,179
Domagaya 13
Donnacona 13-14, 96
Dreams 57-59, 89
Druillettes, Gabriel 146
Drunkenness. See alcohol
DuBoc, Laurent 164
Du Creux, François 54, 106, 111
Duchesneau, Jacques 176
Dumoulin, Pierre 73
Durand, Jean 164
Dutch 20, 55-56, 131, 134, 159. See New Netherland
Du Tertre, Jean-Baptiste 29, 31, 34, 78

E

Earthly Paradise 28, 31, 34. See primitivism
Eden, Garden of. See Earthly Paradise, primitivism
Education 95-96, 165-177, 193-194
English 7, 9, 18, 20, 131, 134, 135, 140, 159, 160, 191, 192. See New England
Entaraha 101
Environment 7, 8, 32, 43, 44, 77, 90, 105, 164, 185, 192, 197
Epidemics. See disease
Equality 30
Eskimos 88, 105, 108
Essomericq 12
Estienne, Henri 13, 23
Etinechikawat, Jean-Baptiste 140

F

Fasting 72
Feast of the Dead 46, 101
Firearms 68, 134-135
Fishermen 8, 12, 44, 108, 110, 121, 122, 161, 190
Five Nations 18, 55, 56, 136. See Iroquois
Fléché, Jessé 51, 66
Florida, settlement in 14, 16
Folle-Avoine 60
Fontainebleau 15

Fort Frontenac 67, 167, 182
Fort Niagara 90
Fox 90, 183
Francis I 14, 42
Franciscans. See Récollets
Freedom 29, 92, 94, 95, 160, 190
Frémin, Jacques 58
Frontenac, Louis de Buade, comte de
  53, 68, 176, 180, 181
Fur trade 7, 12, 55, 68, 92, 93, 110
  121, 133, 135, 154, 157, 184, 192

G

Galinée, René de Bréhaut de 97
Gannensagouas, Marie-Thérèse 75
Gannondaris, Cecile 70, 159
Garcia, Gregorio 19
Garnier, Charles 24
Gendron, François 105
Genebrard, Gilbert 20
Gomara, Francisco Lopez de 17
Gravier, Jacques 53
Grotius, Hugo 20, 133
Guarani 13
Guyart, Marie. See Marie de
  l'Incarnation

H

Hache, Robert 114
Hairiness 23, 24. See wild men
Head trophies. See scalping
Hébert, Louis 171
Hennepin, Louis 21, 25, 57, 65, 67,
  68, 88, 89, 92, 129, 132, 137, 142
  157, 167, 181
Henry II 14
Henry IV 14, 153
Henry of Susa 160
Hispaniola 107
Homosexuality. See sexual morality
Hospitality 8, 85-87, 109
Hospital Nuns 49, 53, 75, 100, 159,
  165, 167, 168, 171
Hôtel-Dieu de Québec 68, 75, 100, 106
Houbou, Guillaume 171
Huguenots 14, 16, 20, 30, 65, 67, 72-74,
  75, 76-77, 125
Hurons 24, 25, 27, 29, 31, 33, 46, 47,
  53, 55, 57-59, 62-66, 85, 87, 90-92,
  101-103, 124, 125, 129, 131, 137,
  138, 140, 141, 144, 162, 164, 171,
  173, 174, 180-181, 183

I

Iberville, Pierre le Moyne, sieur d' 124
Idolatry 16, 42, 76
Illinois 18, 26, 53, 101, 175
Innocent X, Pope 68

Inquisition 51
Iouskeha 44, 59, 61
Iroquois 10, 15, 25, 55-56, 64, 71, 89,
  101, 102, 114, 120, 124, 125, 127,
  129-132, 134-138, 140-145, 160, 167,
  172, 176, 180, 183
Israel, Ten Lost Tribes 20-21

J

Jamet, Denis 124, 154, 178
Jansenists 68, 170
Jesuits 18, 24, 32, 41, 48, 55, 73, 74,
  93, 94, 95, 111, 124, 132, 135, 137,
  140, 156, 161, 164, 167-169
Jewish origin theory 20-21, 45-46
Jogues, Isaac 94, 102, 105, 140, 141, 142
Jouvency, Joseph 58, 131
Juchereau, Jeanne-Françoise 100

K

Kalm, Peter 184
Kickapoos 26
Kidnapping 12, 13

L

La Barre, Le Febvre de 161, 165
Lac des Deux Montagnes 75, 183
Lafitau, Joseph-François 18
Le Hève 170
Lahontan, Louis-Armand, baron de
  24, 30, 111, 132, 143
La Montagne 170, 182
Lalemant, Charles 23, 43, 73, 78
Lalemant, Jérôme 44, 55, 145, 157
Languages 51-53
La Peyrère, Isaac de 21-22
La Rochelle 10, 134
La Salle, Robert Cavelier de 68
Las Casas, Bartolomé de 16
Laudonnière, René de 123
Laurentian Iroquois 13-14, 123,
  128, 184
Laval, Mgr. François de 18, 70, 71, 95,
  111, 112, 159, 170, 171, 174
Le Clercq, Chrestien 44-45, 52, 67, 99
Le Febvre, Thomas 27, 33, 43
Leinhody 110
Liquor. See alcohol
Le Jeune, Paul 3, 25, 34, 42, 43, 54,
  59, 61, 101, 124, 129, 134, 138, 139,
  140, 146, 148, 157, 168, 178
Le Moyne, Jacques 123-124
Le Moyne, Simon 55, 136
Le Roy, Louis 10, 28
Léry, Jean de 17, 30, 67, 147
Lescarbot, Marc 19, 20, 29, 30, 32-33,
  34, 52, 73, 74, 78, 101, 106, 107,
  108, 154
Lorette 69, 161, 181, 184

Louis XIII 15, 96, 166
Louis XIV 15, 95
Louisbourg 123
Lumnius, Joannes 20

M

Magic 62-64
Magnan, Pierre 137
Major, John 15-16
Malouins, See Saint-Malo
Malecite 108, 124, 161
Marie de l'Incarnation 18, 26, 27, 47,
 50, 54, 57, 60, 63, 70-71, 95, 102,
 110, 111, 159, 161, 171, 173
Marie de Saint-Joseph 49
Marie des Neiges 175
Maryland 140. See English
Marsolet, Nicolas 163
Massachusetts. See English,
 New England
Mather, Cotton 74
Mayhew, Thomas 76
Medecine 66, 89, 105-107, 195
Membertou, Henry 51
Meulles, Jacques de 161, 176
Mendieta, Geronimo de 177
Miamis 18, 26, 90
Michilimackinac 20, 135 ,
Micmacs 10, 26, 33, 45, 51, 52, 67, 70,
 78, 86, 92, 93, 99, 106, 107, 108,
 110, 123, 161, 170
Military alliances 7, 12
Millet, Pierre 60, 174
Miscegenation 66, 107-109, 161-165,
 173, 175, 183-185
Miscou 67
Missionary work 7, 41-83
Mocquet, Jean 14, 34, 122
Mohawks 56, 71, 136
Montagnais 14, 25, 33, 62, 67, 101,
 124, 131, 132, 135, 141, 144, 154,
 163, 167, 168
Montaigne, Michel de 14, 17, 27, 28,
 30, 122, 130, 146-147, 153, 190
Montesinos, Antonio de 16
Montmagny, Charles Huault de 111
Montmorency, Henri, duc de 153
Montreal 97, 106, 109, 125, 156, 160,
 163, 175, 179, 180, 182
Mussard, Pierre 76
Mystics, native 69-70, 75

N

Naples 107, 108
Neutrals 78, 101, 102
Negroes 139
New England 67, 73, 74, 76, 113, 127
New Netherland 55, 56, 74, 76,
 131, 142

New York. See English, New England
Nipisguit 67
Nipissings 101, 167
Noble savage, myth of 9, 28-30, 34,
 41, 147, 191
Notre-Dame des Anges 166-168
Normans 10
Noue,Anne de 54

O

O'Gormanthesis 9-10
Oki, See shamans
Onakonchiarroenk, Ignace 70
Oneida 59, 114, 136
Onandaga 56, 136
Origin of Amerindians 19-21
Ossossané 65
Ottawa 44, 78, 90, 101, 128, 135, 144
Oviedo y Valdéz, Gonzalo 17, 23, 110

P

Packiriny, Charles 161
Pagan resistance 44, 47, 53-54. See
 counter-innovative techniques
Panis. See Pawnee
Paris 15, 20, 30, 105, 170
Pasquier, Etienne 22
Patetchoanen, Pierre-Antoine 166
Paul III, Pope 17
Paulmier, Binot de Gonneville 12
Pawnee 139, 183
Pelletier, François 164
Peltrie, Madame de la 49
Peralta, Juan Suarez de 19
Perrot, Nicolas 43-44, 45-46, 86, 89,
 109, 128, 133, 143
Pétuns. See Tobaccos
Pierron, Jean 62, 76
Platform torture 120, 121. See
 barbarism
Poissons, Jean-Baptiste 20
Polygenism 20-21. See Isaac de la
 Peyrère
Pontgravé, François 14, 73
Pontgravé, Robert 73
Popelinière, Henri de la 16
Portuguese 146, 190
Pottawatomie 62
Poutrincourt, sieur de 73, 106, 107
Prairie de la Madeleine 169, 179-180
Primitivism 26, 34, 190, 192
Protestants. See Huguenots
Proprietary rights 159-161, 194

Q

Québec 54, 64, 75, 95, 98, 100, 106,
 134, 159, 162, 163, 166, 168, 178, 180
Quéylus, Gabriel de 111
Quinté 170, 182

R

Rabelais, François 14, 16
Radisson, Pierre-Esprit 143
Racial concepts 136, 153, 158-159,
177-178, 198. See skin colour
Ragueneau, Paul 55, 57, 63, 65, 157
Ratio Studiorum 168
Razilly, Issac de 169
Récollets 24, 25, 46, 47, 50, 55, 60,
65-67, 68, 72, 75, 85, 94, 96, 105,
108, 129, 141, 154, 155, 162, 165-167,
177, 178, 182, 183
Religious images 61-63
Reservations 26, 71, 111, 160-161,
169, 177-183
Ribaut, Jean 14, 16
Richelieu, Armand Jean Cardinal de
29, 155, 169
Roberval, sieur de 14, 16, 22
Rock tribe 65
Ronsard, Pierre de 16
Rouen 13, 14, 30, 111, 166
Rousseau, Jean-Jacques 29

S

Sagard, Gabriel 24, 29, 31, 33, 46, 55,
60-61, 72, 78, 87, 91, 97, 105-106,
128, 141, 148, 154, 178
Saint-Castin, Jean Vincent,
baron de 165
Saint-Malo 13, 14, 107, 108, 161
Sainte-Marie des Hurons 56, 105
Saint-Sauveur 159
Saintonge, Alphonse de 16
Saint-Vallier, Mgr. Jean-Baptiste de
112
Sault St. Louis 161, 179, 180
Scalping 120, 121, 122-127, 140, 148
Scientific knowledge 93-94
Sedentary settlement 26, 54-55, 84-85,
104, 154-161, 165, 177, 178, 194, 196
Segregation 16, 153-185
Seignelay, Marquis de 112
Seneca 56, 58, 71, 92, 97, 136
Sepulveda, Juan Ginés de 14-15
Sesmaisons, Pierre de 164
Sexual morality 12, 31, 59-60, 72,
107-108, 112, 114, 120, 121, 144
Shamans 56, 65, 99, 105, 106
Sillery 106, 140, 161, 169, 178-179
Sioux 26, 90, 138, 183
Sisters Hospitallers. See Hospital Nuns
Sisters of the Congregation 75, 95,
175-177
Skandahietsi, Louis 140
Skanudharoua, Geneviève-Agnès 75
Skin colour 22-23, 33, 139
Slavery 15-16, 123, 136-139, 146.
See Pawnee

Somatic norm image 23, 158, 193
Spaniards 7, 15, 17-20, 70, 107, 108,
159, 190, 191, 192
Stadacona 13
St. Joachim 171
Sulpicians 65, 68, 161, 169-170, 177,
182, 183
Susquehannock 126
Swidden cultivation 55

T

Tabagerres 14
Tadoussac 69, 84, 98, 103, 110, 124,
134, 163, 164, 180
Taigoagny 13
Talon, Jean 95, 100, 169, 175, 182
Tapie de Monteil, François de 132
Tawiscaron, Jean 44
Tegakouita, Catherine 70
Thévet, André 14, 42, 121, 128
Timogona 123
Tobaccos 101, 106
Tonty, Henri de 124
Torture. See barbarism
Trois-Rivières 54, 64, 161, 163, 178, 180
Troyes 14
Tsondihouanne, René 70
Tupinamba 13, 14, 29
Tuscarora 126
Turner thesis 9

U

Ursulines 48, 53, 75, 95, 102, 163,
165, 171-175, 176, 177
Utopianism 16, 18, 28-32, 50, 86,
156, 190, 192

V

Valladolid 16
Venereal diseases 107-108
Ventadour, duc de 48
Vergil, Polydore 76
Verrazano, Giovanni da 12, 13, 23, 144
Versailles 15, 165, 176, 177
Vikings 8, 20, 44, 121
Villegagnon, Nicolas Durand de 14, 16
Viret, Pierre 76
Vitoria, Francisco de 133

W

Warfare 7, 18, 69, 85, 92, 126,
127-138, 194
Wild men 13, 23, 190
Windigo psychosis 146
Witchcraft 58, 60-65, 102-103, 120, 183
Women 12, 25, 26, 32, 33, 76, 77-78,
107, 108, 109, 112, 120, 121, 124,
129, 132, 140, 141, 143, 144, 161-164

Z

Zarate, Agustin de 19
Zummarraga, Juan de 16

207